THE
NON-WESTERN
FILMS OF
JOHN FORD

The Non-Western

CITADEL PRESS   SECAUCUS, N.J.

Films of
JOHN FORD

by J.A. PLACE

dedicated to Michael

ACKNOWLEDGMENTS

Many of the stills came from Larry Edmunds Bookshop and Eddie Brandt's Saturday Afternoon Matinee. For help in locating and viewing films I am gratefully indebted to Bob Epstein and Charles Hopkins of the UCLA Film Archive, David Bradley, Mark Haggard, Walter Clamett of Films Incorporated, and Warner Brothers 16. For typing I thank Nancy Williams and the Steno Pool at College V, UC Santa Cruz. For making this project possible as my doctoral dissertation, I thank my Chairperson, Frank LaTourette, members of the committee Richard Hawkins, Albert Hutter, and especially committee members Richard Thompson and Tim Hunter who gave both moral support and invaluable advice in that stage of the work. To my friends, colleages, and students at Santa Cruz I am gratefully indebted for endless discussion, encouragement and advice, particularly Julianne Burton, Peter Rose, Lorraine Kahn, Allan Plone, Paul Skenazy, and Mitch Meisner. To Michael Hiles I am eternally grateful for facilitating the final, nearly unmanageable steps and for the moral support that made it possible. I will always be indebted to Lowell Peterson for the confidence to undertake the project in the first place, and to see it through the dissertation stage. Above all, I thank my editor, Leslie Donaldson, for her wit, understanding, extraordinary competence, and persistence when only her faith kept us going.

Designed by A. Christopher Simon

LIBRARY OF CONGRESS CATALOGING IN PUBLICATION DATA

Place, Janey Ann, 1946-
    The non-Western films of John Ford.

    Continues The Western films of John Ford.
    1.   Ford, John, 1895-1973. I.   Title.
PN1998.A3F615   791.43'0233'0924   78-12832
ISBN 0-8065-0643-1

CONTENTS

INTRODUCTION

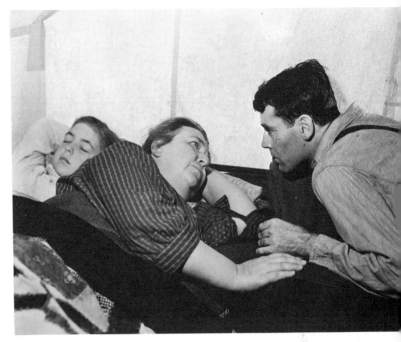

The Grapes of Wrath: a social structure which cannot fill the needs of its members.

They Were Expendable: Ford both affirms and deeply criticizes American values in World War II. (Robert Montgomery)

Today is a time of deep cynicism. Religion, politics, and art all reflect the despair people feel over values they once had faith in and their deep need to somehow replace or renew those impoverished values. These necessarily contradictory needs cannot be reconciled on any level except that of art, and then only rarely. The art of John Ford is newly and continually poignant, uniquely speaking to both the hope and the despair. While he is considered a prophet of patriotism, conservatism, and male heroism, Ford actually speaks most intimately to our deepest fears and desires. His films deal with individuals who find the world in which they live unable to affirm or even sustain them. Even while they are emotionally isolated, they function in the only way open to them, to continue to serve and defend the society which rejects them. Thus Ford performs the nearly impossible dual function of affirming the existing social order and all its mythologies, and profoundly critiquing it in both personal and structural terms. It is to both these operations that we respond today. The ache to substantiate the mores by which we live and the deep sense of their meaninglessness is simultaneously touched and soothed by Ford's art.

Films are said to constitute a history or a mythology of America, especially those which deal as centrally with issues of historical development, ideological questions, and specific events and personages as do Ford's films. While this is certainly true, films are far more than artifacts. They are artistic experiences which retain historical corporality, but are worth attention outside their strict historical context because they can offer emotional experience to an ever-changing audience. It is not the historical meaning or even the surrounding context that we find compelling, but the films themselves—touching and moving new audiences, providing meaningful constructs to questions of individuality, honor, family, duty, love, and continually questioning the values we

History in film: war comedies *What Price Glory* (World War I)
and *When Willie Comes Marching Home* (World War II).

Filming *Judge Priest:* in 1934 Ford recreates the milieu of 1890 small-town America.

have to live by. It is a measure of the artist's vision that a work created fifty or more years ago can continue to offer such rewards. But the work does not stand independently of its original social milieu, nor of the one in which it is newly experienced. It is a product of the relationship between the artist and the culture in which he or she lives, and the experience of art is a relationship between the individual members of the audience and the work, which changes over time.

The relationship between art and its culture is a very complex one which grows even more so when that art is also popular art or popular culture. The relationship is clearly determined by the economic structure of the industry which requires that products of that system fundamentally support its ideological operation, or at least mask any contradictory function. It is a necessary relationship because art must be firmly rooted in its social context in order to have any meaning, and it is reciprocal in that art and society reflect and refract each other in a continual exchange. But the means by which to measure the effect of popular art on its culture are even less adequate than those which measure the effect of the culture on the artist and his/her product. With movies which engage emotions so strongly and often so unconsciously, this is especially difficult. It has led writers to attempt to analyze either their own social milieu or a historical one through the films of the time. The films are inevitably chosen for their value in making the conclusion: the sample is thus "stacked." Such an enterprise is further compromised when a writer uses only those aspects of a film that support his/her analysis, leaving the rest of the film unrepresented. The artistic integrity that makes the film worthy of study in the first place is thus destroyed. Treating film as a mere cultural artifact without artistic relevance must necessarily produce work which does not speak to the most valuable function of a film.

Similarly, attempts to analyze the artist through his or her art while ignoring the social context that informed and, to an immeasurable extent, determined the work are inadequate, especially for a broadly based product of popular culture like movies. How can we study films in a way that leaves out neither their social dimension nor their artistic dimension? In a historical study of works of art and popular culture the cultural context cannot be experienced firsthand and the tools to study that context are inadequate: this is the dilemma. A limited attempt, which accounts for the

continued importance and relevance of films made ten, twenty, thirty, forty or more years ago and thus are remote from our social context, might recognize the great power of films to speak to an audience about themselves as individuals within a social milieu. As long as this communication is immediate, those films will continue to

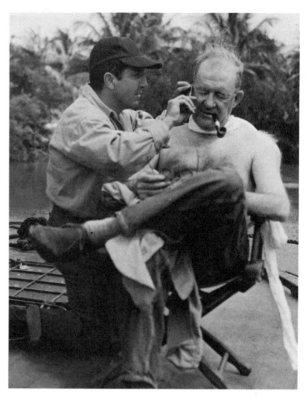

Ford on the set of *They Were Expendable,* 1946.

The Black Watch, 1929. Nearly fifty years removed from our social context.

Ford's films speak of America's relation to its own histories and mythologies: *They Were Expendable.*

Henry Fonda as Wyatt Earp in *My Darling Clementine.*

be seen and function within the current social context. Their relevance gives them a place and an audience within that new context. An attempt to adequately examine the historical context of a given film is inviting but an impossibly huge and difficult project demanding a scope too broad to manage. Thus, the interaction between the film and the current social context might well be a workable place to start. The films that become well known out of their own time generally deal in some way with questions of continued relevance: the loneliness of individualism and heroism, the complexity of loving or being loved, the despair when traditional values lose their meaning. This point of audience interaction with the issues of the film keeps the films newly meaningful to changing social milieus, and it is here that this book will deal with the films of John Ford.

John Ford worked in the film industry from 1914 through 1972. His films were popular and commercial successes throughout that time, and today are shown both for entertainment and for study in universities, repertory theaters, and film institutes. They remain relevant, moving, and immediate for present-day audiences. They speak of America and its relation to its own mythology; Ford's films both helped to create that mythology and to question its values. These films deal with questions of war, politics, work, responsibility. They look back at history and rewrite it according to values whose variance to those of the accepted version of history is made clear in the film. They both affirm our cultural experience and heritage, and question and subvert it. This tension, both satisfying and disturbing, keeps the films potent as is all great art.

Ford directed over two hundred films during his career, and more than a hundred of them are extant. In Volume I, *The Western Films of John Ford*, nineteen films were represented. It would be impossible to give the remaining films even cursory coverage in this volume, and the unequal attention given to the films is thus generally a statement of the author's judgment of importance. The hundred-plus silent films Ford directed are largely lost. There are complete prints of many and fragments of others. Some, thought lost, have been rediscovered in archives all around the world in the last few years, and more will undoubtedly be unearthed in the near future. For reasons of space, and also in the hope that a really complete treatment will be possible when this period of Ford's career becomes more fully visible, no silents are included in this volume.

Our cultural heritage is both criticized and affirmed in *The Sun Shines Bright.*

Hangman's House, 1928: moody, decadent interiors match themes of the tyranny of the past. (June Collyer and Hobart Bosworth)

Genres are defined by their subject matter, *What Price Glory:* a war film. (Dan Dailey as Captain Flagg).

The arrangement of films in this volume is along genre lines. Subject matter determines genre: detective films, musicals, science fiction, Westerns, war films, all belong to a subject category. Genres can be expressed in any range of visual styles, and thus are flexible to changes in the ideology of a given time, and can be active over a very long period of time. Genres become familiar or conventionalized. An audience knows certain things about the character, the situation, the relationship, by having seen these same components countless times before. In Westerns, some of these objects are guns, horses, cattle, costumes. Narrative patterns become conventionalized as well, and thus produce repeated structures within a genre. In gangster films the "one last job" is one such narrative structure. It will inevitably result in disaster, but was intended to give the outlaw just enough money to settle down and stop his life of crime. In Westerns the military theme of the settling of the West by the cavalry is another familiar narrative theme.

These objects and narrative themes do not contain any consistent ideological meaning. Meaning is structured largely by the visual style. The ideological content of genre objects can change, depending upon their presentation in the text, but their conventionality remains consistent. For example, the railroad in Westerns has undergone a radical change in its ideological content through

The Sun Shines Bright: an Americana film.

Meaning is structured by visual style: war in *They Were Expendable* in a system of beliefs.

Shooting *The Long Gray Line.*

The Sun Shines Bright: the rituals of burial are informed by previous use in Ford's films.

the history of the genre. When Ford used it in *The Iron Horse* (1924) and Cecil B. DeMille used it in *Union Pacific* (1939), it was an agent of uncomplicated progress, identified in the former film with Lincoln's persona as a unifier of the nation. The railroad was the means by which to tame and build the wilderness into a democratic garden of peace and plenty for all: an instrument of desired progress, of Walt Whitman's perfect society of man in the wilderness. Later, as illustrated by Henry King's *Jesse James* (1939), the railroad was often seen as a tool of big money interests which would destroy the yeoman farmer of early Western dreams and myths. By 1957 in *3:10 to Yuma,* it was the oppressive instrument which takes a farmer off to jail. In the sixties, Sergio Leone was using Westerns to reverse their previous ideological content: railroads represented the tool which would contribute to the closing off of the frontier, serving money interests and oppressing the farmers by stealing their land. Leone's *Once Upon a Time in the West* (1969) further identifies the railroad with oppressive religion and it is represented as a primary exploitive factor in the West. Sam Peckinpah (in *The Wild Bunch,* 1969) used this genre object in a similar manner. Thus the railroad remains an element of the Western, but its ideological content can change to express new relationships within the dominant ideology of the nation. It is largely in this way that genre films have become the major form for the repeated telling and reformulation of our own mythology.

The tools used to study myth in other cultures are thus illuminating for genre films. Structuralism is such a critical approach. Adopted by Claude Levi-Strauss to study myth in primitive cultures and since recruited to other areas of analysis, structuralism seeks to identify hidden structures which run through many related narrative patterns, such as the variations of a myth or the films of one genre or one director. The repetition of a structural pattern derives meaning not only from its specific context, but also from its earlier or wider use. Levi-Strauss and many subsequent users of this method have restricted its application to narrative. With film we should be able to discover patterned relationships between themes and styles in a director's work. For example, the very expressionistic style of *The Fugitive* creates the theme of abstraction. The narrative story is taken out of the mundane, detailed, miserable world of Graham Greene's *The Power and the Glory,* distanced and rendered visually harmonious. Most of Greene's intentionally ugly and squalid tension is thus destroyed. This process of change is primarily carried out through style, and is similar to the operations of style in other of Ford's films. It is through a study of the combination of narrative, visual style, and the complexity of their interaction, which gives contextual meaning to each element, that the fullest critical work will be done on a director's oeuvre. The relation between repeated elements reveals meaning as important as the elements themselves: the relation between the Billy Priest of *Judge Priest* (1934) and his society, and the Billy Priest of *The Sun Shines Bright* (1950) and his society, informs each film and suggests the direction of the author's work as a whole.

Working within a genre offers a director both confines and attendant freedoms. The existing structures and objects of a genre allow the director the boundaries within which to express a very personal world view which might become too specified and unintelligible without such structures. This helps explain the fact that Ford's most highly regarded films are those which are not very personal *(The Informer, The Graphs of Wrath)*, and the Westerns, which are familiar and accessible through their narrative structures. *The Searchers* and *The Man Who Shot Liberty Valance*, both intensely personal films of a mature artist, have recently acquired critical reputations: when each was released it was considered just another genre film, unworthy of serious consideration. Now that John Ford's critical reputation is very high, even his most personal and least accessible films are reconsidered because the auteur theory has established the importance of studying all the films directed by one person.

Auteur criticism is based on the concept that the director is the primary creative consciousness behind a film. The creative efforts of many people go into the making of a film; the director is the orchestrator of all these contributions. The director is the creator of the visual style of a film, in which so much of the "unspoken" communication lies. Like the study of a writer or a painter, an individual work of a director is illuminated by other works, and progressions can be found over the entire oeuvre. A director's themes and visual motifs can be identified, then studied for change or variation. As important as the narrative themes and motifs of the genre, a director develops his/her own conventionalized patterns. In Ford's war films, the military hierarchy has a specific mean-

John Ford, 1927.

They Were Expendable: shadows representing men and entrapping compositional lines are some of Ford's recurring visual motifs.

13

Window frames separate characters from the objects of their desires

in *The Sun Shines Bright*

and *How Green Was My Valley.*

Iconography conjures a feeling of home in war-torn Phillippines: *They Were Expendable.*

ing that it does not necessarily signify in a war film by another director. These repeated themes can be isolated and observed in their development through his work. In some of his later works (for example, *The Wings of Eagles* and *The Long Gray Line*), as his conventions and their use become more specified without the familiar larger context of a genre like the Western, the films seem quickly dated and difficult for audiences to respond to directly. The military films are controlled by a very timely body of conventions, making *They Were Expendable* a difficult picture because there is much to overcome (World War II from an ostensibly patriotic American point of view) before the deeper structures of the film can be seen. Pictures like these demonstrate that not only is the meaning of the film determined by its style, but visual style can perform an operation of criticism upon the conventional structure of the genre.

Both the auteur theory and the growing interest in generic structures have contributed to the reevaluation of many films which because of their setting within a genre have been denigrated in Hollywood's self-hatred for its most "commercial" products. In fact, this is exactly the area to study for questions of ideology, mythology, and even personal achievement, since it was often in cheaper genre pictures that the director was freer to experiment. Where the studio investment was less heavy, the "front office" did not control the production as carefully.

The conventions of a genre, then, can act as a filter, or a distancing device, like the framework of a myth, allowing both artist and audience the familiarity of the structure and the possibility of expression and interpretation within it. The Western is the most structured, the most conventionalized genre, followed by the musical, the detective picture, the science fiction film and the horror film. Beyond that, a concept of genre becomes so much less structured that there are overlaps and marginal narrative similarities. For Ford, narrative themes and ideological content are most clear in the Westerns, partially because of the conventionalized patterns that can be recruited to his own artistic vision, and partially by their clear "mythic" narrative status which allows more direct expression. Ironically, they seem "less real" instead of the "supra real" they actually are. This artistic vision remains the same when it is not set in the American West, but it becomes less accessible because of its less direct link to the shared

The generic elements of the sea voyage allow Ford to abstract an attraction to death in *The Long Voyage Home.* (John Wayne, John Qualen)

Mythical small town America of Puxatawney, West Virginia in *When Willie Comes Marching Home.*

experience of myth. As it is less confined in the clearly "unreal" world of the Western genre, Ford's mature vision becomes threatening. An audience cannot easily assimilate such a dark vision when it is not mediated by familiar genre structures.

Ford made military pictures, Americana pictures (a genre he nearly defined himself), "national" pictures, always Irish or Welsh, and many that do not fit even into these loose categories. Many overlap—*The Grapes of Wrath* (1940) could be considered a Western, an Americana picture, or in a category all its own. The "political" pictures, *The Last Hurrah* (1958) and *Young Mr. Lincoln* (1939), could constitute their own category, or fit into an Americana genre. The genre categories and their motifs grow looser after the Westerns, and their organization in this volume is not intended as definitive. Not all films are genre

pictures, and there is an element of diminishing return when narrative similarity is sought instead of discovered. The films of the last two chapters have consistence, but not enough to constitute a mappable genre. The films are discussed as individual artistic and popular culture products, as elements in Ford's oeuvre, and as genre films with meaning derived from their shared similarities with both Ford's work in the genre and the entirety of the genre category. The most illuminating of these areas is used with regard to each individual film.

John Ford is the greatest filmic artist America and the world have produced to date. In spite of Ford's continued commercial success, there was a time when such an aesthetic judgment would have been met with derision, and more recently, skepticism. Now it is hardly agreed upon, but is accepted as a valid critical position. There have

In its stylization, *They Were Expendable* is darkly threatening to American imperialist ideology.

The Long Gray Line: military. (Tyrone Power)

Genre comedies: *What Price Glory:* war.

been six books on Ford in English in the last ten years, and countless articles in film and popular journals. They have established such an atmosphere of high critical regard that *Film Quarterly* felt it time to debunk the "inflated" reputation (Winter 1975). Ford's work has thus been the subject of scholarly theoretical articles and of popular criticism, both of which take as an assumption that these films are worthy of such attention. It was not always so. The genre pictures, the popular successes, and the superficial patriotism of many films made Ford difficult for audiences of the sixties and seventies, but the qualities of deep questioning of values while still affirming vital aspects of them kept drawing audiences to these films. They continue to move people emotionally in deeply satisfying ways, even when the articulation of that satisfaction is difficult. And that articulation is the goal of criticism.

The Last Hurrah: a political/Americana film. (Frank McHugh, Wallace Ford)

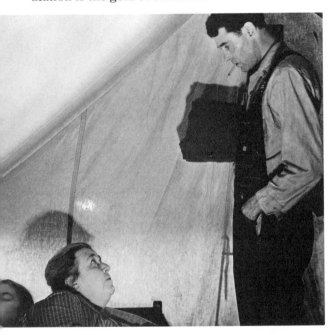

Jane Darwell and Henry Fonda in *The Grapes of Wrath.*

John Ford, circa 1930.

The Sun Shines Bright: the traditional values of the dance are hollowed out, yet speak to deep emotions in its formal precision.

How Green Was My Valley: the visual and emotional theme of isolation and exile from home.

THE AMERICANA FILMS

The Americana genre: rural, small-town America. *The Sun Shines Bright.*

20

INTRODUCTION

The Americana genre is the very opposite from a hard-edged, clearly differentiated genre like the Western. Generally set in a small-town, rural, often Southern pre-World-War-II America, the narrative structures tend to concern families, children growing up, fathers whose jobs are less important than their families. The ideological questions the genre addresses are those of the small town in a rapidly urbanizing country, and the films are thus often nostalgic fantasies. Like the Irish films and Westerns, they are mythlike in that they become a tribute to a time of innocence imagined. Vincente Minnelli's *Meet Me in St. Louis* (1944), Douglas Sirks *Has Anybody Seen My Gal?* (1952), and Henry King's *Margie* (1946) are at the heart of the genre and some of its finest examples. Of the eleven sound films Ford made which belong in this category only five—*The Will Rogers Trilogy, The Sun Shines Bright,* and *Pilgrimage*—are typical, centrally located examples of the genre. With variations, they follow the narrative pattern of conflict in the form of the introduction of outside values and/or power which present a threat to the sociopolitical structure of the town or family. The parameters of the ideological system are the society as conservative (usually the elders), the society as innovative (usually the hero), and the point of struggle, or threat. These are developed during the action of the film and the resolution explores a formulation of these basic interactions.

In *Pilgrimage* the war provides the new physical dimensions, and the mother's acceptance of her son's child the resolution: the family rather than the community is thus affirmed as the basic unit of value. In *Judge Priest* and *The Sun Shines Bright,* the narrative outline is classic, with small-town rural, humane Southern independence struggling to maintain its integrity against corrupt, big-city Northern politicians. The other pic-

The Western: genres are defined by their iconography and narrative patterns. John Wayne in *She Wore a Yellow Ribbon.*

The Grapes of Wrath: nostalgia for small-town values and simplicity.

Eastern forces bring conflict to the rural southern town in *The Sun Shines Bright*.

The Sun Shines Bright: the warm and humane courtroom of Billy Priest: more to the spirit of the law than the letter.

Lost silents: *The Brat*, 1931, an Americana film which affirms the values of the unpretentious poor over the affected society of the rich.

tures all partake of some aspects of the Americana genre elements, but with great variations. In *The Grapes of Wrath* the same process of rural family values—and the existence of the family itself—are under attack by large, mechanized powers. In this very antithesis of a nostalgia film, Ford demonstrates the economic threat forcing a land-bound concept of family to change into a class-based one. The humor in *Tobacco Road* is nearly exclusively at the expense of the poverty-stricken tobacco road farmers who find no value in family themselves; it is an uncomfortable comedy in this genre. Perhaps the most inclusive statement that can be made about the genre is that it has fondness for the people of an innocent, simpler, imagined time, making this lack a serious problem in *Tobacco Road. The Whole Town's Talking* is an inversion in another way: set in the city, it affirms the simpler, kinder personality through the gangster, making an urban newspaper crime comedy an American genre film in the same way Capra did in *Mr. Deeds Goes to Town* and *Mr. Smith Goes to Washington.*

The political pictures, *Young Mr. Lincoln, Prisoner of Shark Island,* and *The Last Hurrah,* constitute a subgenre even while belonging first to the American category. Their specific narrative patterns include a direct use of history: each is based on "real" events whose outcome is known before the film ever starts. Ford uses the rituals of politics, such as the courtroom drama, to create narrative structures which deal with the same value systems as the other Americana films.

The intersection of genre patterns and artist vision is particularly intriguing in this category. Unlike the Western (the genre model), in which it is possible to trace a few structural elements through Ford's use of them and have a schematized but fairly accurate "map" of the direction of his development, in the Americana genre the boundaries are so subject to variation that such an operation is intensely complicated. Further, many films which centrally belong in another genre have a great deal in common with Americana films, such as *The Long Gray Line* and *When Willie Comes Marching Home,* making it difficult to look only to these eleven films for Ford's attitudes toward the themes and ideological operation of the Americana genre. His own evolving vision of America, its mythologies, and the values they impart moved further and further from the lightly cynical but deeply optimistic silent *Just Pals* (1920) and *Pilgrimage* (1933). Will Rogers

Americana genre values in other genres: *The Long Gray Line*

When Willie Comes Marching Home

23

was uniquely suited to simultaneously extending the cynical as well as optimistic aspects of small-town America (the exception is *Dr. Bull,* in which the cynical clearly dominates) as Rogers' ironic wit questioned the values which were then affirmed through the action of the film. But in the Will Rogers Trilogy the insupportable contradiction between the optimism for the future and the deep sense of loss for the Rogers character is heightened. This conflict, basic to all Ford's films, is delineated most clearly in the Westerns because of their highly conventionalized genre language. But likewise in the Americana films, the gulf between the needs of the individual and his society's ability to fill them widens in the later films. The artist's vision is the ideological determinant, and in this regard, his late films in all genres find the values and mythologies of American society a sham and a betrayal of its most valued members.

The Sun Shines Bright, 1953: the gulf between the needs of the individual and his society's ability to fill them widens from *Judge Priest,* 1934.

PILGRIMAGE
1933

Henrietta Crossman as Hannah Jessup in *Pilgrimage.*

CREDITS

Production company: Fox. *Director:* John Ford. *Scenarists:* Philip Klein, Barry Connors, from the story "GOLD STAR MOTHER," by I.A.R. Wylie. *Dialogue:* Dudley Nichols. *Photographer:* George Schneiderman. *Art Director:* William Darling. *Music:* R.H. Bassett. *Recording Engineer:* W. W. Lindsay, Jr. *Editor:* Louis R. Loeffler. *Assistant director:* Edward O'Fearna. *Dialogue director:* William Collier, Sr. 90 minutes. *Released:* July 12.

CAST

Henrietta Crossman (*Hannah Jessop*), Heather Angel (*Suzanne*), Norman Foster (*Jim Jessop*), Marian Nixon (*Mary Saunders*), Maurice Murphy (*Gary Worth*), Lucille Laverne (*Mrs. Hatfield*); Charley Grapewin (*Dad Saunders),* Hedda Hopper (*Mrs. Worth*), Robert Warwick (*Maj. Albertson*), Betty Blythe (*Janet Prescott*), Francis Ford (*Mayor*), Louise Carter (*Mrs. Rogers*), Jay Ward (*Jim Saunders*), Francis Rich (*nurse*), Adele Watson (*Mrs. Simms*).

SYNOPSIS

To keep him from his lover, Hannah Jessop enlists her son Jim in the Army during World War I. When he is killed, her guilt and anger are so strong she will not acknowledge his son until she has gone to France with the Gold Star mothers and seen a similarly possessive mother nearly destroy her son. Hannah returns home to accept what remains of her family.

Pilgrimage is one of Ford's early masterpieces. Few early talkies achieved the visual beauty of silent films as the change placed restrictions and required new techniques for the camera, but *Pilgrimage* is fully realized visually, with evocative planes of light, misty exteriors, and loving photography of the little Arkansas farm. It is a moving, heartwarming story of tragedy and forgiveness, laced throughout with some of the best humor of the period, possible only from a director who loves both the ethnic, uniquely American culture and the French one it clashes with. The Americana genre elements are fully exploited in this encounter. But perhaps most important of all (lacking in some of the early "action" pictures like *The Lost Patrol, Four Men and a Prayer,* and *The Long Voyage Home*), at its heart is the passion of love and sexuality that fires so many of Ford's best films, and the nearly as powerful drive to rebuild the family after destroying it.

Pilgrimage begins as a mild, inverted Oedipal narrative, as Hannah Jessop's (Henrietta Crossman) possessiveness of her son Jim (Norman Foster) confines him—both physically and sexually—to such an extent as to portend disaster. Hannah invokes the Bible on "evil" women and forces Jim to choose between his mother and his lover Mary Saunders (Marian Nixon). To keep him from Mary, Hannah enlists Jim in the army.

The lovers, Jim and Mary, are particularly appealing in their innocence and their persecution. Mary is first framed in the ripples from a stone Jim throws in the pond, and when his army train leaves, we watch that departure and their anguish on Mary's face rather than seeing the train pull out. Mary has kept her pregnancy a secret; she will not add to Jim's burden by telling him.

25

The pivotal scene of the film is filled with touches that might seem trite in the hands of a less skilled director—or an insensitive audience. In the trenches, Jim is the third on a match; then firing starts and Ford cuts to Hannah waking in the night to gasp "Jim!" At that moment, Mary's father (Charley Grapewin) comes to fetch Hannah to help deliver Mary's baby. We have not seen that Jim is officially dead, but all three events portend it more strongly and poetically than the information which comes later—especially the birth of his son at the moment of his death. In many of Ford's films this kind of compensation takes place (*Drums Along the Mohawk, How Green Was My Valley*) as Ford's vision is epic and the forces of that vision (at least in the pre-fifties films) insist on a kind of balance. When the mayor comes the next day to inform her that Jim has indeed been killed, Hannah puts together the pieces of Jim's picture, torn when he defied her over Mary. Ford fades out on this sad, lovely image, then in on a title, "Ten Years Later," where we see the terrible change that has come over Hannah. She is mean to a man whose land she is

buying, and will not let little ten-year old Jimmy play with Jim's dog, who immediately recognizes the boy and runs to him. Her denial of kindness to those around her is easily recognizable as her denial of kindness to herself, and we see the fiercely loving woman inside the nasty, guilt-ridden one. It is the "Gold Star Mothers" journey to France that releases her.

From its very beginnings, when Hannah tells the officers who come to invite her on the trip, "I didn't know generals ever got killed," the trip is filled with humor. The many ethnic groups represented—Jewish, Scottish, Irish, German, Italian, back hills American—provide rich comedy with its roots in Ford's faith in this country's many nationalities. Mrs. Hatfield (Lucille Laverne) is a cruder, lovable contrast to Hannah; their marksmanship and direct manners amuse and outrage the French, and plea an eloquent case for the no-nonsense values of hills people.

Mrs. Hatfield has sensitivity and wisdom as well as broad humor: when Hannah breaks down and tells the others that she had her son drafted and is therefore responsible for his death, Mrs.

The Gold Star Mothers leave for France.

Hatfield understands the extent of such passion and says, "You must have loved your son very much."

Mary comes to see Hannah off, bringing flowers for her to put on Jim's grave, and after a moment's hesitation, Hannah takes them. There is a close-up of their hands touching through the train window as Mary stands on the ground. Later, as Hannah boards the ship to France, a woman whose son is listed only as "missing" these ten years and therefore cannot go asks Hannah to put flowers on a grave for her. This woman softens Hannah by choosing her to ask, and Hannah accepts. The violence and sorrow of war is evoked in the midst of the humor of the trip.

Hannah must relive her own sin before she can be released from its guilt and be reunited with what remains of her family. She does this, without losing any of her tough, hard-edged character, by saving a couple in a similar situation. As she goes walking alone after seeing her son's grave, she finds Gary Worth (Maurice Murphy) drunk and suicidal on a bridge, and takes the young man home, bullying him as she did her son. In the

morning he tells her his mother doesn't approve of his girl, Suzanne (Heather Angel), and later Hannah learns the girl is pregnant. She goes to Mrs. Worth (Hedda Hopper) and tells her not to make the same mistake, not to kill her own son through her possessive love for him. They are thus reconciled, and Hannah has opened her ten-year-old wound to other people, accepting the humiliation and shame for the good it can do others. She is finally able to cry over Jim, and collapses on his grave in tears.

Arriving home, Hannah goes immediately to Mary, begs her forgiveness, kisses her passionately when that forgiveness is offered, and embraces her grandson. She calls him Jimmy Jessop and gives him his father's dog. The last shot is of the three in close-up, a family at last. The great emotion of this scene is the result of the suffering each woman had to endure to achieve it, and we feel that once they have become a family, they will let nothing threaten it again.

Hannah prevents another mother from making the same mistake she did ten years ago in rejecting her son's wife.

THE WILL ROGERS TRILOGY (and THE SUN SHINES BRIGHT)

DR. BULL (1933)

CREDITS

Production company: Fox. *Director:* John Ford. *Scenarist:* Paul Green; from the novel, *The Last Adam*, by James Gould Cozzens. *Dialogue:* Jane Storm. *Photographer:* George Schneiderman. *Music:* Samuel Kaylin. *Recording Engineer:* E. F. Grossman. 76 minutes. Released September 22.

CAST

Will Rogers (*Dr. Bull*), Marian Nixon (*May Tripping*), Berton Churchill (*Herbert Banning*), Louise Dresser (*Mrs. Banning*), Howard Lally (*Joe Tipping*), Rochelle Hudson (*Virginia Banning*), Vera Allen (*Janet Carmaker*), Tempe Pigotte (*Grandma*), Elizabeth Patterson (*Aunt Patricia*), Ralph Morgan (*Dr. Verney*), Andy Devine (*Larry Ward*), Nora Cecil (*Aunt Emily*), Patsy O'-Byrne (*Susan*), Effie Ellsler (*Aunt Myra*), Veda Buckland (*Mary*), Helen Freeman (*Helen Upjohn*), Robert Parrish.

SYNOPSIS

George Bull, the town doctor in a little Connecticut community, has his hands full with a paralyzed young man, a typhoid epidemic (caused by the rich family of the town, the Bannings, and their lumber mill), babies to deliver, confused teenagers to set straight, a persistent hypochondriac, and his own courtship of the widow Carmaker. Sometimes more as Will Rogers than as the character he is playing, Dr. Bull solves all these problems, including the miraculous curing of the paralyzed man with experimental cattle medicine, and, with Janet Carmaker, leaves the ungrateful town which has just "voted" to replace him.

JUDGE PRIEST (1934)

CREDITS

Production company: Fox. *Director:* John Ford. *Producer:* Sol Wurtzel. *Scenarists:* Dudley Nichols, Lamar Trotti; from stories by Irvin S. Cobb. *Photographer:* George Schneiderman. *Music:* Samuel Kaylin. 80 minutes. Released, October 5.

CAST

Will Rogers (*Judge William "Billy" Priest*), Henry B. Walthall (*Rev. Ashby Brand*), Tom Brown (*Jerome Priest*), Anita Louise (*Ellie May Gillespie*), Rochelle Hudson (*Virginia Maydew*), Berton Churchill (*Senator Horace K. Maydew*), David Landau (*Bob Gillis*), Brenda Fowler (*Mrs. Caroline Priest*), Hattie McDaniel (*Aunt Dilsey*), Stepin Fetchit (*Jeff Poindexter*), Frank Melton (*Flem Tally*), Roger Imhof (*Billy Gaynor*), Charley Grapewin (*Sgt. Jimmy Bagby*), Francis Ford (*Juror No. 12*), Paul McAllister (*Doc Lake*), Matt McHugh (*Gabby Rives*), Hy Meyer (*Herman Feldsburg*), Louis Mason (*Sheriff Birdsong*), Robert Parrish, Grace Goodall (*Mrs. Maydew*), Ernest Shield (*Milan*), Paul McVey (*Trimble*), Vester Pegg (*Herringer*).

SYNOPSIS

During election time in a Civil War–conscious Kentucky town of 1890, Bob Gillis, a mysterious figure in the small community, assaults a man for insulting Ellie May, an orphan girl, whose lack of "family background" make her an unacceptable wife for Jerome Priest, a new lawyer just returned home. Thanks to Judge Billy Priest, it is revealed during the trial that Gillis is Ellie May's father, and his heroism in the Virginia Regiment redeems both of them from social disgrace. Billy wins the election, reunites the father and daughter, and makes it possible for Jerome and Ellie May to marry.

STEAMBOAT ROUND THE BEND (1935)

CREDITS

Production company: Twentieth Century-Fox. *Direc-

tor: John Ford. *Producer:* Sol M. Wurtzel. *Scenarists:* Dudley Nichols, Lamar Trotti; from story by Ben Lucian Berman. *Photographer:* George Schneiderman. *Art director:* William Darling. *Set decorator:* Albert Hogsett. *Music director:* Samuel Kaylin. *Editor:* Alfred De Gaetano. *Assistant director:* Edward O'Fearna. 70 minutes. Released, September 6.

CAST

Will Rogers *(Dr. John Pearly)*, Anne Shirley *(Fleety Belle)*, Eugene Pallette *(Sheriff Rufe Jeffers)*, John McGuire *(Duke)*, Berton Churchill *(The New Moses)*, Stepin Fetchit *(George Lincoln Washington)*, Francis Ford *(Efe)*, Irvin S. Cobb *(Capt. Eli)*, Roger Imhof *(Pappy)*, Raymond Hatton *(Matt Abel)*, Hobart Bosworth *(Chaplain)*, Louis Mason *(boat race organizer)*, Charles B. Middleton *(Fleety's father)*, Si Jenks *(a drunk)*, Jack Pennick *(Ringleader of boat attack)*, William Benedict *(Breck)*, Lois Verner *(Addie May)*.

SYNOPSIS

With a newly acquired steamboat-cum-floating-wax-works show, Dr. John Pearly sells his cure-all elixir along the Mississippi. His nephew Duke is accused of murder, and only one eyewitness can prove it was self-defense. Dr. John and Fleety Belle, the swamp girl Duke loves, set off down the river to find him before Duke is hanged. They become involved in a race for Duke's life and the steamboat itself, and use the sure-fire elixir, the waxworks, and most of the boat itself to fuel their win.

THE SUN SHINES BRIGHT (1953)

CREDITS

Production company: Republic. *Director:* John Ford. *Producers:* John Ford, Marian C. Cooper. *Scenarist:* Laurence Stallings; from stories "THE SUN SHINES BRIGHT," "THE MOB FROM MASSAC," "THE LORD PROVIDES," by Irvin S. Cobb. *Photography:* Archie Stout. *Art direction:* Frank Hotaling. *Set decorators:* John McCarthy, George Milo. *Music:* Victor Young. *Editor:* Jack Murray. *Assistant editor:* Barbara Ford. *Assistant director:* Wingate Smith. 90 minutes. Released May 2.

CAST

Charles Winninger *(Judge William Pittman Priest)*, Arleen Whelan *(Lucy Lee Lake)*, John Russell *(Ashby Corwin)*, Stepin Fetchit *(Jeff Poindexter)*, Russell Simpson *(Dr. Lewt Lake)*, Ludwig Stossel *(Herman Felsburg)*, Francis Ford *(Feeney)*, Paul Hurst *(Sgt. Jimmy*

Bagby), Mitchell Lewis *(Andy Redcliffe)*, Grant Withers *(Buck Ramsey)*, Milburn Stone *(Horace K. Maydew)*, Dorothy Jordan *(Lucy's mother)*, Elzie Emanuel *(U.S. Grant Woodford)*, Henry O'Neill *(Jody Habersham)*, Slim Pickens *(Sterling)*, James Kirkwood *(Gen. Fairfield)*, Mae Marsh *(old lay at ball)*, Jane Darwell *(Amora Ratchitt)*, Ernest Whitman *(Uncle Pleasant Woodford)*, Trevor Bardette *(Rufe, leader of lynch mob)*, Hal Baylor *(his son)*, Eve March *(Mallie Cramp)*, Clarence Muse *(Uncle Zach)*, Jack Pennick *(Beaker)*, Ken Williams, Patrick Wayne.

SYNOPSIS

THE SUN SHINES BRIGHT is a remake of much of the same material as JUDGE PRIEST (1934). In spite of the impending election, Billy Priest takes on the defense of a black boy accused of rape, and leads the funeral procession of a prostitute whose return to town, and death, bring the town secret to light. Lucy Lee Lake is united with her grandfather, General Fairfield, and is engaged to the reformed Ashby Corwin. Billy Priest wins the election and the forces of the Confederacy thus triumph over the carpetbagger, Maydew.

When working with Will Rogers, John Ford encouraged him to improvise and change dialogue to better fit Rogers' own personality whenever possible, and this comfortable, creative working relationship is probably responsible for the wonderful, relaxed feel of the films. But equally important and in no way contradictory, the charac-

Will Rogers in *Judge Priest.*

Dr. Bull: Small town America of the early 1920s.

Judge Priest: Small-town America of the 1890s.

Relaxing on the set of *Judge Priest:* left to right, Will Rogers, John Ford, Stepin Fetchit, Hattie McDaniel.

ters Rogers plays in all three films are immediately recognizable as Fordian heroes, caught between the forces of individualism and social commitment.

Doctor Bull (1933) is set in small-town early 1920s America, *Judge Priest* (1934) is set in 1890s, carpetbagged Kentucky, and *Steamboat Round the Bend* (1935—the last and biggest budgeted of the three) also takes place in the 1890s, but although the small-town populism is part of the ideology of the picture, it is largely set on the Mississippi River rather than in a small town. Rogers, in the first two, is a public servant of a kind—a doctor in *Doctor Bull* and a judge in *Judge Priest*—who is in danger of being turned out of office during the course of the film. This threat, which is the form the film's "evil" takes, comes from outside the community in *Judge Priest*—it is the Northern carpetbaggers who are stirring up the town and trying to get the Confederates thrown out of office. They lose the election, and order and social organization is returned to the town.

The social world of Judge Priest is a good one, where evil threatens from without and can be exorcised by the Fordian hero represented by Rogers, whose commitment to his society is his driving force, and who can withstand the demands it makes of him. This film, of the three, is set most clearly in the past for the main character. His sexual energy is released because his wife and children are dead, and the town thus becomes the focus of his energy. Billy's nephew Rome (Tom Brown) becomes his surrogate in the courtship of Elly May (Anita Louise), with the film dissolving from the young couple to Billy's memory of his wife. Rome is thus the most direct beneficiary of Billy's efforts on the town's behalf, but the entire community is "healed" of its tensions and divisions.

Doctor Bull proposes a similar premise: the town is trying to get rid of Dr. Bull (Will Rogers) for "moral" reasons and a crisis strikes that only he can handle: a typhoid epidemic. Indeed, only Dr. Bull and *not* a city doctor can bring them through it: his powers of medicine are nothing short of miraculous and come (as with other Ford heroes) from Dr. Bull's role as the loner in his society. He uses experimental cow serum to cure a young man of permanent paralysis and inoculates the children against the epidemic; but since the evil has come from within the town in the form of the greed of the rich—their mill became diseased

The social world of *Judge Priest*—all members are integrated into the final parade.

Misty shots of the young lovers of *Judge Priest*—Rome and Elly May—are reminiscent of Billy Priest and his wife.

Vera Allen as the widow Janet Carmaker pleads with the townspeople not to replace Dr. Bull as town health official.

and started the epidemic—and the moral pettiness of many in the community, Dr. Bull leaves the town at the end of the film. Like antisocial heroes of Westerns, he leaves the corrupting influences of socialized men to be free, even though control of those forces does lie within his reach. The difference here is a sexual one—he breaks out of a lifetime of repression through the harassment of the very community he has been sublimating his sexuality to serve, and finally asks the widow Carmaker (Vera Allen) to marry him. They leave together: their future is ahead alone, not behind in the town as was Billy Priest's.

In *Steamboat Round the Bend,* the alienation from society (first as represented by organized towns and second by family and sexual contexts) is the most complete of the three films. Rogers, as Dr. John Pearly, wants to be a steamboat captain with his nephew Duke (John McGuire) who meets him with a swamp gal in tow. Dr. John is clearly offended, but when Duke is imprisoned for a murder he committed in self-defense, John and Fleety Belle (Anne Shirley) become a team both in the winning of the steamboat race and the eventual freeing of Duke. There is more erotic physical contact between John and Fleety Belle than with Duke, and he identifies the girl with his dead sister whom he loved (hence his great love for her son Duke) by giving the girl her clothes as he tells her his sister was the most beautiful woman he ever saw. They finally get Duke released through the crisis of the steamboat race, during which they have to actually consume the boat itself for fuel, and John's Pocahontas medicine for combustion in order to win. Duke is released in more of a gesture to their winning than to his innocence. The lack of ritualized "justice" is indicative of an attitude (as in *Dr. Bull*) toward society in which the threat to the characters comes from within the small-town Americana setting. The second, more personal, stage of John's alienation is then set: the last shot of the film is Duke and Fleety Belle in the steering compartment of the steamboat with John, his back turned to the camera and to the young lovers (who represent the world) alone on the deck. His most basic alienation is sexual, and this makes *Steamboat* the most lonely of the three pictures; in *Doctor Bull,* when Bull left the evil little town he had served most of his life, he took his new bride with him. But John is totally alone at the end of *Steamboat.* Like Tom Doniphon in *The Man Who Shot Liberty Valance,* he has contributed to his own alien-

31

Will Rogers as Dr. John Pearly and Anne Shirley as Fleety Belle try to protect Duke from the law in *Steamboat Round the Bend.*

Duke—John McGuire—in prison as his only chance to prove his innocence seems lost.

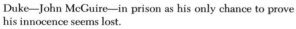

Steamboat Round the Bend.

33

The courtroom in *Dr. Bull:* a theatrical camera style.

On the set of *Judge Priest.*

ation by providing his own rival who takes "his girl" away.

Visually, the three films are fairly unexpressive and consistent in their use of the theatrical precepts of camera style. Most clearly in *Doctor Bull,* the film begins "setting the stage" with a long shot on the railroad station, which pans over to the town itself, and the film ends with an opposite similar shot of the town, panning over to the train upon which Dr. Bull and his new wife are leaving. Will Rogers is introduced as on stage, entering a medium long establishing shot of his home, shot from an audience perspective, from stage right rear, and actually pauses for a moment as though to announce his presence to the audience and receive their applause. Throughout all three films, the camera is in service of the action, only rarely expressing a point of view.

In *Judge Priest* also, the film opens and closes with theater-like establishing shots: it opens in the courtroom on a close-up of Judge Billy Priest reading the newspaper, pulling back to reveal the entire stage upon which much of the film will be played. It ends on the parade, which has combined all the good forces of the town through Billy Priest's exorcising of the evil forces of the North, marching full front toward the camera in an enclosing, self-concluding long shot. There are many beautifully composed shots in *Judge Priest,* as in all Ford's films, but they tend to be inanimate in the Will Rogers trilogy.

Steamboat Round the Bend opens on the boat, establishing the locale and stage of the play, and ends with the boat, having resolved the conflicts and leaving John alone and alienated, even from his family. There are again, a few evocative shots, like the one tracking shot (one of the few subjective shots in the three films) down the aisle of the courtroom finding John and Fleety Belle alone in the pews after Rome has been convicted. The issue of point of view is the primary one that links the three pictures visually: throughout, the point of view is that of a theater audience, even when that audience is taken inside and allowed to move around. The camera is generally in the service of narrative action, not emotional expressivity. It is this largely stable, eye-level, third-person point of view camera style that characterizes the three pictures, and it is the use of a greater emotional intensity of visual style in *The Sun Shines Bright* that deeply personalizes the later film.

Between *Judge Priest* (1934) and *The Sun Shines Bright* (1953) the subject matter remains

The courtroom in *Judge Priest:* David Landau as Bob Gillis is accused by Senator Horace K. Maydew (Berton Churchill).

Judge Priest: Elly May with Rome and with an unwelcome suitor. The camera style is stable, eye level, and from a third person point of view.

the same, but the narrative dynamic becomes more interior, the formal qualities are more expressive, and the entire visual and thematic mise-en-scene is darker in *The Sun Shines Bright.*

In *Judge Priest* an imperfect but stable and good community is presented. There is nostalgia here for a lost past in the form of the pre–Civil War times, which lie with few of the trappings of defeat on the little town. It is a time remembered of glories and greatness, and its outcome does not seem to have imposed any serious restrictions on the town. We are as near to Ford's perfect society in America in this film as we are in *Drums Along the Mohawk:* in the Western there is more of a future to look forward to, and in *Judge Priest* more of a past to look back on, but in both films we are as close to that *actual* past that so many of Ford's Westerns and Americana films take as their point of reference.

The sense of time becomes much more complicated in *The Sun Shines Bright,* with both the original relation to the past of the town's late 1800s changed and the additional perspective of 1953 on the thirties, an almost inescapable tangent to a remake by the same author. In this case it is more than incidental: the use of Stepin Fetchit (as Jeff Poindexter) in both films would seem to indicate a comment on the earlier film. The Civil War plays both the same role it did in *Judge Priest,* that of a starting point for much of the comedy of the film and a well-spring of Southern glory, and a new role in *The Sun Shines Bright.* It is a marker of defeat which brought in the carpetbaggers who threaten the town and its entire way of life. The election is between a carpetbagger lawyer who wants to dishonor the somewhat fragile Southern glory, and he employs methods that leave no doubt about the fate of the town in his and his cronies' hands. There is truly something at stake there, unlike *Judge Priest,* in which the outcome of the election has serious consequences for Billy Priest (Will Rogers), but generally few for the town. He stands for a more humane law than his opponent Maydew (Berton Churchill), with tolerance and an eye "more to the spirit of the law, not the letter," but Maydew is little more than a blustering fool. The Maydew (Milburn Stone) of *The Sun Shines Bright* is a potent danger, and removes much of the relaxed enjoyment of the society that gives the earlier film its gentleness.

Not only is the near-perfection of the late nineteenth century lost and only a memory in *The Sun*

The stable, good community of *Judge Priest.*

A similar unconflicted community in Ford's *Drums Along the Mohawk,* 1939.

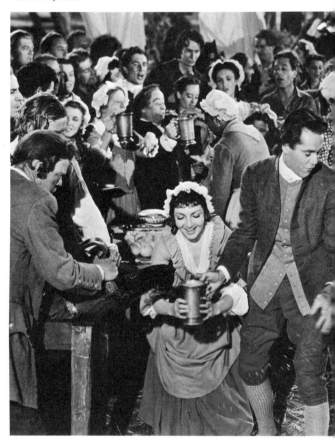

Stepin Fetchit plays Jeff Poindexter in *Judge Priest.*

Civil War loyalities—and adversaries—are kept alive in the southern small town of *The Sun Shines Bright.*

In *The Sun Shines Bright* something is truly at stake.

Ford creates the troubled memory of the near perfection of the nineteenth-century community in *The Sun Shines Bright.*

Shines Bright, but there is an additional element of alienation (both for the audience and the artist) in that the 1930s are gone as well. The time in which the artist could create such a balanced and gently virtuous and happy society has been lost, and in the 1950s this rather thirtyish film becomes even further removed from our ability (and his own) to see Ford's America as he saw it in the thirties.

The nostalgia in *Judge Priest* which gives the film much of its depth and nearly all (except for the greater but vaguer past of the Civil War) of its meaningful roots in its own past, comes from Billy Priest's dead wife and child. In nearly the only formally thoughtful scene in the film, he gazes at his wife's picture, is reflected in its circle to emphasize his spiritual nearness but physical distance from her, and his loneliness is almost unbearable. It is this loneliness which deepens him and makes his character so receptive to the hidden value in others: it is the same kind of loneliness of Nathan Brittles (John Wayne) in *She Wore a Yellow Ribbon.* It fills him with something so personal an audience can find the same loneliness in themselves, and gain solace from their own isolation through his. The present lovers in *Judge Priest,* Rome (Tom Brown) and Ellie May (Anita Louise), dissolve into the past; becoming Billy and his wife, and his need for his own past becomes so strong he goes to visit her in the graveyard, talking to her with as much ease as Brittles does to his wife Mary.

John Wayne as Nathan Brittles at his wife's gravesite in *She Wore a Yellow Ribbon.*

37

This is nostalgia of a very specific sort. Billy Priest's looking backward in the 1934 film and his present sense of loss are rooted in something very specific and understandable, and most importantly, something from *without* himself. It does not lessen the power of that past, but its specificity, which he makes clear to Rome when he tells him about the loneliness of his life as Ellie May is framed in the background of the shot, separates it from the nostalgia of *The Sun Shines Bright.* In the later film, there is nothing specific (except a vague sense of the time itself and his part in it) to relate Billy's alienation to. His sadness, which seems much more pressing than that of the earlier Billy Priest, is all-pervasive and comes from within himself. It comes from a sense of loss of something so nameless it cannot even be represented except through his intimate connection with the past of the town, with death, and with a tolerance in dealing with those the rest of the town consider unworthy.

The final scenes of *Judge Priest* and *The Sun Shines Bright* illustrate their relationship to their time and their Billy Priest. In the early film, after the triumph of the election in the afternoon, Billy Priest, with the minister (it is interesting to note that in the later film Billy actually *becomes* the minister of his people as he gives the funeral sermon for Lucy's mother) at the head of the parade, pulls in the black sheep Bob Gillis (David Landau), and all are joined in a tracking shot, moving forward in hope and triumph. In the later film, however, Billy Priest sits alone at night after hearing the results of the election. The people of the town pass by his house in the darkness and pay their respects to him, first the Blacks, to whom he seems closer than to the good people of the town who wanted to lynch the boy. Then the rest of the people come, singing and offering him their thanks, but he remains alone in the darkness and cannot join them; and they remain visually separated into class and color-defined groups. Lucy Lee (Arleen Whelan) and Ashby (John Russell) whose union is the only hopeful sign in the film, stand together and watch him, but even they cannot enter into his company, or bring him into theirs. He is alone, moved to tears by their friendship, but still alone.

The film ends with Billy walking away from the camera in darkness into his lonely house. He has not brought the same degree of harmony and unity to his town and to himself that characterized the earlier film. Like nearly all of Ford's later her-

The loneliness of Billy Priest in *The Sun Shines Bright* is deeper than in *Judge Priest* and unspecified; it comes from within and links him to the victims of the town.

Judge Priest—the triumph of justice and faith in the community as Bob Gillis is judged innocent.

Billy Priest literally becomes a lay minister at the prostitute's funeral.

The Victory parades: in *Judge Priest* Billy marches in the sunny afternoon, in *The Sun Shines Bright* he stands alone in the dark.

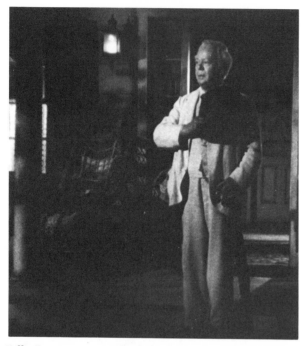

Billy Priest is unremittingly alone at the end of *The Sun Shines Bright.*

oes, his later Billy Priest is an individual who gives his life to his society, but cannot get back from it the value he requires. He becomes a solitary existential figure who acts from a sense of need and of self, not from any hope of fulfillment. And he remains alone. In the Westerns, what these men have lost is easier to represent: the women they love, which stand for any real connection to life itself, or the ability to believe in the very future they continue to build.

The darkness of the film is mirrored in the relationship of Lucy Lee and Ashby. There is a wildness in his past that we never know, but we feel it in his visual representation; e.g., the dark silhouette in his window. It makes him an outsider in the town and it casts a darkness over everything he does. Lucy Lee has a similar darkness: she lives with Dr. Lake and calls him "Daddy Lake," but knows he is not her real father. Her need to know her parentage does not come from a desire for social standing, but to know who she is in the most personal sense. In *Judge Priest,* Rome is without any kind of darkness in him: he comes home a new lawyer, jokes with Aunt Dilsey, and pursues Ellie May with no inner conflict. The only effect of her lack of a father is to make her the butt of crude jokes among the men and reduce her social standing so that Rome's stuffy mother will not permit the marriage. There is nothing from within the characters driving for the solution of the mystery, and no darkness to it when it does come out. Ellie May's father was once in prison, but distinguished himself in the Civil War, thus wiping out any previous dishonor. There is no stain on the lovers when their problems are solved, no lingering implications for the future.

The Sun Shines Bright is fraught with such implications. Lucy Lee's identity and its coming to light involve the entire town in a painful lancing of a very old wound, and only Billy's guidance through its cleansing bring the town to a "health" which is the resolution of all the narrative themes of the film. These themes are stated economically and linked visually by Billy in the first moments of the film: The first shot is of the steamboat with "Vote for Billy Priest" on it, a statement of the narrative structure which will provide the film with a problem and its resolution. The second shot is of Billy and Jeff balanced in a long shot of the town. Establishing this arena—the town itself —Ford cuts then to a medium shot of the two, still in balance and with black women in the background behind them. Thus Billy is immediately

The darkness of *The Sun Shines Bright* is mirrored in the relationship of Ashby and Lucy Lee.

Lucy Lee looks over Billy's shoulder at the key to her mysterious past.

...ee and the portrait of her parents.

The General assumes his rightful position as Lucy Lee's grandfather at her disgraced mother's funeral.

Lucy Lee's identity coming to light unleashes violence.

Billy Priest and Jeff Poindexter.

41

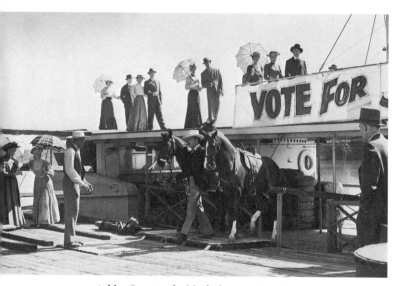

Ashby Corwin, the black sheep, arrives home.

Dorthy Jordan as the prodigal woman of shame returning home to see her daughter before she dies.

Billy Priest is the only one to recognize the dignity of Molly Cramp, society's outcast.

represented as the stability of the town and linked with its black members. Ford then cuts to a long shot of Ashby, then to Billy, and back to a medium shot of Ashby. His catalytic function is thus premonished, and the point of view we will share in the film is firmly established as Billy's.

Ford's vision has always included a notion of defeat and dishonor whose acceptance could dignify and purify the sufferer. Lucy's mother's (Dorothy Jordan) shame and alienation from the society dignifies her and her daughter when she returns in the face of it to see her daughter one last time. Ford's love of the South comes in part from the very nature of its defeat; but more from its characterization in his films as feminine. The qualities of beauty and dignity in the face of defeat, courage of a sort that does not come from possessing superior force, personal retention of honor and humility when society's dictates would not allow honor: these are the values Ford seems to hold most real, not the masculine values of the sort represented by military victory. This is realized in the funeral which joins not only the family, but the town itself and its past. This ritual unites all: the lovers, the family, the town, its glorious past in the Civil War, and is presided over by Billy, who even brings the prodigal Ashby to prayer on his knees. But it still leaves Billy Priest alone, perhaps because his identification and understanding of the ritual is greater than anyone's.

Billy of *The Sun Shines Bright* is more removed from his surroundings and closer to the poor and outcast of society than is the Billy of *Judge Priest.* It is to him that the doctor goes with his information about the dying woman (Lucy's mother), and only to him that the old general will talk. His connection with the past is not only one of sharing in its darkness, but of having the wisdom and tolerance to understand it. The people who are "good" and those who are "bad" are much less delineated in this later film. The people who walk in Lucy's mother's funeral procession are first the prostitutes of the town, then Lucy herself, and then Billy and Ashby. These first are the ones most lacking in social prestige, yet they have more value in Ford's world than the rest. This increasing distance between Ford's value of a character and his own society's value of him (except of heroes, whose value remains fairly constant) marks his increasing failure to believe that society can fill a person's needs which arise out of living in that society.

The lynch mob is representative of this society,

Billy is responsible for the joining of the factions of the town at the funeral: Lucy Lee and the prostitutes.

The funeral procession.

Billy with Dr. Lake and with the General: everyone goes to him with their trouble and loneliness.

and although they have come from north of town and do finally offer their apologies, their very existence in the film as an organized group of people (a masculine group) comments on the society to which they belong. It seems curious that, while remaining true to the racial sterotypes of the times (as does their representation in *Judge Priest),* in *The Sun Shines Bright* the black characters are, like prostitute Mallie Cramp (Eva March) and Lucy's mother, the persecuted people of the town for whom Billy Priest gives his finest and most personally dangerous efforts. The young black boy (Elzie Emanuel) in his innocence and the dignified Uncle Ples (Ernest Whitman) seem more crucial to Ford's image of the Black in the South than does the repetition of Stepin Fetchit in his role from the earlier film. The black women at the church who sing for the funeral may seem to fit a stereotype, but there is more dignity in their mass than in any white group in the film, and Ford's portrayal of this may seem awkward today. But when they pass Billy's house at night, there can be no doubt that they are among the film's most valued characters, along with the prostitutes, the suffering mother, and the orphan girl Lucy and her returned, reformed lover Ashby. Billy Priest is closer to these rebels and misfits than to the stable society of the town.

43

In the earlier film, the only socially reprehensible characters are the pompous Maydew and the snobbish Mrs. Priest, but they are shown to stand outside of the common run of the town, thinking themselves above it and in reality in need of a dressing down, which they get. But the point of reference in the early film is that normal society; in the later one it is the misfits. It is these very different groups that the Billy Priest of each movie is identified with, and that the artist himself is allied with.

The Sun Shines Bright is one of Ford's last films to be set in America without the distancing device of also being set in a more formal genre than Ford's own American mythology. It is therefore a kind of final statement on this kind of film, and is at the same time more personal (it is his favorite film) than the genre films, as it goes deeply into his own creation—first *Judge Priest* and the

Americana films of that period of his career, and then to the limits of his own feelings about America. In a film like *The Quiet Man* he escapes into the past of another country, which is more laden with the rituals and traditions that illustrate the depth of meaning a society has in the life of its people, but in *The Sun Shines Bright* he has dipped into his own past of feeling about this country, used his rituals of death, dance, family tradition, and the traditions of a Civil War to work through this final statement. It is a dark statement, in which a man finds too little in his society's values to validate his life. Even after bringing about the kind of unity and health that signified hope in *Judge Priest*, he remains alone at the end of this film, alienated visually from both the audience and from the community he nurtured: he moves into the past as it moves into the future he made possible.

The lynch mob—Billy saves them from their own violence.

44

The outcasts for whom Billy gives his all—and to whom he is the closest: Lucy Lee's mother, Molly Cramp, and the Blacks of the town.

The endistancing formal precision of *The Sun Shines Bright:* Ashby, Lucy Lee and the General.

The formal, icy beauty of the dance.

THE WHOLE TOWN'S TALKING

1935

Edward G. Robinson plays both the notorious gangster Mannion and the meek newspaperman Jones.

CREDITS

Production company: Columbia. *Director:* John Ford. *Producer:* Lester Cowan. *Scenarist:* Jo Swerling, from the novel by W.R. Burnett. *Dialogue:* Robert Riskin. *Photographer:* Joseph H. August. *Editor:* Viola Lawrence. *Assistant director:* Wilbur McGaugh. 95 minutes. Released February 22.

CAST

Edward G. Robinson (*Arthur Ferguson Jones: "Killer" Mannion*), Jean Arthur (*Miss "Bill" Clark*), Wallace Ford (*Mr. Healy*), Arthur Byron (*Mr. Spencer*), Arthur Hohl (*Detc. Sgt. Michael Boyle*), Donald Meek (*Mr. Hoyt*), Paul Harvey (*J.G. Carpenter*), Edward Brophy (*"Slugs" Martin*), J. Farrell McDonald (*WQarden*), Etienne Girardot (*Mr. Seaver*), James Donlan (*Howe*), John Wray (*Henchman*), Effie Ellsler (*Aunt Agatha*), Robert Emmett O'Connor (*Police Lieutenant*), Joseph Sawyer, Francis Ford, Robert Parrish, Frank Sheridan (*Russell*), Clarence Hummel Wilson (*President, Chamber of Commerce*).

SYNOPSIS

When a notorious killer escapes from jail, a meek newspaper clerk—his double—is reluctantly dragged into heroism, aiding in the killer's apprehension and discovering his own dangerous personality, which wins him the girl he has loved from afar.

It is impossible to discuss *The Whole Town's Talking* without reference to its production. It is a totally unsuitable film for Ford. It looks as though it began as a Frank Capra project (although Mr. Capra was never involved) and the script resembles a Capra script; the direction does not fit such a story and is definitely not in the best tradition of Ford. The narrative dynamic rests on comic twists, mistaken identity, police and bureaucrats as incompetent fools, and has a lightness that fits the *Mr. Deeds Goes to Washington* comedies of Capra but is never found in a Ford film.

The one element in the film that seems meaningful to Ford (and not exclusively—it appears in Capra's *It's a Wonderful Life*) is the idea that two totally different personalities exist in the same person. Jones and Mannion (Edward G. Robinson) are different characters, but both are played by the same actor and as the film progresses they get closer and closer to each other until they switch identities at the end. Jones is the tender poet whose love for his "Cymbeline" (Miss Clark, played by Jean Arthur) does not give him courage to approach her, so he steals her picture and sends her poems that she finds mushy and offensive. Our visual introduction to Miss "Bill" Clark is a tracking shot which leads her as she enters the office, tossing her cigarette away on the floor and bursting through the door on a wave of assurance and confidence. She is excited by the idea of a man like the killer Mannion, but when she realizes she is with him in Jones's apartment, she is terrified.

When Jones first learns he resembles the notorious killer, he looks at himself in the mirror, searching his face for clues to a killer character.

With the comic, classic visual motif of a man seeing his "shadow" reflected in a mirror, Ford creates the most visually exciting scene in the film. Similarly, when Jones sees Mannion in his apartment, they stand on the opposite sides of the room, light between them and darkness surrounding each one: they are the two sides of a reflection. The two grow closer together when they both author Mannion's life story for the newspaper. When Jones gets drunk, having been somewhat liberated by contact with his "shadow," his repressions leave him and he becomes the tiger Miss Clark suspected in him. He grabs her, kisses her, then leaves for an unheard-of afternoon off. Finally Jones takes Mannion's identity in order to save himself, Miss Clark, his aunt (Effie Ellsler), and Mr. Hoyt (Donald Meek). Mannion is killed by his own men, who think he is Jones, and the real Jones leaves for Shanghai with Miss Clark.

The Whole Town's Talking is a light, entertaining film. Its failing is not necessarily a major one: it is simply that when the credits say "directed by John Ford," one can confidently expect more than a light, entertaining film. This is one of the few films which will disappoint that expectation.

The comic, classic visual motif of a man confronting his "shadow."

Jones and Miss Clark.

Jones is center frame for nearly the first time after "capturing" Mannion.

Jones and his secret love "Cymbeline"—Jean Arthur.

Escaped gangster Mannion intrigues Miss Clark as his look-alike Jones looks on with envy.

PRISONER OF SHARK ISLAND

1936

CREDITS

Production company: 20th Century-Fox. Director: John Ford. Producer: Darryl F. Zanuck. Associate producer-scenarist: Nunnally Johnson, from the life of Dr. Samuel A. Mudd. Photography: Bert Glennon. Art director: William Darling. Set decorator: Thomas Little. Music director: Louis Silvers. Editor: Jack Murray. Assistant Directors: Edward O'Fearna. 95 minutes. Released: February 12.

CAST

Warner Baxter (Dr. Samuel A. Mudd), Gloria Stuart (Mrs. Peggy Mudd), Claude Gillingwater (Col. Dyer), Arthur Byron (Mr. Ericson), O.P. Heggie (Dr. McIntyre), Harry Carey (Cdt. of Fort Jefferson, "Shark Island") Francis Ford (Corporal O'Toole), John Carradine (Sgt. Rankin), Frank McGlynn, Sr. (Abraham Lincoln), Douglas Wood (Gen. Ewing), Joyce Kay (Martha Mudd), Fred Kohler, Jr. (Sgt. Cooper), Francis McDonald (John Wilkes Booth), John McGuire (Lt. Lovell), Ernest Whitman (Buckland Montmorency "Buck" Tilford), Paul Fix (David Herold), Frank Shannon (Holt), Leila McIntyre (Mrs. Lincoln), Etta McDaniel (Rosabelle Tilford), Arthur Loft (carpetbagger), Paul McVey (Gen. Hunter), Maurice Murphy (orderly), Jack Pennick (soldier who sends flag messages), J.M. Kerrigan (Judge Maiben), Paul Stanton (orator), Maurice Murphy (orderly), Whitney Bourne, Robert Parrish.

SYNOPSIS

After unwittingly aiding Lincoln's assassin, Dr. Samuel Mudd is condemned to life on an island prison in a mock court trial. An outbreak of yellow fever nearly decimates the island: Dr. Mudd regains both his dignity and his freedom when he saves both guards and prisoners.

Like Young Mr. Lincoln, Prisoner of Shark Island depends on our knowledge of certain versions of history for both its narrative logic and its myth-creating power. This history is recruited selectively to rewrite the myths. First is the legend of Lincoln as healer and unifier: the first scene of the film is the end of the Civil War. Lincoln (Frank McGlynn, Sr.), shot in low angle on a balcony, asks the band to play "Dixie," humorously claiming it as contraband of war. With the cut to the theater poster of the play with John Wilkes Booth, Ford underscores our knowledge of the fateful event with ominous music, and finally treats the assassination with the tenderness he reserves for his most beloved characters. As with the death of Mary O'Donnell in The Long Gray Line, we simply see the president's arm drop from the camera position behind. Not until he is dead do we approach him in a medium close-up full front, and that dissolves into a beautiful, immortalizing texture which is like a portrait. The fatherly, healing Lincoln is conjured, with only the comic grandfather (in a beautiful track back from close-up to long shot to reveal that he is lecturing only to his tiny granddaughter, Martha) to swear it never was a question of slavery, but only States rights. Dr. Samuel Mudd is quite reconstructed in his opinion of Lincoln as the commander-in-chief who defeated his beloved South, and sincerely tells Booth, "I guess Old Abe's all right after all. He's the only salvation we Southerners can look for—him and God's mercy." He even knows instinctively that Booth is not all right, saying he "smells of snakes" after the actor leaves his house. The Lincoln myth is thus maintained, even transferred to Mudd by virtue of his profession as healer which is the mainstay of Ford's Lincoln politically. But within that construct, Ford is then free to criticize the apparatus of law and of the North that he finds dehumanizing and brutal, using his Lincoln surrogate, Dr. Mudd, as its victim.

Ford creates a double knowledge, and focuses on process rather than action and narrative outcome in the same way he does in Young Mr. Lincoln, They Were Expendable, and other films. He begins Prisoner of Shark Island with a title that explains that Mudd was vindicated and his name cleared, so that we never have any fears about the outcome of the narrative: justice will prevail. Thus justice and law are separated, as they so often are in art which seeks to reconcile the actual workings of the society, and the ideals of that so-

Warner Baxter as Dr. Samuel Mudd in *The Prisoner of Shark Island.*

ciety: in other words, to create myth. In many films Ford criticizes this process implicitly and thus undermines it, but he was not so successful in this process in the early films, and *Prisoner of Shark Island* does not really contain such a critique except in certain moments. The law of the Yankee court has no pretentions: the prisoners are treated like dangerous animals, with hoods over their heads; dirty, rumpled clothes rob even Mudd of the class status his profession gives him. They are shackled, pushed and shoved, and Ford presents their trials ritualistically so that the outcome is known and the individual case has no relevance. The court of army men is told by its superior that the "object is not guilt or innocence, but to save the Union." They are to ignore trifling technicalities of law and that "obnoxious creation of law—reasonable doubt." As he walks to the window where a mob of rabble is yelling, he directs the court that "the voice of the court must be the voice of the people." There is no question of the role of justice in the courtroom.

There are two values in addition to that of doctor/healer which combine to make Sam Mudd a proper hero for the myth Ford weaves in this film. One is that of the South: Mudd is a "Southern gentleman" that even the rebellious, frightened black guards can recognize and trust. Trust means

obey in the film, and while it is entirely proper to criticize the racism of the assumption, it is necessary to recognize the kindly, paternal, committed, and responsible aspects of the attitude in a Fordian world view. The values of the South are most seen in the Mudd family, which is the other, perhaps primary unit of meaning in Ford's work—at least until late in his career. The little family of Samuel Mudd is a feminine one, with his beautiful long-haired wife, his feisty and lovely little girl, and nearly senile grandfather (Claude Gillingwater). They are composed as a family together threatened by irrational and brutal forces from the outside, and much of the saving wit and grace of the film resides in the boundaries of the family. Bert Glennon's breathtaking photography, which turns the Dry Tortugas prison into a fairyland of light and shadow, also creates beautiful depth-of-field integration in the Mudd household, a visual metaphor for the ease of space and play they have together which we see and feel in their joking interactions.

As the embodiment of the values of justice, the South and the family, and also as victim to their antithesis, Mudd becomes the agent of both his own salvation and that of the plague-stricken prison. Not only does he get the Blacks back to

The prison at Dry Tortugas: the guards show the new inmates the shark-infested moat.

work, he finally forces the supply ship to land, a feat outside the power of the commander of the prison. More importantly, Mudd becomes a sort of agent of nature, calling down a cooling storm which blows away the yellow fever. He completely subjects himself to the people who were his jailers, the storm, and his profession, to the point of total collapse, and is thus redeemed. Even the unbelievably sadistic guard who was his particular torturer wants to be the first to sign the pardon appeal for the doctor.

The reunion of the families—both Mudd and Buck—creates the closure that is particularly satisfying in a film with such a semicircular structure in which the end is stated in the beginning (Mudd vindicated) and the values violated in the beginning have all been reinstated: those of family, the South, justice, and the lack of legal process by which they have been reinstated (rather Mudd gives himself up to his tormentors, and thereby commands the forces of nature and justice itself) is far more ideologically dangerous than the 1930s racism of the film. It is the same kind of falsification as the end of the Civil War in the first scene of the film: the hero figure has joined opposing forces for their own good and the bloody process and its dark underlying reasons have been repressed.

Dr. Mudd during the yellow fever plague on the prison island; a doctor again in the crisis.

YOUNG MR. LINCOLN

1939

The vast majority of Ford's films actively deal with the creation of myth, or at least the value of myth. The Westerns are generally most direct, because the constructs of that genre are uniquely suited to the expression of American mythic values. *My Darling Clementine* is perhaps the most direct of all the Westerns, since it deals with a *known* myth: it is not simply expressing the values of the culture but rewriting the Wyatt Earp/Doc Holliday myth. This is also true of *Young Mr. Lincoln* which because of its historic/political relevance, becomes more weighted in its mythic expression that any other of Ford's films.

CREDITS

Production company: Cosmopolitan-20th Century-Fox. *Director:* John Ford. *Executive producer:* Darryl F. Zanuck. *Producer:* Kenneth Macgowan. *Scenarist:* Lamar Trotti, based on the life of Abraham Lincoln. *Photography:* Bert Glennon. *Art directors:* Richard Day, Mark Lee Kirk. *Set decorator:* Thomas Little. *Costumes by Roger Music:* Alfred Newman. *Musical director:* Louis Silvers *Editor:* Walter Thompson. *Sound effects editor:* Robert Parrish. 101 minutes. Released: June 9.

CAST

Henry Fonda (*Abraham Lincoln*), Alice Brady (*Abigail Clay*), Marjorie Weaver (*Mary Todd*), Arleen Whelan (*Hannah Clay*), Eddie Collins (*Efe Turner*), Pauline Moore (*Ann Rutledge*), Richard Cromwell (*Matt Clay*), Ward Bond (*John Palmer Cass*), Donald Meek (*John Felder*), Spencer Charters (*Judge Herbert A. Bell*), Eddie Quillan (*Adam Clay*), Judith Dickens (*Carrie Sue*), Milburn Stone (*Stephen A. Douglas*), Cliff Clark (*Sheriff Billings*), Robert Lowery (*juror*), Charles Tannen (*Ninian Edwards*), Francis Ford (*Sam Boone*), Fred Kohler, Jr. (*Scrub White*), Kay Linaker (*Mrs. Edwards*), Russell Simpson (*Woolridge*), Charles Halton (*Hawthorne*), Edwin Maxwell (*John T. Stuart*), Robert Homans (*Mr. Clay*), Jack Kelly (*Matt Clay, as child*), Dicky Jones (*Adam Clay, as child*), Harry Tyler (*hairdresser*), Louis Mason (*court clerk*), Jack Pennick (*Big Buck*), Steven Randall (*juror*), Clarence Wilson, Elizabeth Jones.

SYNOPSIS

Ford weaves Lincoln's youth, loss of Ann Rutledge, choice of law profession, and early cases into a mythic tapestry that resonates in our knowledge of the rest of the Lincoln history.

Henry Fonda as Abraham Lincoln.

Henry Fonda as Wyatt Earp in *My Darling Clementine:* Ford tells another known myth.

On the set of *Young Mr. Lincoln* with cinematographer Bert Glennon.

Springfield, Illinois: small-town America

The "high society" dance: Mary Todd in her environment.

Lincoln as both a character and a genre object has special relevance for Ford. From *The Iron Horse* (1924) through *Cheyenne Autumn* (1962) Lincoln's physical presence or spiritual presence in a photograph is conjured to indicate a paternal, unifying authority. He directs the adventurous steps that will unify the nation with the railroad in the silent film, and is a source of inspiration for the Secretary of the Interior trying to unite the Cheyenne nation with the powerful white nation in the last Western Ford made. He is inscribed with virtues of mediation, strength, authority, and a special kind of insight whose source is clear in *Young Mr. Lincoln.* Lincoln functions as a raison d'être even though he dies as the film begins in the *Prisoner of Shark Island.* Thus Lincoln is a central obsession with Ford. Through this film, which most centrally concerns the creation of the values that Ford ascribes to Lincoln, the use of the Lincoln myth in other films (and related myths like Wyatt Earp) is better understood.

Young Mr. Lincoln begins with the myth. The film opens on the poem, in which questions to which we know the answers are posed. We are thus alerted that a general *awareness* of the history (not simply the history itself) is going to be incorporated into the story, not ignored as in *My Darling Clementine,* where the story is played "straight" and not self-consciously set in the past. *Young Mr. Lincoln* assumes and depends on audience awareness of the myth, yet at the same time, it rewrites it according to Ford's special vision of Lincoln, his role in America's history, and the forces that directed Lincoln. The poem sets up two dynamics; one is a series of either/or questions, and the other is a limiting function—the film will act out the myth according to some principles and against others: it will be a rewriting, not a telling. What is left out or repressed in such a rewriting becomes fully as important as what is included, especially in a process as self-conscious as the one in this film.

Three actions are taking place from the film's beginning and must be separated before they can be clearly seen. First is the rewriting of the myth, second is the creation of values (and the negative aspect—the leaving behind of values and history that are normally part of the myth) to be affirmed by this rewriting of the myth, and third is the complex function of critiquing the first two. This third function, carried out at a formal level of visual style, is what makes the best of Ford's films so much richer than most: it both affirms and critiques the values by which we live.

The poem and backward-looking structure are not the only indications that knowledge of the myth on the part of the audience is assumed. In the first scene, in which Lincoln gives a speech (both to us and to the people in the film) his first line is, "You all know who I am." We do indeed know who he is—both in the film and in our history, and the comment calls upon both categories of knowledge, thus setting the self-aware mechanisms so necessary to the function into motion. The characterizations of Mary Todd (Marjorie Weaver) and Stephen Douglas (Milburn Stone) also rest on a knowledge of Lincoln *outside* the film but necessary to it. Thus the film relies on external knowledge of the myth, but through Ford's choice of determinants of the rewriting, the values of the myth are redefined. This retelling is experienced especially powerfully because it calls upon knowledge shared by the audience but external to the film. We become implicated in its reformulation as Ford directs us to selectively supply knowledge about the characters and their history.

The creation or recruitment of values is the ideological function of the film. Following the poem, this tends to be a series of binary oppositions, either/or choices, which immediately restrict the subtlety and nuance of the values represented. This is the usual ideological operation of myth: though the conventionalized, schematized representation of narrative, complexity and ambiguity are far less important than ritual. The narrative pattern of ritual (i.e., the nature - season rituals of death and rebirth that have both pagan and Christian examples of myth) must be constant, and schematized or abstracted from the complications of everyday experience. Thus they are nearly binary systems where operation masks contradiction and function often as a repressive force in a culture—the Catholic Church in Latin America, for example. Ford treats the Lincoln myth in this manner in the narrative, then critiques its ideological function formally.

In *Young Mr. Lincoln* this operation is represented graphically in the choices he makes: they are not masked but clearly represented, and all are immediately (because of our knowledge) recognizable as being determined, or operations of fate. The first is the acceptance of the law book from the mother (Alice Brady) in exchange for supplies, which not only is fated, but sets up determined, valued relationships: the mother is the giver of the law. The second determined choice is whether he will go into law: the spirit of Ann

Rutledge (Pauline Moore) and a stick "decide," but since we already know the outcome, this simply functions to further implicate Ann (and sexuality) in the decision. She then becomes another inscription in the Lincoln myth: a dead first love who retains important parts of a mythic hero is often part of the legend.

Lincoln's role as mediator is insisted upon in a series of oppositions. His first law case is handled with intelligence and finally force ("Did you fellas ever hear 'bout the time I butted two heads together?"), and all parties are satisfied in the end. The money which changes hands is exactly right for Lincoln's fee, and his unifying function has been introduced. A somewhat irrational aspect of that function has also been introduced—the case is resolved not simply "by the law," but by Lincoln's threat and ability to carry it out. At the fair, this unifying function is again illustrated: he will not decide between the two pies he is "judging," and simply keeps taking a bite of one, then an-

The system of exchange is established: the pioneer mother gives Lincoln books for trade goods.

53

Lincoln with the soon-to-die Ann Rutledge in her environment.

Lincoln's first case—a mixture of judicial insight and the threat of physical violence.

Lincoln "judging" the pies: refusing to choose.

other, as the scene finally fades out. His force and irrational character are also demonstrated, however innocently. He wins the rail-splitting and he cheats by using a mule to win the tug of war for his side. In spite of his profession, unifying fairness and calm, he is even at this point shown to be not dependent upon logical, rational, knowable precepts. He is further the unifier in the main drama of the film: he refuses to consider one son guilty and split the family, and it is here that Lincoln demonstrates his greatest insight. He doesn't win the case with fancy legal maneuvers but with divine inspiration via the mother, who gives him the almanac. This element of irrationality is an important aspect in the myth, but relative to history, perhaps the expected metaphor of the family for the nation is of even greater value in terms of its absence. This film about the great unifier and mediator (in harmony with Ford's vision of Lincoln) does not even mention what the majority of the audience might most easily associate with Lincoln the president: the Civil War and the tearing of the nation. Only his unifying function is suggested in his "innocent" playing of "Dixie." The *repression* of this violent aspect in the reworking of the myth and the inscription of its opposite value—unification—describes exactly the repressive ideological function of myth, and it is reversed on the formal level in this film.

Another important aspect of the historical myth which is repressed in *Young Mr. Lincoln* is that of the work process. Not only do we see very little of the political in this film (one speech, after which we do not even know or care if he has won the election; Stephen Douglas; and a few references to his career, past and future), but the process by which Lincoln becomes a lawyer and a politician is telescoped into the transition of a dissolve. The point is not that hours and years of hard work could have been shown, but that this repression leads to the second important variation of the myth. Lincoln is a mythological figure because of a special state of being, not a state of becoming. He is a passive, removed figure in the narrative from the first shot; he already *is* (in history, our knowledge, and in myth) at that moment and is very little different at the end. At one point in the trial he says, "I may not know much about the law, but I know what's right!" This is the crux of the myth: he *knows,* he *is.* he does not *learn;* that which he learns does him little good. But what he *knows* on intuition saves his clients, will win him Mary Todd over Stephen Douglas—who knows

Potential violence during the attempted lynching: Lincoln prevents it through force first, then persuasion.

Lincoln is abstracted through visual style to another level of representation.

Lincoln as an actor contemplating his own myth.

Politics in *Young Mr. Lincoln:* the process and its result are devalued.

law—and will take him to his fate on the abstracted hill of destiny. He has a special connection to God himself. In the Lamar Trotti screenplay he actually talks with God as he walks off at the end of the film. Thus his value comes not from his culture, but from above. He is essentially a visitor, like most mythic heroes, and certainly like Wyatt Earp in *My Darling Clementine*. In the absence of the political along with the painful Civil War and the process of work and achievement based in such a cultural process, these important elements of the historical myth become internal shadows of repression, and function to structure the narrative and its process of rewriting for the viewer. Lincoln thus becomes less a historical myth and more a cultural one, in which the facts of history which root the character in "becoming" are repressed, characteristics of greatness are detached from their generation, and a mode of being unrelated to social processes is defined.

Ford often uses Fonda for the mythic character who simply is—notably in *My Darling Clementine* and this film, less so but still strongly in *The Grapes of Wrath*. Fonda has the ability when directed by Ford, to express the strength, authority, but abstraction required by such a figure. He can seem detached, a sort of a divine vessel which forgoes real human contact (in *Young Mr. Lincoln* it is taken from him with Ann's death) in favor of divine contact. It is a passive, static, yet graceful and inspired position. Perhaps above all, it is characterized by *being* rather than becoming: the character is unchanged from the first shot to the last, and he is not affected in his decisions or actions by the motives, drives, or ideas of other people.

The narrative, then, is a standard one: the myth is rewritten to remove those problematic processes of work and failure; everything that does not affirm the values of the culture is repressed and the hero is removed from a historical context. The ideological operation offers knowledge as a divine gift, the repression of sexuality as a way to such divine gifts, mothers as handmaidens of God's word, and force as the right of those who know. It suppresses objection based on logic and work, and teaches us history is not a process of men and women but of larger-than-life *men* whom we can understand only on faith and acceptance. This is often the function of popular culture, to suppress and rework various myths and thereby to console, offer faith-based explanations, and repress those disruptive and sexual elements that would not fit well into a hierarchical society. There are many reasons films fill this function: the huge amount of money required to make them, thus giving the power structure a real stake in their impact on people, the ideological control exercised on both an implicit and explicit level by the people and institutions who control the money. But there is room for protest, or subversion, and it exists at the level of the form. A director can question and critique, and sometimes even condemn (as Douglas Sirk does in his melodramas of the fifties) the values offered by the narrative of the film. Ford's best films do this, and his later ones (*The Wings of Eagles, Seven Women, Liberty Valance*) often do it at the level of the narrative itself, which may be one part of the reason that they're so badly understood now and were ill-received when they were made. In *Young Mr. Lincoln,* like most of Ford's films of this time containing such a critique (*The Grapes of Wrath, How Green Was My Valley, My Darling Clementine*), the critique functions through a process of abstraction which involves the audience in a constant process of "becoming aware" of the work of the narrative.

The character of Lincoln, through whom this process is carried out, is abstracted and removed from the narrative of the film first by our awareness of the myth and Lincoln's "real" place in history. Further, music, composition, focus, acting, movement within the frame, and chiaroscuro all function to visually and emotionally remove Lincoln and create at least two levels (sometimes three) of which we are simultaneously aware. Lincoln seems to exist on a different level than that of the action of the film. He drops into the film to narrate (but not really *act* in—thus his posture of being is questioned) his own story from time to time, but is rarely fully integrated into the narrative of the film. He illustrates and comments on the film from without, often merely "watching over" the stylized action out of the events of his life, often "narrating" or walking through those events, but generally not belonging to the level of action.

The first view we have of Lincoln is premonished by low music. It immediately removes what will follow from the preceding level of pompous, overacted, tongue-in-cheek speechmaking; we see Lincoln reclining in a chair carving a piece of wood. The shot is an introduction, a static shot acquainting the audience with the actor who will play the part. In this case it is Lincoln who will play the part of Lincoln, immediately abstracting him from the rest of the film. He rises slowly, moving with the thoughtful deliberateness which will continue to isolate him from the rest of the film by the necessary slowing down of action that his movement dictates. He is getting into his part —we see the process of the actor preparing, but with the added dimension that it is for his role as himself that he is preparing. Throughout the film, most notably in the murder sequence and the trial scenes, Lincoln hangs nearly suspended on the side of the frame, watching the action, both to function as the determining influence which makes it possible and necessary, and to stand nearly motionless waiting for his cue. In the murder sequence he follows the crowd to the site without sharing their excitement, hangs back by the little family in his dark clothes and hat as the townspeople mill around in the background, and steps in at his cue to take his position in the narrative.

In the courtroom, Lincoln is often static, framing two sides of the shot by his dark outline. His foreground dominance is not part of the action, but determines it. In other shots, he moves restlessly on another level from the action of the trial, either above it (as when he goes up the stairs and leafs through some books with the trial going on around him, sitting down on the rail as though taking a rest from his role) or below it sitting down on the little steps that lead up to the jury box while John Felder (Donald Meek) is giving an impassioned speech. This movement is in opposition to the general movements of the court, as well as to the expected movement of his character within the scene. There are shots which compose Lincoln to resemble a bust of himself, and one in which he is draped horizontally across the frame while questioning a witness. This deliberate failure to conform to expected visual composition calls attention to the difference in the elements of the frame. The contradiction between what the narrative would seem to demand—formal courtroom composition—and what Ford presents us with visually requires the audience to become aware (to varying degrees), and thus constitutes a critique.

From the day Lincoln rides into town on a mule to set himself up as a lawyer (the scene itself looking like a highly stylized reenactment) his clothes set him apart from the rest of the people through chiaroscuro: he is abstracted in black and white with no gray at all; others, even when dressed in

black and white, contrast with his austerity. The costume itself is clearly a costume, with the stovepipe hat no one else wears a self-conscious prop in terms of the film. It is, however, primarily in the play of light and dark that his costume places Lincoln on a different level from the rest of the film: when he is first in his office settling a case the white of his shirt seems to collect light and glow with it, while the black of his vest contrasts it. In the night with his coat on he is appropriately like a spirit belonging to another world.

Lincoln is played with a detachment unmatched by any other character. In the courtroom scenes it is contrasted for humor (as well as for purposes of removing Lincoln from the level of action) with the overly enthusiastic and emotional investment in the case by the prosecuting

The courtroom drama.

Burning the barrels after the parade.

lawyer. With J. Palmer Cass (Ward Bond), the trap is set and sprung in a manner that underscores the process of acting out that Lincoln demonstrates through most of the film. His detachment from the action of the film is a part of the scene: Lincoln already *knows* (both the answers to the questions and the entirety of the story of his life). But there are moments in which Lincoln seems to forget his role in his life and simply plays or remembers the life. In the balcony scene

Selecting the jury: Lincoln "knows" who will be fair to his clients.

Lincoln visits the little farm of the pioneer family who have become his surrogate family.

with Mary Todd (Marjorie Weaver) he seems lost in memory as he gazes at the river (which has come to mean Ann Rutledge to him) and is framed with Mary just barely visible behind him. He seems not simply removed from Mary Todd and the dance into a reverie of *his own,* but also abstracted from the scene itself onto his level of Lincoln (rather than Lincoln playing Lincoln). It seems that not only has he forgotten Mary Todd for the moment, but he has forgotten the movie, the re-enactment of some of his life, in favor of his life itself.

As the film draws to a close, Lincoln becomes totally abstracted to the level he has functioned on through most of the film, and the level of action falls away. When he walks out of the courtroom toward the door where the "people are waiting" he is already removed from the people around him (even while he speaks to them). Mary Todd cannot quite touch him, and Stephen Douglas refers to history: they will be opponents again, and he will not make the mistake of underestimating Lincoln again. As Lincoln walks on, the people do not exist. We experience them as the actor does—hearing only their cheers, but the cheers are reserved for the "real" Lincoln. They have no place on the level the film is moving towards. Only the family appears once more to take their leave of the man and the myth, and then Lincoln walks off into the storm and even out of the film itself. Taking his place is a bust of himself, then the statue. The abstraction is total at this point; the "actor" Lincoln has returned to the level of statue and myth, having left it on one plane (but never moved from it on another) to narrate and illustrate this version of his story.

The constant split between Lincoln and the narrative is a self-conscious device which insists upon the necessity of becoming aware—of questioning both what is inscribed in the created myth and what is being repressed. Unlike Douglas Sirk, Ford is not clear in his denunciation of the ideology of the narrative (at least at this point in his career), but his insistence in visual terms that the viewer at least be aware of the process of mythmaking and the values affirmed and repressed is at least as powerful (if less easily articulated because it is visual) as those elements of the narrative which construct the myth. There is an unusual amount of freedom to perceive both functions simultaneously in Ford's films, and to experience them according to the subjectivity of the viewer.

After the murder: all the participants are there, but only Lincoln can find the real relationships between them.

THE GRAPES OF WRATH

1940

CREDITS

Production company, 20th Century-Fox. *Director:* John Ford. *Producer:* Darryl F. Zanuck. *Associate producer-scenarist:* Nunnally Johnson, from the novel by John Steinbeck. *Photography:* Gregg Toland. *Art directors:* Richard Day, Mark Lee Kirk. *Set decorator:* Thomas Little. *Music:* Alfred Newman. Song, "Red River Valley," played on accordion by Dan Dorzage. *Editor:* Robert Simpson. *Sound:* George Leverett, Roger Heman. *Sound effects editor:* Robert Parrish. *Assistant director,* Edward O'Fearna. 129 minutes. Released, March 15.

CAST

Henry Fonda (*Tom Joad*), Jane Darwell (*Ma Joad*), John Carradine (*Casey*), Charley Grapewin (*Grandpa Joad*), Dorris Bowdon (*Rosaharn*), Russell Simpson (*Pa Joad*), O.Z. Whitehead (*Al*), John Qualen (*Muley*), Eddie Quillan (*Connie*), Zeffie Tilbury (*Grandma Joad*), Frank Sully (*Noah*), Frank Darien (*Uncle John*), Darryl Hickman (*Winfield*), Shirley Mills (*Ruth Joad*), Grant Mitchell (*guardian*), Ward Bond (*policeman*), Frank Faylen (*Tim*), Joe Sawyer (*accountant*), Harry Tyler (*Bert*), Charles B. Middleton (*conductor*), John Arledge (*Davis*), Hollis Jewell (*Muley's son*), Paul Guilfoyle (*Floyd*), Charles D. Brown (*Wilkie*), Roger Imhof (*Thomas*), William Pawley (*Bill*), Arthur Aylesworth (*father*), Charles Tannen (*Joe*), Selmar Jackson (*inspector*), Eddie C. Waller (*proprietor*), David Hughes (*Frank*), Cliff Clark (*townsman*), Adrian Morris (*agent*), Robert Homans (*Spencer*), Irving Bacon (*conductor*), Kitty McHugh (*Mae*), Mae Marsh, Francis Ford, Jack Pennick, Peggy Ryan, Wally Albright.

SYNOPSIS

Returning home from prison, Tom Joad finds his family and others like them driven off their small tenant farms by large companies who can farm vast tracts of land more economically. The Joads, with Casey, the preacher who lost his calling, make the difficult journey to California, but once there find the promises of work empty. They finally find work, only to realize they are strikebreaking. Tom discovers Casey is a leader of the strikers, and when the owners kill Casey, Tom takes up his role. He leaves his family to do labor work, and they go on with faith in "the people."

The basic unit of emotional value in Fords' oeuvre, which is threatened and must be affirmed through some process during the course of a film, is some variation of the family. It is often a military family: the army in the cavalry picture, the navy in *The Wings of Eagles* and *They Were Ex-*

On the road: the family of *The Grapes of Wrath.*

Jane Darwell as Ma Joad and Dorris Bowdon as Rosaharn.

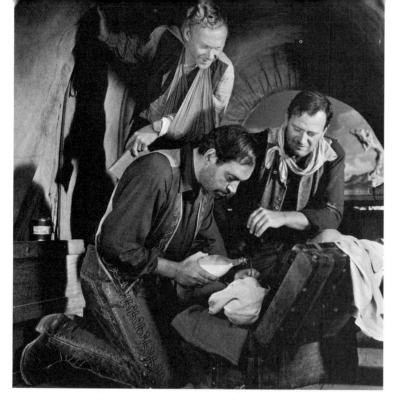

The makeshift family of Ford's *Three Godfathers*, 1948, with Harry Carey, Jr., John Wayne, and Pedro Armendariz.

The nuclear family in harmony with the environment: *Drum Along the Mohawk*, 1939.

The road: generally vertical, describing a path west and into the future.

pendable, sometimes a national family: the Cheyenne nation in *Cheyenne Autumn*, a combination of the Irish nation and a nuclear family in *The Quiet Man*, sometimes a makeshift family which is formed to create meaning where none exists, as in *Three Godfathers* and *Stagecoach*. In the early pictures, like *Drums Along the Mohawk*, the nuclear family (represented in *Drums* by Gil and Lana Martin) is in harmony with the larger context of society (i.e., the building of a community in the wilderness). In the later pictures, the nuclear family is in conflict with and nearly destroyed by the structured context, as in *The Wings of Eagles* and *Rio Grande*. The society cannot fill the needs of individuals within it, either inside or outside of the family context. In some of Ford's darkest pictures, the social structure of value fails altogether for the characters with whom we identify, and the family construct—even so self-fulfilling a construct as the wartime navy in *They Were Expendable*—cannot redeem it.

In *The Grapes of Wrath* the basic unit of the personal family is threatened by economic and spiritual terrors which it must overcome by transforming itself into an abstracted notion of class instead of the nuclear family unit. The Joad family itself must be broken apart (through Grandpa's (Charley Grapewin) then Grandma's (Zeffie Tilbury) deaths, through family members leaving, and finally, by Tom's (Henry Fonda) departure in order for the larger structure of class to be forged, and this abstracted notion of class unity is an expression of the political, religious, and mythical levels of the film. It is remarkable that out of one of the bleakest books written on America, Ford was able to create a populist vision that is less conflicted in its resolution than nearly any of his films after 1939 and most of those that came before.

The mythology of *The Grapes of Wrath* is insistently American, yet functions also at the level of a religious and political ritual structure. The road metaphor illustrates both these levels: while it is abstracted through visual representation to stand for the road into the future, traveled by an entire class of people, it is also specifically Route 66 across America. The visual abstraction is carried out first by its constant vertical compositional lines in the frame—our first view of the film is an extreme long shot of the vertical road which nearly bisects the frame. Tom (Henry Fonda) as a faceless, nameless, everyman walks down the middle of the road. This composition extends and enlarges the significance of the recruited (from reality and from our shared mythology) significance of the road, and the frequent use of similar compositions continues this process. The pattern of travel also becomes abstracted as the Joad family moves across the United States: Ford continually begins a new leg of the journey with a long shot of the truck on the road, cuts to a closer long shot of the family, and then moves in for the specific action required by that scene. These sequences, coming at regularly increasing intervals throughout the film, form a visual pattern which indicates repetition beyond that which is shown. Through this pattern their journey is expanded to represent all Okies leaving home, and even to modern man's alienation when he and his family are uprooted from the land. The real road signs from New Mexico, Arizona, California, and the faithfulness to the physicality of such a journey root the parable in a specific American consciousness, and the two levels of the metaphor function simultaneously.

The last shot of the film carries on the journey towards unity visually with a final image of the road which represents the future illuminated by the beautiful sunset and marked by a sign post center frame. It is an abstracted image, as the whole movement of the film has been one of abstraction from a physical reality to a mythic one, in which the metaphor of the road combines with the political and religious level shift to express the unity and survival of an entire class through the journey of one family.

The music of *The Grapes of Wrath* is made up entirely of American folk tunes: the credits roll over "Red River Valley" and "Home on the Range," both of which occur with other traditional songs throughout the film. This too serves to root the film in its specifically American context, and to refer to a past which is our shared mythology represented in the songs and music.

The entire concept of the family—its roots and its identification—undergoes radical transformation through the course of the film. Muley (John Qualen) expresses the concept of the family as defined by its land: he cannot leave it and goes mad when forced to alter his relationship to his land. The film cuts back from the wild animal eyes of Muley, lighted from below in the dark, to a flashback of his family losing their land. This exterior scene is lighted in high key, flat, natural light, emphasizing the contrast with the earlier, crazed scene of Muley. In the final shot of this

The Joads on the road: homeless, rootless and alienated from the land.

"The road" is specifically Route 66.

61

Muley: the very low-key lighting on his face and unbalanced composition immediately characterize him as a little crazy.

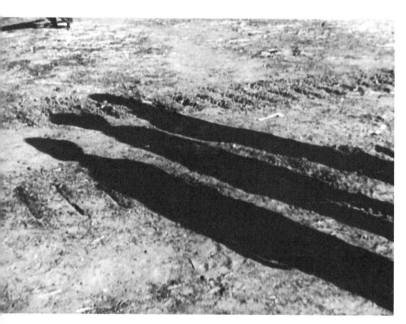

Muley's family as mere shadows representing the thousands thrown off their land.

Grandpa has to be dragged off the land; here shadows encircle and threaten him.

scene, Ford pans from a medium long shot of the family down to their shadows as the Caterpillar rolls over their flattened house. Their experience comes to stand for the experience of all dispossessed tenant farmers. Only those who can survive being uprooted from the land can travel the road into the future: Grandpa wants to be left behind on his land, and is framed in a circle of light with the rest of the family (who will force him to leave) as dark, ghostlike shadows around him. He does indeed die within a day of being uprooted from the land, and his last gesture is to take a handful of earth. Grandma dies next, in a gesture of sacrifice for the continuation of the family as Ma (Jane Darwell) disregards her impending death and the rituals that should surround it for the sake of the family traveling across the desert and into the future.

Ma articulates the landbound concept of family that must become a thing of the past: she tells Tom that when they were on the land, the family had a boundary to keep them together. Without it they are drifting off, and dying, and the family is losing the structure which gave it the value it possessed in the past. Through the journey a new concept of family is being forged, one which must destroy the old, but which will be better able to cope with the problems raised by industrial and agrarian development and progress.

The family unit is inadequate to deal with the forces that cause its destruction: from the very first representation of the banking interests, they are impersonal, removed, out of reach of the farmers. The man who tells Muley to get off his land remains in his car, simply another agent like the car itself or the Caterpillar tractors, immobile and not responsible. Ford cuts back to the man in the same machinelike pose—removed from the land by his car—from shots of the family on the land. He is a visual constant in contrast to their changing defensive positions, but like the Caterpillar operator who comes to fell their house, he is simply a representative, not "someone to shoot." The huge, impersonal, economic and all-pervasive nature of the problem renders the family impotent, and in order to deal with it at all, a new form of unity must be created. It is the work of the film to carry this out at the level of class.

The changing, mechanized world is represented by cars (as the headlights seeking out Muley, Tom and Casey [John Carradine] as they hide out on Joad land) and by the Caterpillars. The montage of their march across the land is in low

The Joad family at Grandpa's gravesite. The old man could not survive off the land.

The rejoining of the family: from the excited, animated close-ups of Ma and Tom, Ford cuts to a delicately formal greeting in meeting shot.

Muley's flashback: the banker, an agent of the machine, blocks off and dominates the composition.

Muley's family: static and helpless in the face of the impersonal threat.

Muley and the land: "being born on it, working it, and dying on it—that's what makes it our'n, not a scrap of paper!"

The caterpillar tractor montage is Russian in its extreme low angles and dynamic movement.

The advance of the machine on the helpless farmers.

angle, building image after image to give power and strength to the machines. The emotional sum of these shots is infinitely greater than the parts because of the montage construction. When a neighbor appears as the driver of the tractor, it is as though he were swallowed up by the machine; the structure of its dynamic determines him rather than the reverse.

The agents of economic interests are always characterized by their relation to cars: they have a control over mechanization that the Joads (with their continually breaking-down truck) do not. In the labor camp the Joads first encounter the labor contractor and a policeman sitting on a car, surrounded by the workers. It defines their difference visually by separating them. The car is a more direct agent of the violence of oppression when it is driven at top speed through the crowd, oblivious of their safety, directly at the camera. It is an image of rape, and indeed, a *woman* is killed.

The visual lines of the film carry out this same theme of the relation of the characters to their environment. In the epic, Ford's usual narrative mode, the characters determine the environment; it is an expression of their actions and inner motives. It is significant of the modern movement in narrative that the characters are at the mercy of immutable environmental forces. In *The Grapes of Wrath,* horizontal and vertical lines compose traps and barriers to the people who have no means by which to alter them. They are combined to form an environment that is unyielding and not subject to the control of the characters. Tom especially, as representative of his class, is constantly trapped in constructions which block him off from the side, the back, and the front. In the camp when he wants to take a walk, in extreme close-ups when police or inspectors threaten him, in the scab labor camp where the long lines of houses block off the sides and horizons of the frame, Tom is constantly cut off by the lines of the composition. In one such composition of a close-up of Tom, the framing pushes his head against the top of the frame and grips it in a visual vise comprised of the car's rear-view mirror in the front and the intersection of lines behind him. Only in the government-run camp are the lines open and unconfining.

Thus *The Grapes of Wrath* is a remarkably "modern" film, in which the characters do not determine the narrative dynamic through their actions and personalities, but in which a truly radi-

cal critique of the possibilities of individual action is questioned and the need for new concepts which are difficult, painful, and leave certain traditions behind is affirmed. The traditions are not simply ignored, but deeply mourned. As in mythical ritual, the process of mourning relieves some of the pain of leaving. When Ma is preparing to leave her home, Ford extends the scene in depth but not in screen time by cutting back to various close-ups of Ma as she goes over her possessions. In a particularly poignant shot, she looks sadly into the past through her reflection in an old mirror, holding up earrings. Ford holds on the shot, then cuts to a medium shot as she give these, too, up to a past she must leave behind.

Representatives of the owners—and agents of the machine they never leave—dominate and control the camp visually.

The police car cuts viciously through the transient camp.

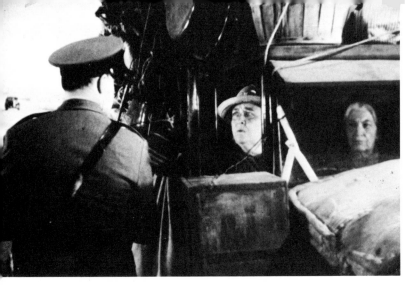

When Ma is framed with the inspector, she is dominated by his bulk and authority, but when Tom is in a similar composition, they have a more "equal" visual relationship. His ability to take on the burden of rebellion is thus established visually.

Tom caught in a visual vise of intersecting lines—the visual representation of his trap becomes more pronounced during the film.

While still mourning the loss of the family and its land as the basic structure of society, Ford nonetheless maintains the need for new concepts of work, class and land. The long shots of huge orange groves are not bounded by entrapping lines, and offer a hope for a future relationship to the land for the people. The class of workers will have the same relationship to the land that the family of farmers had to theirs; and this implies a structure and power to the working class that has its roots in a Marxist analysis of the relations of production.

The political and religious issues of the film are quickly combined in the person of Casey. He has "lost his calling," recognizing that there are no clear-cut moral issues outside the material base of people's relation to their world. There is no right or wrong, he tells Tom, "They's just what folks does." As the firm economic structure of the society around him collapses, so does his faith. The problems of the land cannot be solved by any easy, local answer, and he is too responsive to the real needs of his people to preach a doctrine which ignores their suffering, which he recognizes as economic, not moral, in origin. Thus when asked to pray for Grandpa, he prays for the living, not the dead, and Ford cuts to a shot of the children who are the future. Casey ceases to be a minister of God, and in the killing of a woman because the one worker asks for minimal rights in the camp, he becomes a minister of the people. He (and Ma, for different reasons) doesn't look back when the Joads are leaving their land, for his future lies in the labor work of California: he leaves behind only his lost faith.

Casey is a Christ figure, as even his initials J.C. indicate, and following Christian mythology, he is martyred to his cause. He takes the place of the so-called troublemaker when the woman is killed, happy and smiling for the first time. Later, he is killed for his labor work, but not until he passes his mission on: Tom has been linked to Casey by their "outsider" status from the very first scenes, and in the final ones before Casey dies, they are further joined through lighting and composition. Tom is fated to take Casey's place, which he does first by the "mark" of his conversion—the wound which will identify him as one of the strikers. Thus the religious aspects of the film are first secularized by Casey, and then further shifted to the level of myth by their focusing in Tom, who has been the outsider and the potential mythical hero from the beginning.

Tom in another visual trap: the flashlight beam reveals and threatens him.

Ma leaving her memories behind.

Casey is the searcher for his lost faith.

The huge, ordered farms of California.

Tom is increasingly abstracted into the mythical leader of his people.

When the Joads learn there is no work in town, Tom walks into close up, carrying the focus with him. Responsibility rests on him.

Tom is a tiny figure silhouetted in the glorious panorama—he now represents an entire class of people and has ceased to be Tom Joad: he is a mythical figure.

In the construction of the mythical hero, Ford used not only the visual devices of lighting, camera angle, and movement open to a director, but also the iconography of actors and their personas. Henry Fonda's persona is suited to representing the hollowed-out, mythic hero who is capable of being filled with meaning beyond that of a specific character. In *My Darling Clementine* he is abstracted to represent mythical forces in the West, and in *The Grapes of Wrath* he plays a similar role. Through the film, his status as outsider (he is first introduced as a released murderer returning home) remains intact even when reunited with his family. The primary device for maintaining this distance is to frame Tom separated from the rest of the family: he often walks into close-up from a medium shot of the family, carrying the focus with him. At the end of a scene Ford generally cuts to or focuses on Tom. This both distances him from the rest of the family and implicates him in the action of the scene: when it has been one of injustice, which it generally is, Tom thus becomes implicated in the solution. He is thus formally fated to take Casey's place as spiritual and actual leader of the movement.

In the final sequence of the film, there is a shift of levels back to the beginning: Tom first emerged as the faceless figure on the vertical road, and he leaves in a similar composition: he is in long shot, walking away from the camera as he first came towards it. The "I'll be there" speech expresses verbally his break already premonished visually with the family and its implications for a larger concept of family. Tom has thus become the secular Christ figure, dispersed over the entire class of workers: he tells Ma he'll be there when a child is hungry, when injustice is done, when men are forced to strike. He must lose his specificity (his own identity) to take on this larger one, and Ma must function as the agent to give it to him. In earlier scenes in which he talked of leaving, the camera cut between them expressing their disagreement, but in their final scene together they are in two-shot, as Ma finally understands what he must do. Having taken up Casey's burden of leader of his people, he must sacrifice his personal family connection.

This is a move to a larger unit class from the family, but it is also another giving up of identity, which is unique to Ford. The earlier, landbound concept of family is feminine in Ford's universe. It is specifically through its feminine character that the family takes on the nurturing values which are at one with its relation to the land. Women are the constant, the "stream of life" as Ma describes it to Pa (Russell Simpson). They live continuously, whereas men live in a series of jerks. Like the South of *Rio Grande, The Horse Soldiers,* and other Ford films, the family of *The Grapes of Wrath* is warm, nurturing, continuous, the carrier of tradition, and feminine. And like the South, it is fated to be destroyed by the war (the Civil War in the Westerns) and by progress. A less rich, more mechanized, masculine structure (the Northern government of carpetbaggers in the Americana pictures) of social order must be given way to, for only in its new and discontinuous hardness, its willingness to give up tradition and emotional value, can the problems of modern alienation be controlled.

It is Ma who holds the family together, a burden she shares with Tom when he comes back. She is directly responsible for Grandma's unacknowledged death, and a camera movement renders this explicit. When they are in the inspection station, the camera pans from a close-up of Grandma, even now dead, to a close-up of Ma, urging the men to let them go across. Later, she shares this burden with Tom but still excludes the rest of the family. This sharing is carried out visually as they approach the "promised land." The old truck must be pushed the last part of the journey, then Pa steps out in long shot and the film cuts to a long shot from his point of view of the valley. All of the family run to see it except Ma, whose point of view of their backs we share, involving us in her position. The film then cuts back to her: she is separated from the rest of them by the horizontal fence in the lower part of the frame, and by the long, low angle which places her far back in the composition. She is isolated from the rest of the family by the terrible burden of knowledge she has taken on herself, sacrificing Grandma so that the family could cross the desert without the interference a dead body would certainly cause them. She then sits in medium shot on the running board; her direction of sight seems to be looking for some means of integration with the family, and the weight of the composition throws the viewer's attention as well towards the family off in the distance looking at the valley. Ford then cuts to the shot of Ma alone again, then to a closer shot in which Tom detaches himself from the group and walks toward her, still in long shot. He joins her in the earlier composition of Ma by the truck in medium shot, and Ma rises to

Grandma's death: Ma's responsibility is emphasized visually by the flashlight beam in her face.

The responsibility structure of the family: Ma, carrying Grandma's death alone, cannot join the others until Tom joins her and shares the responsibility.

Strikers' families: literally behind bars.

Ma and Pa: "We're the people."

walk into low angle medium close-up. Tom thus shares her knowledge and the integration is expressed visually. He has the ability to be a support to her, and with that Ma assumes her full importance as she walks into a low angle close-up with Tom behind.

The government camp is a heaven for the Joads and for their class. In it they can be a family again, and Ford uses his iconographic integrating sign of a dance to illustrate the safety and ritual aspects of the camp. But this is only an island, one which Tom must choose to leave in order to carry on with his work. He and the family would have remained safe there, but it becomes a political decision to leave, an indication that the local level populism is not enough of an answer to deal with the forces that threaten the class of workers. The outside is too strong structurally for the camp to fully defend itself against, and the economic base of the oppression of the workers is not adequately dealt with in such an isolated structure, given the enormity of the outside world which has been described visually and thematically as an oppressive trap for the entire class of people.

Ma accepts the new definition of family based in class in her "We're the people" speech, which identifies the Joads as archetypes of the poor of America. This marks the end of their journey insofar as it has an end: the shift in the concepts of the family from the personal to the class, through the agencies of the economic and the political, unifies the film on visual and thematic levels, making it one of the most far-reaching and powerful statements about the relationship of the personal to the political and religion to myth in all American art.

In the last shot, the entire journey is abstracted and the movement of the film is unified on a mythical level.

70

TOBACCO ROAD
1941

The "poor white trash" of *Tobacco Road:* Gene Tierney as Ellie May, Charley Grapewin as Jeeter Lester, and Ward Bond as Lov Bensey.

Jeeter Lester—poised between dignity and degeneration.

CREDITS

Production company: 20th Century-Fox. *Director:* John Ford. *Producer:* Darryl F. Zanuck. *Associate producers:* Jack Kirkland, Harry H. Oshrin. *Scenarist:* Nunnally Johnson; from the play by Jack Kirkland and novel by Erskine Caldwell. *Photography:* Arthur C. Miller. *Art directors:* Richard Day, James Basevi. *Set decorator:* Thomas Little. *Music:* David Buttolph. *Editor:* Barbara McLean. *Sound effects editor:* Robert Parrish. 84 minutes. Released: February 20.

CAST

Charley Grapewin (*Jeeter Lester*), Marjorie Rambeau (*Sister Bessie*), Gene Tierney (*Ellie May Lester*), William Tracy (*Duke Lester*), Elizabeth Patterson (*Ada Lester*), Dana Andrews (*Dr. Tim*), Slim Summerville (*Henry Peabody*), Ward Bond (*Lov Bensey*), Grant Mitchell (*George Payne*), Zeffie Tilbury (*Grandma Lester*), Russell Simpson (*Sheriff*), Spencer Charters (*employee*), Irving Bacon (*teller*), Harry Tyler (*auto salesman*), George Chandler (*employee*), Charles Halton (*Mayor*), Jack Pennick (*Deputy Sheriff*), Dorothy Adams (*Payne's secretary*), Francis Ford (*vagabond*).

SYNOPSIS

The poor white trash of Tobacco Road maneuver each other for food, a car, and a wife.

The unusual mixture of broad comedy (including parody of those values Ford treats most seriously throughout his career) which often borders on the cruel, and yet essential dignity of Jeeter Lester (Charley Grapewin) and his wife Ada (Elizabeth Patterson) in their refusal to leave their land, has been difficult for audiences and critics—then and now—to accept. The proposed reasons are many: the stage play contains much broader sexual humor that had to be somewhat repressed

in the film, although Ford certainly makes the nearly silent, sensual Gene Tierney as Ellie May seem the embodiment of titillating degenerate sexuality. The "unreality" of the characters might come across better on the stage than through the intimacy of film, especially with Arthur Miller's lush photography. Perhaps in 1940, following *The Grapes of Wrath* (with which it is invariably compared), *The Long Voyage Home,* and followed by *How Green Was My Valley,* all deeply serious pictures, people were not expecting the unique, perverse, and conflicting sensibilities of *Tobacco Road.*

The film begins with a backward-looking narration by Jeeter on Tobacco Road years ago—a time when people and land were rich and great together. "All that they were, and all that they had, is gone with the wind and the dust." This sadness and loss is echoed when Jeeter and Ada talk about their children, who never write and whose names they can't quite remember. The values of family so prevalent in Ford seem also gone with the dust. The old folks are unremittingly alone at the end—Ellie May is gone, Grandma (Zeffie Tilbury) has wandered off, and no family ties even to the land are represented as enduring. Dude (William Tracy) berates his parents without mercy, telling them gleefully that they will be thrown off their land. Thus what has been most valued in Ford's artistic vision is meaningless and even cruel in this film; nearly all values are inverted. Only dignity and individualism, which are difficult to recognize in the face of the parody, are left intact.

The degeneration of the poor white trash of Tobacco Road includes greed and theft from relatives—even one's own children: Jeeter steals the turnips from Lov Bensey (Ward Bond) and tries to sell Dude's and Sister Bessie's (Majorie Rambeau) car. No one works, and in spite of the banker's analysis that individual farming of this land cannot be profitable, the people are presented as lazy and irresponsible). Practical values are perverted: Dude cares only for the car horn and within one day has reduced it to a wreck. Bessie spends every cent of her money and has none left to save Jeeter and Ada from the poor farm. Human values are even more parodied: Lov can't understand the relation between his wife Pearl running off and his treatment of her; Dude marries for the car, religious sister Bessie marries for barely repressed lust. The poor folk of Tobacco Road are like children, and it is somehow appropriate (if grating) that Captain Tim (Dana An-

Opposite page), The dignity, loneliness, and poverty of tobacco road is made achingly beautiful by Arthur Miller's cinematography.

The joining of Sister Bessie and the Lester family—more through the car than through the marriage.

Family loyalties: Jeeter Lester tries to steal and sell Sister Bessie's car, Lov Bensey floors Duke, and Lov's turnips are stolen.

drews), son of Captain John, is a paternalistic, fond, but stern provider to Jeeter.

It is not the film's intention that these characters be taken seriously, but it is difficult to remain in a farcical sensibility when the formal aspects of the film are "serious" and deeply beautiful. The mise-en-scene of a film always informs the narrative at the very least and enriches, critiques, or creates another level of expression at the most. In *Tobacco Road* the two are clearly in unproductive conflict. The visual style is in harmony with the serious moments in the film: when Jeeter and Ada talk of their children; when they walk toward the poor farm in the twilight. It enriches their dignity and utter resistance to any change which is not on their own terms, and it softens the bleakness of the alienating individualism and the loss of all family ties in the film. It does more for their retention of dignity and beauty than does the script, and through this treatment they become characters we can love and understand. But the broad humor of the rest of the film is not well served by such a style. *Tobacco Road* was made during a period of Ford's career characterized by an almost expressionistic style. The exaggeration of lighting, shadow, and drama at the formal level is a rich technique that lends grandeur. It can enlarge and deepen the emotional qualities of the film, providing a nonverbal articulation which can resonate in a viewer, adding a mythic and a deeply personal dimension at the same time. In *How Green Was My Valley, My Darling Clementine* and *The Grapes of Wrath* this style is most fully able to inform the entire film, and these are among Ford's very finest films. *The Informer* and *The Fugitive* are the most expressionistic of Ford's works, and in these films the visual style sometimes is so overwhelmingly powerful that it cannot inform the narrative but only observe it. The problem with *Tobacco Road* is not with the material or censorship, but lies in the basic, profound and above all unproductive contradiction between the material and its presentation, in the formal dimension of the film. This tension leaves the mise-en-scene beautiful but empty and nearly meaningless, informing only a few scenes: the material is out of harmony with itself and its audience.

The beauty of the visual style is at odds with the narrative— Duke throws rocks at his mother.

74

The mise-en-scene is in unproductive conflict with the comic, farcical narrative.

Slim Summerville as Henry Peabody—hiding out from Sister Bessie.

Jeeter and Ada Lester facing the poor farm—the material of *Tobacco Road* is out of harmony with its presentation.

THE LAST HURRAH

1958

CREDITS

Production company: Columbia. *Director-producer:* John Ford. *Scenarist:* Frank Nugent; from the novel by Edwin O'Connor. *Photographer:* Charles Lawton, Jr. *Art director:* Robert Peterson. *Set decorator:* William Kiernan. *Sound:* Harry Mills. *Recording Supervisor:* John Livadary *Editor:* Jack Murray. *Assistant director:* Wingate Smith, Sam Nelson. 121 minutes. Released: November.

CAST

Spencer Tracy (*Frank Skeffington*), Jeffrey Hunter (*Adam Caulfield*), Dianne Foster (*Maeve Caulfield*), Pat O'Brien (*John Gorman*), Basil Rathbone (*Norman Cass, Sr.*), Donald Crisp (*the Cardinal*), James Gleason (*Cuke Gillen*), Edward Brophy (*Ditto Boland*), John Carradine (*Amos Force*), Willis Bouchey (*Roger Sugrue*), Basil Ruysdael (*Bishop Gardner*), Ricardo Cortez (*Sam Weinberg*), Wallace Force (*Charles J. Hennessey*), Frank McHugh (*Festus Garvey*), Anna Lee (*Gert Minihan*), Jane Darwell (*Delia Boylan*), Frank Albertson (*Jack Mangan*), Charles FitzSimmons (*Kevin McCluskey*), Carleton Young (*Mr. Winslow*), Bob Sweeney (*Johnny Degnan*), Edmund Lowe (*Johnny Byrne*), William Leslie (*Dan Herlihy*), Ken Curtis (*Monsignor Killian*), O. Z. Whitehead (*Norman Cass, Jr.*), Arthur Walsh (*Frank Skeffington, Jr.*), Helen Westcott (*Mrs. McCluskey*), Ruth Warren (*Ellen Davin*), Mimi Doyle (*Mamie Burns*), Dan Borzage (*Pete*), James Flavin (*police captain*), William Forrest (*doctor*), Frank Sully (*fire chief*), Charlie Sullivan (*chauffeur*), Ruth Clifford (*nurse*), Jack Pennick (*policeman*), Richard Deacon (*Plymouth Club director*), Harry Tenbrook, Eve March, Bill Henry, James Waters.

SYNOPSIS

Irish-Catholic long-time Mayor Frank Skeffington (Spencer Tracy) runs for one more term, thus mobiliz-ing the forces of old, Protestant money (the aristocratic members of the Plymouth Club) against him and his reforms for the poor. Skeffington asks his nephew Adam (Jeffrey Hunter), a fence-sitting sports writer, to "observe" this "last hurrah," which ends in failure even though his opponent, Kevin McCluskey (Charles FitzSimmons) is nothing more than a comic, ineffectual puppet. Skeffington has a heart attack following his defeat, and dies surrounded by his friends (and some enemies). He comforts them as he dies, leaving the world of the film an empty place indeed without his presence.

The passing of a time of greater struggle, greater possibility, greater value, and above all, greater men than the present is capable of bringing forth, is the theme of some of Ford's most wistful, gently moving films: *She Wore a Yellow Ribbon, How Green Was My Valley, The Man Who Shot Liberty Valance,* and *The Last Hurrah. The Last Hurrah* does not have the bitterness and irony of *Liberty Valance,* nor is it emotionally devastating as is *How Green Was My Valley.* Thematically it has most in common with *She Wore a Yellow Ribbon,* which also is temporally situated at the very edge of the time whose passing it chronicles and mourns. Visually, it is the darkest and most enclosed of any of these films, reminiscent of *How Green Was My Valley,* but lacking the soft quality of the darkness in the earlier picture. This may have more to do with the difference in the "look" of the two studios for which the films were made, *Valley* for 20th Century-Fox, which was not noted for its dark, crisp blacks, and *Hurrah* for Columbia which was; but whatever the reason, there is a perceptual effect resulting from intense contrast between light and dark in *Hurrah* that stylizes the film.

The Last Hurrah is surrounded by darkness. It opens and closes the film, beginning with the credit sequence (which is composed of scenes from the film of the campaign parade at night) and ending with Frank Skeffington's (Spencer Tracy) death, also at night. There are constantly dark foreground objects imposing themselves in the frame, and vertical lines of dark walls, curtains, and doors blocking off the scene within the frame. Darkness itself, in addition to dark objects, functions in this way, as when the scene is lighted to be illuminated from the middle of the set backward, leaving the foreground dark. Spencer Tracy himself offers physical manifestation of this contrast when he is dressed in a dark suit, framed against a dark background, with his white hair

Spencer Tracy as the old-time politician Frank Skeffington in *The Last Hurrah*.

The Last Hurrah is surrounded by darkness: the victory parade for McCluskey.

glowing in the strongest light existing in the frame. This all gives an impression of the past: in his office when he calls Adam (Jeffrey Hunter) in to see him, Skeffington is surrounded by organized vertical and horizontal lines of darkness. His office seems to exist out of time, and when Adams leaves, turning to say good-bye to his uncle standing in the door, Skeffington is metaphorically "framed in the past" with his office behind and on the sides of him, situating him from the camera's viewpoint behind Adam in enveloping darkness.

This darkness does not necessarily forbode sinister or unhappy events; it roots the film in the past, and encloses it there. Like the portrait of Skeffington's dead wife Kate which dominates his home, it does not function to cast a pallor over the scene, but simply to draw him backward into a time we know only through these remnants of it still existing in the present. Skeffington is of a time that is rapidly vanishing: he tells Adam that his kind of politics, and he along with it, is on the way out. Unlike the passing of a better time in *The Sun Shines Bright,* however, in which the "old-time" politician wins the election but is isolated in heart-wrenching loneliness at the end of the film, in *The Last Hurrah* the representative of that better time does not mourn his passing (and he does die, unlike Billy Priest in the earlier film). The loss is for the city and the people of the present, not for the man who has known a more meaningful life, who is confidently leaving it, surrounded with love and without regrets.

An impression of the past is created through the use of darkness, enclosed interiors, and classical balanced composition.

Adam (Jeffrey Hunter) puts the traditional rose before the portrait of Skeffington's deceased wife Kate which dominates the home.

Skeffington's campaign: back rooms and deals.

Skeffington is usually center frame and encircled by contrasts in light and dark: he is the center of the universe of the film.

We feel that loss through the point of view of Adam, who is the one left alone and without comfort at the end of the film. His observation of the "last hurrah" is required in an interestingly self-conscious way: not only does the filmaker need such a sensibility (a man of the present but without the direct ties to the politics of the present, or the persons of the story), but the character (Skeffington) himself requires it. Skeffington calls Adam in to observe his campaign as though he were aware it will end as it does. Adam alone of the characters in Skeffington's political entourage or in his family possesses the detachment and capability to filter the experience and understand the significance of it. He is a confident, aloof character in the beginning, with no real allegiance to either side. Through his observation of Skeffington's life and purpose, he comes to love the old man and finally participates in his life at the end of the film. Adam alone feels the defeat coming: as the others cheer at early returns and explain away the implications of poor results, Adam isolates himself from the rest of the company as he feels the disaster coming.·

Like the child in *How Green Was My Valley,* Adam does not become part of the picture until the very end, when he takes over Skeffington's tribute to his wife by putting a fresh rose under her portrait. His detached observation and gradual involvement mirrors our own, and as a narrative device the character is an inspiration. Like the lieutenant who loses the girl at the end of *She Wore a Yellow Ribbon,* his increased loneliness and suffering brings him closer to the old man. Adam is totally alone at the end of the film: his wife is incapable of responding to the poignancy of Skeffington's death, and aside from his friendship with his uncle, he has been presented as a solitary character. His is the loneliness we also feel with the death of the past we yearn for; like him, we must go on living.

The values of an imagined past are thus affirmed through Skeffington, and those of the present found wanting through Adam and the action of the film. *The Last Hurrah* is in many ways closer to the Will Rogers Trilogy than to the other political films, as the magnetic central character is left behind by a lesser order than he once was responsible for. The values of small-town America, with its humanism, individualism, and justified trust in its political process and politicians, are gently mourned as the new order takes over.

As in previous films, the passing of the better

Only Adam among Skeffington's supporters senses the inevitable defeat.

Junior—Skeffington's son—is a monumentally lesser man who brings his "shy" girlfriend to campaign headquarters.

The comic "dirty deal": Skeffington wins a bank loan for low-income housing by making the moronic son of his adversary honorary Fire Chief.

life is a passive act. The present which will supplant it is not more forceful, more powerful, or even mildly attractive compared with the past. No exterior force causes its passing; rather, it is inherent in the character of nostalgia for a better time that the time slip through one's fingers. The time itself becomes old-fashioned and the impotence of that which will take its place neither hastens nor slows its passing. This is represented by the young men who will take over. Skeffington's son (Arthur Walsh) is nearly moronic, not only unaware of his father's rock-foundation-like role in his own life, but so irresponsible and unresponsive to his father's needs that he forgets to vote for him, and then desecrates Skeffington's campaign headquarters with his "shy" girlfriend. When the going gets rough, he makes an excuse and leaves, just as he cannot accept the fact of his father's death until it is upon him and devastates him. Similarly, Norman Cass Jr. (O. Z. Whitehead), son of Skeffington's most powerful and articulate opposition (in contrast to the ridiculous Amos Force, played by John Carradine), is even more moronic, if possible, than Junior. He lisps, is addicted to fancy hats, and provides the fodder for his father's defeat on the issue of a hospital loan.

The political rival who defeats Skeffington, Kevin McCluskey (Charles FitzSimmons), is depicted as a pompous fool, dishonest in the simplest and most fundamental terms. He deceives the public as to his "happy home," posing with a dog he neither owns nor likes, with a portrait of the Cardinal on his wall. He does not defeat Skeffington, the time simply passes to a more superficial present demanding silly, inconsequential men to carry it out. It is perhaps a weakness of the film that the present which will take over is shown to be so very vapid, and the old politician —who we are told is hated by many people for his "old-style" methods, and who loses the election— is so totally dedicated to the cause of the people and their welfare.

There is some indication that the lack of a precarious background breeds lesser men. As Monsignor Killian (Ken Curtis) tells the Cardinal (Donald Crisp), the best of the young men are no longer going into politics. Once it was one of the few ways the poor immigrants could rise out of the slums, as Skeffington did, and their challenge to the "bluebloods" fired them with life and energy lacking in the young men of the present. The encounter at the stodgy old Plymouth Club, while hilariously weighted against its members, pro-

79

The campaign: Skeffington and his people.

vides a contrast in class that mirrors the struggle of the political race. Now that the people have the city because of the efforts of Skeffington and men like him, there is an air of unconcern which will return it to the aristocrats. This rather naive, idealistic, Populist-oriented political analysis is both contradictory in the film itself (making Skeffington an untarnished hero of the people, yet chronicling their choice of another, lesser man) and without much intellectual weight, but its only function is as a narrative device: in actuality, Skeffington loses because his time is passing and the present is no longer worthy of him.

Skeffington's past is the one being mourned in *The Last Hurrah.* We know it through him and through Adam's love for him, and we glimpse it in his trip to the slum in which he was born. Wistful lullaby music plays as he and Adam stand in the darkness, enclosed totally by it, and talk of the men who came from this beginning with him. We see it in his wife's portrait and his love for her memory, which includes Maeve (Dianne Foster), Adam's wife, who resembles Skeffington's wife Kate. Skeffington's defeat is the beginning of the close of this past. It is foreshadowed in the campaign headquarters, where darkness seems to in-

trude on the young men in their white shirts counting the votes, and it stands before us as Skeffington stands, white hair glowing, before the TV cameras. He calls them in closer to him and announces he will run for governor; it is a "triumphant defeat," as the TV commentator calls it. Then he walks home alone, and McCluskey's triumphant parade passes him by going in the other direction, a visual metaphor for Skeffington and his time receding into the past as the present marches by. It is a powerfully moving shot as the dark, solitary figure moves counter to the raucous, bright parade, and we move with the solitary figure, both because the camera does, and because we know what the victory parade stands for. This is the first step in Skeffington's death, which is unlike any other death in Ford's films. In *The Sun Shines Bright* the underlying fear, alienation, and sense of dread comes from the elemental fear of death, which is never faced in the film directly. In *The Last Hurrah,* Skeffington's proximity to death is made clear throughout the film—he is constantly near it and it holds no dread for him. He is totally confident and in control in the presence of death: at Minihan's wake he moves with ease between the dead man (commenting on how much

Skeffington's last hurrah: a glorious defeat.

Skeffington at Minihan's funeral: he is comfortable in the presence of death.

better he looks than he ever did in life), the widow (comforting her by falsifying his memory of her husband and helping her without offending her Irish dignity by offering her money his wife "left" her when she died), the political implications of the event, the hilarious old woman (Jane Darwell) who is a regular at funerals, and finally the mortician, whom he "convinces" to charge the widow only $35 for the lavish funeral he has put on without consulting her. He is neither awed nor shaken by death, and our sense of comfort in his own death comes from the fact. He is still very much in control during his own death, comforting his friends, especially the childlike Ditto (Edward Brophy) for whom Skeffington has so much affection, joking about Junior's "sense of timing," refusing to let the Cardinal "confess" to him, and even "rising from the grave" to answer Maeve's father's comment that he would have lived his life very differently if he had another chance. The sorrow we feel at his passing is gentle and comfortable—it does not strike deep into our own fear of death as does *The Sun Shines Bright*, and the last shot ends the picture in an enclosing, dignified, tabloid-like composition in darkness. The camera tracks out of the darkened house, and stops just outside the door, looking in through it, with the side of the house blocking off one side of the frame, and beautiful shadows molding the magnificent staircase. Skeffington is above in the bedroom, serene and surrounded by love, comforting us in our sorrow with Adam that the time of such men is gone forever.

Skeffington's own death: he peacefully comforts his mourners.

With Skeffington's death the time of such men is gone forever: through camera point of view we, like Adam, are left deserted and alone.

THE
WAR FILMS

INTRODUCTION

The genre of war films is concerned most directly with questions of ideology rather than myth. Heroism, relations among men, loyalties to cause and country—these are the issues of the genre. Personal values always refer first to the group needs and individual codes are subsumed by the group's safety and/or honor. The historic definition of the genre is strictly determined although variable: World War I, World War II, now Korea (Sam Fuller's *Steel Helmet,* 1951, for example), and soon, probably, Vietnam. Like the Western, the genre is clearly defined both in easily recognizable *real* time periods and subject matter, and the two have a similar proximity to history in that the current interpretation of the settling of the West or the winning of the wars generally becomes the ideological context of the genre film, whether it is to support or criticize that interpretation.

War films are an extraordinarily direct expression of the polarities of chaos and order. The antagonistic tendencies in these opposite directions are an issue of all art and are often represented through psychological chaos and health, composition in painting and architecture, or harmony in music. In war films, the war itself, the battles and explosions, along with the concomitant real (the artificial social structure) or threatened (danger to an entire society) socioeconomic order represents the terrifying chaos. The rigidity of the military hierarchy which replaces family and friendship ties, the highly coded and unquestioned values of heroism are generic attempts to reinstate order in a chaotic world, and above all, to give the chaos meaning. Ford's comic war films—half of those he made in the genre—perform a similar operation. Although none shows the physical chaos potential of war to be a threat, comedy itself is an agent of chaos—defused and rendered safe. The use of comedy allows for the incorporation of the

The War Film genre: action and heroism in the battle for cause and country.

World War I: James Cagney in *What Price Glory.* World War II: Robert Montgomery and John Wayne in *They Were Expendable.*

an Dailey in *When Willie Comes Marching Home:* a mock ortrait of the heroic fighter pilot from a small-town comedy.

Order imposed on the chaos of war: cadets marching in *The Long Gray Line.*

chaotic into the war film dynamic without creating a polarized structure.

However, in the war genre, Ford's most pressing personal questions—male-female relationships, individualism in conflict with social determinants, criticism and creation of national attitudes and mythology—lack a full articulation. War takes men (and women) out of the established social order, and although nearly all war films attempt to reconstruct some variation of that structure, in Ford the surrogate family construct is nearly indistinguishable from that of his other films. One important difference is that the parameters (priorities, relations among members, and emotions) of such a grouping are artificial and fragile. Maintenance of the social construct has to occupy much of the work of the film, rendering Ford's close examination and criticism nearly impossible.

The ideological dimension of Ford's criticism is muted in the war genre, and only in three films does it find full expression. The intersection between genre and auteur shifts in the eight war genre films Ford made. In *They Were Expendable, The Long Gray Line,* and *The Wings of Eagles* his priorities completely overwhelm the generic tendencies. Comedy subverts many generic elements as well as Fordian themes in *When Willie Comes Marching Home, What Price Glory* and *Mr. Roberts,* and comedy gives *Submarine Patrol* a nice balance with little tension between later conflicting tendencies. *The Lost Patrol* is abstracted out of the genre through the setting, and it becomes a general parable with more biblical overtones than references to any specific war. *The Long Gray Line* is a military picture rather than a war film. The two genre are often indistinguishable because of shared conventions and subjects, such as the use of the military as a social unit, actual wars, and U.S. history. There are no battles shown directly in *The Long Gray Line*: the military with its special codes of behavior and relations among men functions as a social, not a fighting, unit. When the men leave the Point to go to war, they leave the frame of the film. Like *The Wings of Eagles, The Long Gray Line* is an epic, encompassing at least fifty years of the life of a man and of the nation.

Tyrone Power as Martin Maher, agent of natural disorder in the rigid order of West Point.

The fragile artificial social structure created in the midst of war: *They Were Expendable.*

Martin Maher (Tyrone Power) and other immigrants to the U.S. are mustered into the rigid order of the core.

The military surrogate family: James Cagney as the stern "father" in *What Price Glory.*

Young officers as brothers at the fragile dinner party of *They Were Expendable.*

Donna Reed as a battlefield nurse, and as a girl-back-home symbol for the fighting men.

The comic side of war: Dan Dailey can only "fight" on the safe home front: *When Willie Comes Marching Home.*

Comedy in *The Long Gray Line:* Old Mr. Maher (Donald Crisp) informs Marty (Tyrone Power) of "the great deed we've done this day" when Martin Maher III is born.

WHEN WILLIE COMES MARCHING HOME

1950

CREDITS

Production company: 20th Century-Fox. *Director:* John Ford. *Producer:* Fred Kohlmar. *Scenarists:* Mary Loos, Richard Sale, from story, "WHEN LEO COMES MARCHING HOME," by Sy Gomberg. *Photography:* Leo Tover. *Art directors:* Lyle R. Wheeler, Chester Gore. *Set decorators:* Thomas Little, Bruce MacDonald. *Music:* Alfred Newman. *Orchestration:* Edward Powell. *Editor:* James B. Clark. *Assistant director:* Wingate Smith. 82 minutes. *Released:* February.

CAST

Dan Dailey (*Bill Kluggs*), Corinne Calvet (*Yvonne*), Colleen Townsend (*Marge Fettles*), William Demarest (*Herman Kluggs*), James Lydon (*Charles Fettles*), Lloyd Corrigan (*Mayor Adams*), Evelyn Varden (*Gertrude Kluggs*), Kenny Williams (*musician*), Lee Clark (*musician*), Charles Halton (*Mr. Fettles*), Mae Marsh (*Mrs. Fettles*), Jack Pennick (*Sergeant-Instructor*), Mickey Simpson (*M.P. Kerrigan*), Frank Pershing (*Major Bickford*), Don Summers (*M.P. Sherve*), Gil Herman (*Lt. Commander Crown*), Peter Ortiz (*Pierre*), Luis Alberni (*barman*), John Shulick (*pilot*), Clarke Gordon, Robin Hughes (*Marine officers*), Cecil Weston (*Mrs. Barnes*), Harry Tenbrook (*Joe, taxi driver*), Russ Clark (*Sgt. Wilson*), George Spaulding (*Judge Tate*), James Eagle (*reporter*), Harry Strang (*sergeant*), George Magrill (*Chief Petty officer*), Hank Worden (*choir leader*), John McKee (*pilot*), Larry Keating (*Gen. G. Reeding*), Dan Riss (*Gen. Adams*), Robert Einer (*Lt. Bagley*), Russ Conway (*Maj. J. A. White*, Whit Bissell (*Lt. Handley*), Ann Codee (*French instructor*), Ray Hyke (*Maj. Crawford*), Gene Collins (*Andy*), James Flavin (*Gen. Brevort*), David McMahon (*Col. Ainsley*), Charles Trowbridge (*Gen. Merrill*), Kenneth Tobey (*Lt. K. Geiger*, Maj. Sam Harris (*hospital patient*), Alberto

Dan Dailey as Willie: the first to enlist from Puxatawney, West Virginia.

Morin, Louis Mercier (*Resistance fighters*), Paul Harvey (*officer*), James Waters, Ken Lynch.

SYNOPSIS.

Bill Kluggs, first to enlist from Puxatawney, West Virginia, is disgraced when his proficiency as a gunner returns him to his hometown, as a trainer. He desperately requests an overseas assignment as neighbors, family, and even dogs treat him like a shirker. Finally he is sent on a secret mission, recovers vital information, and is decorated all in the space of thirty-six hilarious hours.

89

Dan Dailey as the all-American boy going off to war—complete with trombone and Best Girl.

Bill is an increasing embarrassment to his once-proud father as he fails to be shipped out of his home town.

The comedies are all immediately distanced from war by the predominance of the comic narrative themes over the usual serious action and ideological issues of war. On this level, they practically cease to function as war genre films, retaining only the physical links of history and setting. *When Willie Comes Marching Home* takes as its central problem the redemption of individual pride and respect to Bill (Dan Dailey) in his hometown, Puxatawney, West Virginia. After being the first to enlist, Bill becomes a figure of ridicule, stationed as a gunnery trainer in his hometown as others go off to war and heroism. This is accomplished—complete with return of adoring best girl—when he is sent on a secret mission which produces vital information and Bill receives a high brass reception, his fourth recommendation for the good conduct medal, and an overseas assignment.

The small-town comedy is often as sharp and fast as that of Preston Sturges's comic war film, *Hail the Conquering Hero.* During Bill's introductory voice-over, his father passes the plate in church, grimacing at a reluctant donor until he capitulates—only to reach in for change. Bill is an all-American boy, complete with trombone and Best Girl (Colleen Townsend). His pilot training foreshadows that of Spig Wead in *The Wings of Eagles;* like Spig, he lands in an officer's tea party on his first solo. But once he is shipped back home to train recruits, the parody becomes irresistible: Bill and Marge, dramatically, tragically in love at the nearness of his imminent departure overseas, become embarrassed and irritable as he remains longer and longer. The neighbors begin to dislike him for his "safe" job. "You here again?" his father asks, as he becomes an embarrassment to the family. Bill is framed in the background and extreme side of every shot at returning hero Charlie's party. When he cannot take the neglect and jibes any longer, his misery nearly becomes too much to be supported by the comedy. He walks away from the party and a tiny dog bites his leg. Bill's anger (and Dan Dailey's clumsy-comic near fall) are perfect to cap the scene.

Bill's heroism is as accidental and undeserved as his ignominy. In a backstage musical setup ("Where will we ever find a gunner!?" "I'm a gunner, Sir." "You *are!*?"), Bill is sent on a mission at the last minute. Failing to hear an order to bail out, Bill wanders up through the plane to find himself alone, and jumps just in time. French patriots rescue him from his messy tree landing and

Bill helps *his* girl prepare for returning war hero Charlie's party—a picture of comic ignominy.

The unlikely hero: Bill accidentally lands in French Resistance hands.

test whether he really is a Yankee; "What does the Lone Ranger say?" In a sequence nearly repeated in *What Price Glory* Bill and a beautiful French girl (Corinne Calvet) are the principals in a pretend wedding staged to get Bill out of France. On his trip back to the states, everyone gives him liquor and denies him sleep as he recounts the story to every important officer in Britain and the U.S. Home finally, Bill is chased by the same dog, assaulted as a prowler by his father, and accused of desertion by all.

Bill again requests a transfer to combat duty—and is again refused.

The unlikely Resistance organization: Yvonne determines the authenticity of Bill's story.

The utter lack of determined relationships in this film is what marks its comic genius and annihilates its generic preoccupations. In many ways it "fits" better into the Americana genre classification. The values of the small-town family are affirmed far beyond the necessity of the war. Even when they are convinced the banging on the door is MPs, come to arrest Bill as a deserter, Marge swears her love and his father prepares to defend the door. Perhaps the time period—1950–1955—in which the three war comedies were made speaks to their ideological function. There was no longer a war effort to be supported and validated, and the nearness of the war left the ideological homogeneity of the nation pretty much intact. With few doubts to defend against, the needs of war—either specifically or generally—recede and the comedy of *When Willie Comes Marching Home* is welcome. *What Price Glory,* two years further away from this postwar ideological unity, and *Mr. Roberts,* five years further removed, contain proportionally increasing mixtures of comedy and themes more central to the war film genre. *When Willie Comes Marching Home* is nearly pure; it has no traumatic and complex issues of loyalty, death, or patriotism with which to contend.

Bill is knocked unconscious in his unsuccessful attempt to break into his own house after "heroically" carrying war secrets through dangerous enemy lines.

Bill as accidental and successful undercover agent is questioned to exhaustion by the military brass of two continents.

Hierarchy is easily restored in a 1950 free of serious contradictions about the war.

92

The overnight hero back home: even his father and Best Girl can't believe his story.

To the incredulity of his family, Bill is cited for bravery instead of arrested for desertion.

WHAT PRICE GLORY
1952

What Price Glory: the love/hate relationship of Capt. Flagg (James Cagney) and Sgt. Quirt (Dan Dailey) is the core of the film.

CREDITS

Production company: 20th Century-Fox. *Director:* John Ford. *Producer:* Sol C. Siegel. *Scenarists:* Phoebe and Henry Ephron, from play by Maxwell Anderson and Laurence Stallings. *Photography* (in technicolor): Joseph MacDonald. *Art directors:* Lyle R. Wheeler, George W. Davis. *Set decorators:* Thomas Little, Stuart A. Reiss. *Music:* Alfred Newman. *Orchestration:* Edward Powell Song, "My Love, My Life," by Jay Livingston, Ray Evans. *Editor:* Dorothy Spencer. 111 minutes. *Released:* August.

CAST

James Cagney (*Capt. Flagg*), Corinne Calvet (*Charmaine*), Dan Dailey (*Sgt. Quirt*), William Demarest (*Corporal Kiper*), Craig Hill (*Lt. Aldrich*), Robert Wagner (*Lewisohn*), Marisa Pavan (*Nicole Bouchard*), Casey Adams (*Lt. Moore*), James Gleason (*Gen. Cokely*), Wally Vernon (*Lipinsky*), Henry Letondal (*Cognac Pete*), Fred Libby (*Lt. Schmidt*), Ray Hyke (*Mulcahy*), Paul Fix (*Gowdy*), James Lilburn (*young soldier*), Henry Morgan (*Morgan*), Dan Borzage (*Gilbert*), Bill Henry (*Holsen*), Henry "Bomber" Kulkovich (*company cook*), Jack Pennick (*Ferguson*), Ann Codee (*nun*), Stanley Johnson (*Lt. Cunningham*), Tom Tyler (*Capt. Davis*), Olga Andre (*Sister Clotilde*), Barry Norton (*priest*), Luis Alberni (*the great-uncle*), Torben Meyer (*mayor*), Alfred Zeisler (*English colonel*), George Bruggeman (*English lieutenant*), Scott Forbes (*Lt. Bennett*), Sean McClory (*Lt. Austin*), Charles FitzSimmons (*Capt. Wickham*), Louis Mercier (*Bouchard*), Mickey Simpson (*M.P.*), Peter Ortiz, Paul Guilfoyle.

SYNOPSIS

In a little French village, Capt. Flagg and Sgt. Quirt battle the Germans and each other over Charmaine and their long past together.

The innocent—Robert Wagner—whose death is the ritual sacrifice to seriousness in the film.

What Price Glory revolves around the love/hate relationship of Capt. Flagg (James Cagney) and Sgt. Quirt (Dan Dailey). Questions of professionalism and dedication to the cause are certainly touched upon, as each man respects the other in the midst of comic fighting or semiserious war missions, but these themes are assumed rather than validated. Even on the battlefield, their quest for a living German officer is sabotaged by every enemy officer dying on their hands, and likewise Quirt's leg wound is a subject for comedy. The traditional war film sacrifice—generally, as in this film—of the most innocent and deserving boy, is fulfilled in Lewisohn's (Robert Wagner) death which then must be inflicted on his beautiful young fiancée, Nicole (Marisa Pavan). These are, however, the most serious confrontations with the weightier questions of war. So accepted is the "old boy" aspect of war that the final decision is Quirt's: will he stay and marry Charmaine (Corinne Calvet) or will he follow Flagg to war, bad leg, medical leave and all?

Quirt and Flagg validate each other as neither the woman nor the war does. Quirt's pronouncement to Charmaine that the profession of soldier is something like a religion is closer to the boy's club mentality of war-is-glory than to Ford's sensibility. The mutual love of Flagg and Quirt for Charmaine makes obvious Quirt's loyalties. His love would not have escalated to near marriage if it were not shared by Flagg. Both men father the "little boys" who march off to war, sharing a professional competence that joins them as "parents." "Wait for baby!" Quirt yells to Flagg, and limps off to join the company as the picture ends.

Only the death of Lewisohn, and Flagg's talks with him of marriage ("I was saving myself—for what? From what?" says Flagg), introduce some of the tension of a war film. Since *What Price Glory* lacks the total comic commitment of *When Willie Comes Marching Home*, this tension is needed but is inadequate. The lack of a compelling texture into which to place the characters rests in the visual style of the film. Ford was in a transitional period visually in 1952. *The Quiet Man* looks like his earlier work and *What Price Glory* uses the static, functional style of later films like *The Wings of Eagles*. In the later films the style functions to abstract and flatten the themes which Ford is draining of their traditional meanings. But in *What Price Glory* this style does not inform the narrative themes. The characters

Comedy at the front: Flagg and Quirt confront a French citizen more concerned with his dinner than with the war.

The sexual battleground: Capt. Flagg and Charmaine.

The comic near-marriage: Sgt. Quirt and Charmaine.

have very little interior dimension to be enriched visually. Even the visual excitement of the expected battle scenes which could infuse the generic expectations of the film is denied in obvious studio static camera setups and editing. The style is too functional to criticize the content on the one hand or to enrich it on the other, creating a virtual stage play appearance without any of the advantages of theater. It is a film that takes its generic themes too lightly for a serious picture, and takes its comedy too casually for a satisfying comedy. Add to this a static and dull visual style and *What Price Glory* is a likable (because the two leading characters are likable) but neither moving nor complete film.

The flat, static visual style and obvious sound-stage set informs neither the comedy nor the serious war film themes in *What Price Glory*.

MISTER ROBERTS
1955

CREDITS

Production company: Orange Productions–Warner Bros. *Directors:* John Ford, Mervyn LeRoy. *Producer:* Leland Hayward. *Scenarists:* Frank Nugent, Joshua Logan; from the play by Joshua Logan and Thomas Heggen, and the novel by Thomas Heggen. *Photography* (in Warnercolor and CinemaScope): Winton C. Hoch. *Art director:* Art Loel. *Set decorator:* William L. Kuehl. *Music:* Franz Waxman. *Orchestration:* Leonid Raab. *Editor:* Jack Murray. *Assistant director:* Wingate Smith. Exteriors filmed in the Pacific. 123 minutes. *Released:* July 30.

CAST

Henry Fonda (*Lt. [jg] Roberts*), James Cagney (*Captain*), Jack Lemmon (*Ensign Frank Thurlowe Pulver*), William Powell (*Doc*), Ward Bond (*C.P.O. Dowdy*), Betsy Palmer (*Lt. Ann Girard*), Phil Carey (*Mannion*), Nick Adams (*Reber*), Harry Carey, Jr. (*Stefanowski*), Ken Curtis (*Dolan*), Frank Aletter (*Gerhart*), Fritz Ford (*Lidstrom*), Buck Kartalian (*Mason*), William Henry (*Lt. Billings*), William Hudson (*Olson*), Stubby Kruger (*Schlemmer*), Harry Tenbrook (*Cookie*), Perry Lopez (*Rodrigues*), Robert Roark (*Insigna*), Pat Wayne (*Bookser*), Tige Andrews (*Wiley*), Jim Moloney (*Kennedy*), Denny Niles (*Gilbert*), Francis Conner (*Johnson*), Shug Fisher (*Cochran*), Danny Borzage (*Jonesey*), Jim Murphy (*Taylor*), Kathleen O'Malley, Maura Murphy, Mimi Doyle, Jeanee Murray-Vanderbilt, Lonnie Pierce (*nurses*), Martin Milner (*shore patrol officer*), Gregory Walcott (*shore patrolman*), James Flavin (*M.P.*), Jack Pennick (*Marine sergeant*), Duke Kahanamoko (*native chief*).

SYNOPSIS

A palm tree symbolizes the crazy authority of the captain on a cargo ship in the Pacific during World War II. Mr. Roberts rebels, hurls it overboard, and when he is transferred to a battleship and killed, Ensign Pulver repeats his act and assumes his position.

As a group, the comic war films seem less like Ford than any other. And of these, *Mr. Roberts* least bears his personal stamp. Ford shares direction credit with Mervyn LeRoy; he suffered a gall bladder attack and had to leave the picture after exteriors were shot—many in Hawaii's beautiful Kaneohe Bay where for years Ford anchored his own yacht, *The Araner,* used in the filming of *Donovan's Reef.* Ford told Peter Bogdanovich that the "forced comedy" inside the ship wasn't his, and one story has it that he and Henry Fonda, who also played the title role on stage and had very definite ideas about it, so disagreed that they actually fought. It was the last time the two worked together.

The action of *Mr. Roberts* is as removed from World War II as is *When Willie Comes Marching Home.* The ship that never sees action becomes a microcosm for the Navy men. The Captain (James Cagney) is a despotic authority. Mr. Roberts is trying to get off the cargo ship and into the shooting war while taking care of the men, who are like children as they fight over liberty, women, and booze. The ridiculous palm tree is a kind of school flag, the focal point of authority and rebel-

James Cagney as the Captain and Henry Fonda as Mr. Roberts.

The men of the cargo ship look for disrobing nurses instead of enemy ships.

lion. Within this rather standard construct, Joshua Logan's play gives the characters so much life and humor that it infuses a light treatment of a heavy subject with just enough seriousness to deepen the treatment without overwhelming the comedy. Ford and LeRoy's direction, especially Ford's panoramic exteriors, give the film a dimension similar to the immediacy endemic to theater but impossible on screen, whose lack so often accounts for the lifelessness of plays that become films.

Mr. Roberts is a rational force in the chaotic, irrational world of comedy. The Captain is an exaggerated comic figure, a repressive authority obsessed by a palm tree, the men are slapstick figures, and Ensign Pulver (Jack Lemmon), a fast-talking wheeler-dealer whose best laid plans generally go wrong. The backbone of the film, which makes the comedy possible, is Mr. Roberts' integrity, however inappropriate in this crazy context —and Pulver's acceptance of it when Mr. Roberts leaves. Mr. Roberts takes the war seriously. In spite of his desire to see action, he sacrifices himself for the men by entering into a dishonorable agreement with the Captain by promising to not request transfer and to respect the palm in exchange for some liberties for the men. According to the film's established moral framework there is no need to keep it, but Mr. Roberts does, and the palm tree stands unmolested as a symbol of the pact. It is the men who bring about Mr. Roberts' transfer, and when two letters come—one from Mr. Roberts, full of praise, paternal pride, and love for them, and the other a notice of his death —they post the one from him. Finally Pulver faces seriously the directive to take care of the men. Throwing the palm tree overboard, as Mr. Roberts did in the beginning, he fully assumes Mr. Roberts' position and completes the dramatic movement.

The death of Mr. Roberts and passing on of the rational, rebellious, honorable character gives this film a grounding in the values worthy of the sacrifice of a man's life that *What Price Glory* lacks. It introduces a melancholy, tragic note of an actual world which validates the comic one of the film.

Jack Lemmon as Ensign Frank Thurlowe Pulver.

The Documentaries

Robert Montgomery in *They Were Expendable:* on the surface a heroic PT boat squadron leader.

John Wayne: A war film and Western icon. *They Were Expendable.*

Ford is often regarded as a superpatriot, a backward-looking man who shares the paternalistic, imperialistic view of our government toward the rest of the world and the less privileged of our own land. He has been accused of sexism because women are often agents of conservatism and clearly secondary in traditional forms of power to men through most of his films. Critics have interpreted his Westerns as reinforcing the inhumane values and priorities that conquered the plains and decimated native Americans, his war pictures as glorifying imperialist wars, and his Americana films as valorizing racism and oppressive individualism. A deeper look at these films reveals a far more complex, often radical, and nearly always liberating view of the world. With Ford's critical and popular reputation high, these charges are less often leveled today. But there is still overwhelming prejudice against many of the historical subjects Ford used in his films and misunderstanding of the complexity of his interpretation.

This difficulty is magnified with regard to the documentaries. They were made primarily in the service of the country at war. *Sex Hygiene* (1941), *Battle of Midway* (1942), *Torpedo Squadron* (1942), *December 7th* (1943), *We Sail At Midnight* (1943), in World War II; *This is Korea* in 1951, *Korea* in 1959; and he produced *Vietnam! Vietnam!* in 1971. *Chesty* (1970), his last film, was a film about war. The tensions and contradictions that inform the subtleties of his fiction films are largely absent from these assignments. It is difficult to see them all—Peter Bogdanovich reports that *Torpedo Squadron,* eight minutes long, was filmed by a cameraman shortly before the Battle of Midway about life on a torpedo boat. All but one man was killed in the battle, and Ford edited the footage into a film seen only by the families of the dead men. *We Sail at Midnight* was edited into a film from composite footage shot by other people, and *December 7th,* according to Ford, was largely Gregg Toland's project. *Battle of Midway* was spectacularly filmed by Ford him-

99

World War II in *They Were Expendable:* a "glorious" battle at sea.

self in the midst of the battle: he was wounded but went on shooting. The film received an Academy Award as America's first war documentary. The Korea and Vietnam films were edited from already existing footage.

These short films (with the exception of the absurd and wonderful *Sex Hygiene* with its "Fordian moments" in a very explicit and puritanical treatment of venereal disease) were not projects over which Ford had a great deal of creative control. They were often shot primarily in uncontrolled situations—war—and/or already shot before Ford joined the project. Their propaganda purpose is the overriding one; there are many interesting moments one can recognize as Ford, but these are often perverted when viewed now, so closely are the films tied to their historical time and purpose. One such moment is Jane Darwell's emotional, patriotic narration of the hometown boys going off to war in *Battle of Midway.* The attempt to create a bond between the folks

back home and their symbolic sons, brothers, and sweethearts fighting the war is reminiscent of the personalization of large struggles in Ford's fiction films, but in *Battle of Midway* it is too heroic and straightforward. Only in the documentaries does Ford assume wholehearted acceptance of wartime patriotic values. This is of course appropriate to these projects, but makes clear that we must look elsewhere for the subtle poet of America's glory and failures.

Sex Hygiene, a project over which Ford did have control, is outrageously funny in its elaborate distancing of the audience from its nearly unspeakable subject, its wartime, anti-female puritanism, and rather amazing in the careful structure which drives its points home. It opens with a *very* long title role explaining what we will see, then cuts to a dramatic sequence in which one man's unsavory desire to "go to town" results in an outbreak of "cases." The men are asked to see a film on the subject. Ford has immediately cushioned the impact of the subject matter and cut away at the self-consciousness of the audience: we are not watching a film on venereal disease, we are watching *them* watch a film on venereal disease. He provides still another introduction to the subject, this time by a doctor in the film-within-the-film. A very scientific attitude is taken as he explains the functioning of the body. This is all peppered with frightening facts, "chances of a man coming into contact with syphilis are one in ten," and cuts to the horrified men, again reminding the audience that they are experiencing this only indirectly. By the time Ford gets to the shots of the disease itself, the audience has been adequately distanced: self-consciousness and embarrassment will not obscure facts.

The presentation of a value system with those facts is hardly subtle but very effective. Venereal disease harms a whole company and the war effort itself, and a man's primary responsibility is to his company. Thus when the first man "goes to town," the rest of the men are shot in a group, an arm draped across another's shoulder, disapproving of their comrade's need. The end titles again take up this theme: "You don't need sex to be a good sport," and "Your organ will not be harmed by abstinence." The value system is inculcated through a more insidious means in a puritan anti-sex and anti-woman bias. The man who goes to town is shown exiting a room, picking up his still burning cigarette on the banister as he buckles his belt: this has hardly been a fulfilling, sensual experience. When the doctor in the film-within-the-film refers to women, his words and tone are contemptuous. He advises the men to "keep something between you and the germs of venereal disease by using a good rubber," treating women as simple carriers of disease. "If the woman has syphilis or gonorrhea, and she probably has . . ." He refers to women's secretions as "pus-like," and unsurprisingly his strongest directive is ab-

stinence. The only sure way to prevent VD is to not come into any contact with it. The moralistic, paternal attitude has a clear, frightening effect on the men who wipe sweat from brows and grimace at the screen.

The film is really ingenious and effective in its unquestioned ideology. While hardly a film to study for Ford's artistic vision, it is interesting for its Fordian devices in the service of information and values. His last documentary, *Chesty* (1970), is about the career of Ford's old friend, Lewis B. Puller, the most decorated Marine in the corps. There are the Ford tracings: narration by John Wayne, lots of marching footage, war footage, sentimental visual links to Robert E. Lee in Chesty's visit to his grave, military ritual and pageantry. But the film does not have either the personal dimension and conflicting subtleties of his narrative films or the wartime energy and immediacy of the war documentaries. It is a sad last film for an artist of Ford's vision.

The documentaries are not the place to look for Ford's most deeply held ideas on political issues, social and individual values, and the priorities of a culture. These films can only be considered as fragments, made outside the medium—the Hollywood narrative film—that was Ford's. They were made under condtions that allow for the least artistic expression—wartime, financed by the Navy, often shot or edited with someone else in charge, their purpose dictated before their conception. Like Ford himself in interviews, the documentaries rarely exhibit the complexities and liberating contradictions of the best of the fiction films, although they nonetheless often bear his imprint. Better to look to *They Were Expendable* for his thoughts on World War II, *Young Mr. Lincoln* for America's history, and *The Wings of Eagles* for a portrait of a man who chooses the military for his career.

End of the lost battle in *They Were Expendable:* a critique of the sad beauty of defeat.

THE LOST PATROL

1934

CREDITS

Production company: RKO Radio. *Director:* John Ford. *Executive producer:* Merian C. Cooper. *Associate producer:* Cliff Reid. *Scenarists:* Dudley Nichols, Garrett Fort, from story, "PATROL," by Philip MacDonald. *Photographer:* Harold Wenstrom. *Art directors:* Van Nest Polglase, Sidney Ullman. *Music:* Max Steiner. *Recording Engineer:* Glen Portman. *Editor:* Paul Weatherwax. Filmed in the Yuma desert. 74 minutes. *Released:* February 16.

CAST

Victor McLaglen (*The Sergeant*), Boris Karloff (*Sanders*), Wallace Ford (*Morelli*), Reginald Denny (*George Brown*), J. M. Kerrigan (*Quincannon*), Billy Bevan (*Herbert Hale*), Alan Hale (*Cook*), Brandon Hurst (*Bell*), Douglas Walton (*Pearson*), Sammy Stein (*Abelson*), Howard Wilson (*flyer*), Neville Clark (*Lt. Hawkins*), Paul Hanson (*Jock Mackay*), Francis Ford.

SYNOPSIS

During World War I a desert patrol loses its leader and thereby its bearings and its mission. Unseen Arabs kill them one by one in an oasis until only a crazed would-be religious savior, the Sergeant, and one man are left. With rescue moments away, two are killed and only the Sergeant is left to confront the finally visible Arabs and then the British patrol.

The Lost Patrol is abstracted from the World War I desert battle even before it is fully defined. Our first view of the patrol is a long shot of their shadows in the desert; they are phantoms before they are soldiers. Ford then cuts to the title that identifies the time and place, then back to long shot as the leader of the patrol falls dead. His face is never seen; he is simply the bearer of direction and purpose for the mission whose death leaves them lost. The Sergeant (Victor McLaglen) knows nothing: within five minutes into the film "lost" is their physical condition and it becomes apparent that it is their moral and spiritual condition as well.

The film speaks directly to the question of spiritual condition through the character of Sanders (Boris Karloff), but it is difficult to determine exactly what it says. At first, Sanders' concern for the dead seems pitted against the Sergeant's concern for the living. The Sergeant walks away from Sanders' long-winded speech during a burial scene which prefigures the one in *The Searchers*. "Put an amen to it," he says. Although the Sergeant has no idea of where they are or where the patrol should be going, Sanders' leadership is not much better. From the first he appears a little off balance, saying to one man (after still another burial), "You're a gentleman, you have breeding. You must have faith," as the men relieve their fear and preoccupation with death by telling stories of

The soldiers of *The Lost Patrol* are phantoms in the desert—like the Arab enemy—before they are individuals.

Victor McLaglen as the Sergeant and Boris Karloff as Sanders, the religious fanatic.

The burial in the desert prefigures a similar scene in *The Searchers*.

The men of the Lost Patrol.

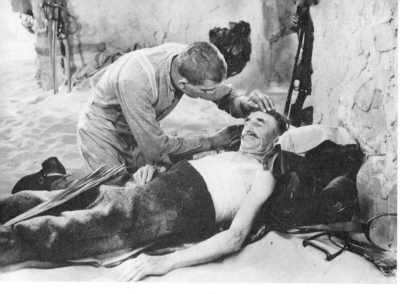

Sanders (Boris Karloff) impotently tries to save the soul of a dying man.

The Sergeant (Victor McLaglen) is responsible for the men but incapable of saving them.

The Sergeant and the innocent boy—first to die.

life and sex. (Actually, neither the gentleman nor the breeding is borne out by his remarks, which are alternately racist—"The Malayan girls are a little dark,"—and sexist—"They should be poisoned before they're twenty-one.") Sanders' concern with the souls of his comrades never does them any good. Indeed, he harasses a sick man with his crazed mission to save the man's soul before he dies. Sanders grows increasingly alienated from any reality until he must be tied up to keep him from self-destruction. He escapes his bonds and walks off in a robe, cross in hand, to his death at the hands of the Arabs.

The Sergeant, the only character without a name, is similarly of little use to the patrol. He feel a strong responsibility to the men's safety, from the innocent boy who is the first to die to the last survivor, but he is incapable of carrying it out. Indeed, he is even responsible for an additional death—that of the pilot who lands and then is shot as he walks toward the men. Although he tries to revenge his buried men when the Arabs finally appear, shooting and laughing crazily as he calls to the dead patrol, the Sergeant manages only to save himself.

For nearly all of the film the Arabs are an unseen, unheard, unknowable danger. They are sometimes identified with eerie music or blowing wind over the desert, but their only real mark is the death of another man. We know the men—one plays music, one talks of a wife and son (only two months old, and they have been away from Britain for over a year—the other men exchange looks but remain silent), one is rich. But the Arabs are not even a traditional enemy in a war—they cannot be engaged. They seem to characterize some malevolent force of nature, but why it should visit itself upon the men of the "lost patrol" (first causing them to be lost) is extremely unclear. While there is certainly no requirement that all answers be spelled out, when an allegory is set up (as it immediately is in the visual presentation) its participants and their mutual relationships become the issue of the film. Within that structure, there is ample room for ambiguity and subtlety, but that structure is largely missing from *The Lost Patrol.* Apparently the men face their own destinies, but how this involves the twisted religious elements and the Sergeant as a responsible leader and sole survivor is unclear. It is not until all the men have died that the Arabs show themselves to the Sergeant, and in spite of cutting which connects the airplane, the British troops, and Sanders, these implied relations are murky. Only the historical setting and the military definition of the group are genre elements. The war aspects of *The Lost Patrol* are not carried out even at the level of allegory, making this film's placement in the genre tenuous at best.

Tensions rise among the men as the unseen enemy picks them off one by one.

The Lost Patrol has the iconography of a religious parable: Boris Karloff as a Christ in the desert.

SUBMARINE PATROL

1938

Perry Townsend—The Rich Punk—joins the Navy.

CREDITS

Production company: 20th Century-Fox. *Director:* John Ford. *Producer:* Darryl F. Zanuck. *Associate producer:* Gene Markey. *Scenarists:* Rian James, Darrell Ware, Jack Yellen; from the novel, THE SPLINTER FLEET, by John Milholland. *Photography:* Arthur Miller. *Art directors:* William Darling, Hans Peters. *Set decorator:* Thomas Little. *Costumes:* Gwen Wakeling *Music director:* Arthur Lange. *Editor:* Robert Simpson. 95 minutes. Released: November 25.

CAST

Richard Greene (*Perry Townsend III*), Nancy Kelly (*Susan Leeds*), Preston Foster (*Lt. John C. Drake*), George Bancroft (*Capt. Leeds*), Slim Summerville (*Ellsworth "Spotts" Ficketts*), Joan Valerie (*Anne*), John Carradine (*McAllison*), Warren Hymer (*Rocky Haggerty*), Henry Armetta (*Luigi*), Douglas Fowley (*Brett*), J. Farrell McDonald (*Quincannon*), Dick Hogan (*Johnny*), Maxie Rosenbloom (*Sgt. Joe Duffy*), Ward Bond (*Olaf Swanson*), Robert Lowery (*Sparks*), Charles Tannen (*Kelly*), George E. Stone (*Irving*), Moroni Olsen (*Capt. Wilson*), Jack Pennick (*Guns McPeck*), Elisha Cook, Jr. (*"Professor" Pratt*), Harry Strang (*Grainger*), Charles Trowbridge (*Admiral Joseph Maitland*), Victor Varconi (*chaplain*), Murray Alper (*sailor*) E. E. Clive.

SYNOPSIS

Rich and spoiled Perry Townsend III is assigned a sub chaser in World War I. He falls in love with a poor girl, and along with a crew of misfits, sees action in Europe and proves himself to be "regular" in spite of his class.

Submarine Patrol is primarily a comedy that relies on conventional genre and filmic characters and their relationships: the rich punk who must learn to be one of the men after joining the Navy,

Submarine Patrol: World War I

The lovers of *Submarine Patrol:* Richard Greene as Perry Townsend III and Nancy Kelly as Susan.

106

the poor beautiful girl he loves, her father who tries to prevent their match, the military-civilian antagonism, and the comic situations that arise from such a characteristic setup. Ford does not deepen the characters or their relationships to any great extent, nor does he raise questions endemic to the genre. *Submarine Patrol* remains a light film whose charm comes from gentle, naturalistic comedy.

The crew of the sub chaser to which Perry Townsend III (Richard Green) is assigned is an engaging array of men who have no commitment either to the Navy or to the war. Cookie runs his restaurant in town, another man drives a taxi, "Professor" Pratt (Elisha Cook, Jr.) keeps his specimens on board ship as he studies for his Master's Degree. The men know so little about shipboard procedure (confusing fore and aft) that they are a comedy team until Capt. Drake (Preston Foster) arrives and shapes them up. They are types, not characters with pasts and futures, but they are given a breadth that nearly compensates for the lack of depth.

Capt. Drake is a man with a past—he was relieved of an earlier command because of "cowardice." Extenuating circumstances (as in *Fort Apache*) are implied but never explained, and he remains a figure of mystery as he sets out to redeem himself with his new command. Perry Townsend also has a past of a sort, in that he is rich and spoiled. He must also be redeemed by proving himself when rank and privilege are taken away, a common narrative pattern which in fact validates the class concept of the greater worth of the rich. The theme that the rich are no better than anyone else is often introduced and then co-opted in this way. First, he/she is exposed as spoiled, lacking in both humility and common sense. But the rich character is the focus of the narrative, and when he/she is "reconstructed," i.e., learns humility, the character is clearly superior to the rest of the people of the film. The attributes of the "common" people are accessible and merely "added on" to the more valuable, *inherited* rather than achieved advantages of the rich. The aristocracy based on money is thus validated after a very slight slap on the wrist, and because it is a co-optation process, only the slap, not the validation, is immediately recognized.

The comedy of *Submarine Patrol* is not based on situation, as in *When Willie Comes Marching Home*, but neither does it spring from characters as dynamic as in *Mr. Roberts*. It relies on charac-

Inside the sub chaser during a hit.

ter types (rich punk, poor girl, Italian hotel manager who cries when happy or sad, comically serious student). The crazy race to get a message to Susan (Nancy Kelly) in Italy, past her civilian ship Captain father (George Bancroft) and his maniacal first mate (John Carradine, played with all his single-minded religious, demonic prissy potential) and all of the wonderful, hilarious complications which ensue, form the comedy which is the real heart of the film.

The war is never a great concern in *Submarine Patrol*. It is the device through which Perry and Capt. Drake prove themselves, and Perry and Su-

"Seaman" Perry Townsend III and Captain Drake (Preston Foster): the civilian and the naval officer.

The war: never the primary concern in *Submarine Patrol*.

Preston Foster as Captain Drake.

Tension between Susan's father (George Bancroft) and her lover Perry Townsend.

The mise-en-scene of war: fog makes the mine search even more dangerous.

san's father become friends, but it is never dangerous or threatening to the men. Unlike *They Were Expendable,* which internalizes and abstracts the war through an unseen enemy, the Germans appear in *Submarine Patrol* for one sequence and provide the film with nearly all its serious content. Ford takes us inside a German sub when it is hit, showing us not a demonic enemy, but people like the men of the sub chaser. When the wreckage floats to the surface and a disappointed recruit asks, "Don't we cheer or something?" the men take off their hats in a sad salute to the dead Germans. This is the most contemplative scene in the film, and without laboring its anti-war message, the sequence refuses to be viewed in a triumphant, patriotic context. Later, in *They Were Expendable,* Ford would critique the rituals and assumptions of war which remain intact in this film without his approval.

The men of the sub chaser do not become the kind of family Ford's military unit often does, but there is rich comedy provided by the contrast between the recruits and the professional Navy men, a standard integrating device when such a family is formed in any group, be it the cavalry or the Navy. "Professor" mistakes a garbage can for a German sub, and is later very hesitant to call out when he really does spot a sub. When Capt. Drake calls for volunteers on a dangerous mission, Cookie steps forward to get the hell off the ship, and all the men step forward with him in a unanimous "volunteer" gesture much appreciated by the Captain. The men act as a unit to affirm the new family of Susan and Perry when they join Perry to shout from their ship across New York Harbor to Susan in her boat.

Submarine Patrol's generic elements are mostly visual. When the sub chaser leaves New York Harbor, the men gaze up at the Statute of Liberty and pay their respects to her and what she represents in silence. The faces of the men against the harbor sky and the line of boats as they leave the safety of the shore indicate eloquently the uncertainty, sacrifice, and danger of the war they must fight. '

George Bancroft, as the civilian ship captain, saves the day when the sub chaser is hit.

THEY WERE EXPENDABLE
1945

CREDITS

Production company: MGM. *Director-producer:* John
Ford. *Associate producer:* Cliff Reid. *Scenarist:* Frank
W. Wead, from book by William L. White. *Photography:* Joseph H. August. *Special Effects:* A. Arnold Gillespie. *Art directors:* Cedric Gibbons, Malcolm F.
Brown. *Set decorators:* Edwin B. Willis, Ralph S.
Hurst. *Music:* Herbert Stothart. *Editors:* Frank E. Hull,
Douglas Biggs. *Second-unit director:* James C. Havens
(rear projection plates by Robert Montgomery). *Assistant director:* Edward O'Fearna. 136 minutes. *Released:*
December 20.

CAST

Robert Montgomery (*Lt. John Brickley*), John Wayne
(*Lt. Rusty Ryan*), Donna Reed (*Lt. Sandy Davis*), Jack
Holt (*General Martin*), Ward Bond (*Boots Mulcahey*),
Louis Jean Heydt (*Ohio, flyer in hospital*), Marshall
Thompson (*Snake Gardner*), Russell Simpson (*Dad,
chief of shipyard*), Leon Ames (*Major Morton*), Paul
Langton (*Andy Andrews*), Arthur Walsh (*Jones*), Donald Curtis (*Shory*), Cameron Mitchell (*George Cross*),
Jeff York (*Tony Aiken*), Murray Alper (*Slug Mahan*),
Harry Tenbrook (*Larsen*), Jack Pennick (*Doc Charlie*),
Charles Trowbridge (*Admiral Blackwell*), Robert Barrat (*General*), Bruce Kellogg (*Tomkins*), Tim Murdock
(*Brant*), Vernon Steele (*doctor*), Alex Havler (*Benny*),
Wallace Ford, Tom Tyler.

SYNOPSIS

In the losing battle of the Phillippines near the end of
World War II, a PT Boat Squadron is slowly destroyed
as it faces the violent death of war and the agonizing
breakdown of the military structure in the Pacific.

Bounded by quotes from General McArthur at
beginning and end, *They Were Expendable* en-

Director John Ford and W.L. White, author of the book on
which *They Were Expendable* was based.

John Wayne as Rusty: a film about defeat.

joys a strange proximity to the war which is its
subject. It was made before the war was really
over, although the outcome already was clear, and
takes the experiences of Lt. John Bulkeley, a personal friend of Ford's, as its source. With both the
national and personal nearness to the war, this is
Ford's most direct war genre film. Yet, like the
other war films he made, *They Were Expendable*
uses only the genre elements, not its themes, and
actually has more in common with his later, more
rigorously interior and despairing films than it
does with other films of the genre.

The breaking down of the military structure from the beginning to the end of the film: Robert Montgomery as Brick
and John Wayne as Rusty.

Wounded Boots Mulcahey (Ward Bond) says
good-bye to his commanding officer Brick.

The hierarchical family of the military: Doc's (Jack Pennick) retirement party.

Robert Montgomery as Brick is isolated by focus which indicates the distance his command requires.

110

The quote which opens the film in the form of a title card, "The tragedy has ended. The victory has been won," acknowledges the result of the immediate past with which the film will deal. This releases the film to seek its own temporal boundaries, since its history in 1945 was well known and Ford is thus not committed to telling the story of the entire war. The part he chooses to focus on was over and was a very small part, which itself ends in defeat. The last quote from MacArthur is the famous "We shall return," made long before the first quote and expressive of the film's greater concern for the experience of war than for its result.

Generally in war genre films this process involves the formation of military relationships and the bond of working for a common goal greater than any individual could attain. The military provides a structure for both hierarchical and pseudo-family relationships and order in the chaos of war. In *They Were Expendable,* however, that structure is broken down both physically in the losing battles and psychologically through its failure to provide the men with a reason to be fighting.

The film begins in order and regularity. The PT boats cutting through the water are grace itself, and Brick (Robert Montgomery) is established in close-up (though isolated from his background through focus) as the stable commander of the PT boat unit, with the lines of men and generals expressing the chain of command and order of the Navy. Scenes in the officers' club and Doc's (Jack Pennick) retirement party continue in even lighting, indicating normalcy, with natural shadows and stable compositions. The announcement of war brings the beginnings of chaos and isolation and finally breakdown for the PT units. First Brick is cut off from the regular chain of command visually by the glass doors of the war room, then passes through a long corridor alone to rejoin his men. The unit is immediately isolated from the rest of the Navy and the meaningful war effort.

Brick as commander maintains a degree of distance from all his men but Rusty, and it is that distance which gives such poignancy to the farewell when Boots Mulcahey (Ward Bond) calls him by his nickname "Brick." It is a required distance; only through it can Brick make decisions that will cost the lives of an unknown number of his men and only through the distance of command can the men give the unquestioning loyalty

The necessary loneliness of leadership: Brick and the Admiral.

demanded by the war effort. Brick must become a somewhat removed figure for the men, lacking in the personal dimension and accruing the iconographic significance necessary for giving orders to men who may die for the safety of the unit. This hierarchical, increasingly impersonal structure escalates up the ranks: Brick occupies the same relationship to the Admiral that his men do to him, and the Admiral is a more remote, lonely figure than is Brick. General MacArthur is the furthest expression of this distance of leadership: his name alone is awesome to the men, and he is photographed like a mythical figure. We see him only from a distance. He walks in long shot alone while his family walks ahead of him and his men follow behind. It is as though his loneliness and necessary isolation are so great they cannot be bridged at all. It is a function of his level of command that he must maintain that distance. He must be remote in order to lead, and that leadership causes a nearly intolerable distance between himself and other men. It is both self-generating and a community necessity which can only be crossed on a professional level, as when he shakes hands with Rusty and Brick, the camera remaining at a distance, or on a ridiculous, worshipful level that maintains the distance by its own ignorance, as when the sailor asks MacArthur to autograph his hat.

Along with the loneliness of leadership and the necessary lack of a personal dimension, there is

111

Brick and Rusty: their friendship forms a bond that is at the heart of the film.

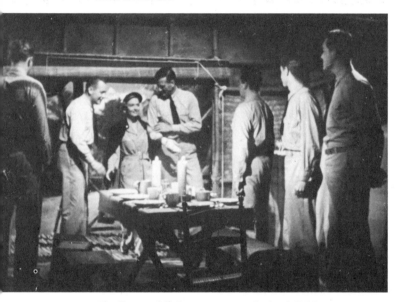

The "stateside" dinner party in the battlefield: an attempt to recreate a feeling of home.

Brick and Rusty: there exists between them a tender vulnerability.

an element of vulnerability in Ford's leaders that exists in direct proportion to our ability to perceive it. General MacArthur is a mythical figure throughout the film, both in his visual presentation and in his effect on the men. He functions almost outside the family of the military because he is the head of it for the audience (in "real" life) as well as for the men, and none of us can get close enough to him to see the vulnerability in which he must share. The Admiral (Charles Trowbridge), however, shows this side to the camera when he sends for Brick and tells him of the impending disaster in the Philippines. He is a little man who now looks old and suddenly physically frail and weak in the darkness, nearly unable to carry the burden of decision that rests on him. It is in Brick, however, that we most intimately know this "other side" of the power of leadership, exposed through his friendship with Rusty (John Wayne). Brick must submerge his individuality in concern for the PT boat squadron, and cannot allow himself the excesses of Rusty in pursuit of glory that has more personal necessity in it than commitment to the cause. Rusty would endanger the mission and his future usefulness by hiding his blood-poisoned arm to take part in the first action the squadron sees, and it is Brick who must pull him back in line. There is a bond between the two men that must submit to various external controls, and it then becomes moving when they transcend those controls, however briefly. After Rusty kicks a bucket in frustration and Brick rebukes him with "does that help?" Brick then kicks it as well in one of the few eruptions of rebellion in him. It joins Brick and Rusty, however comically, for a moment which seems more real than their professional camaraderie. There is a tenderness about their friendship that is fragile and indescribable, but is at the heart of the film. It has roots more in homosexuality than in paternal affecton, but it is not the kind of love that denies any other. When Brick stands in the dark on the porch watching Sandy (Donna Reed) and Rusty, the love that exists between Rusty and him includes, rather than excludes, him from their company. This scene and the dinner party for Sandy make use of a verbal shorthand that sounds corny today, but is as useful as the nicknames for the crew (Rusty, Brick, Shorty, Long, Dad, Boots, Ohio, Slug) in communicating a feeling between people that can only be referred to: to get any closer to it would be to destroy it.

Brick has no one besides Rusty. Without him,

one could imagine Brick never talking to anyone except in accordance with his rank. He has no family except that of the film, the military, and as he must watch them die and scatter, his isolation is presented through a tender vulnerability only Rusty can touch. When his boat, the last of the PT boats, is turned over to the army, Brick wears shorts and this costume alludes to his vulnerability better than any words could do. Rusty discovers Brick: each man thought the other was dead. There is a quick interchange, a grasping of arms and a playful slap, that comes after their initial greeting and indicates their barely controlled joy at finding each other again. The physical contact between them is a shorthand for their feelings: when Brick leaves Sandy and Rusty alone after the formal dinner, he touches Rusty in a near embrace as he goes, and when they leave together in the plane at the end of film, Brick holds Rusty, his arm around his shoulder. It is a love that cannot be articulated and is not limiting, but that reveals itself by partially mitigating Brick's loneliness and isolation.

Death in *They Were Expendable* is neither glory-filled nor brutally meaningless, the two extremes with which it is usually depicted in war films, depending on the attitudes toward war. In the Ford film, both possibilities are there, balanced as to deny neither. The war itself is abstracted in such a way as to internalize the battle: there are no enemy soldiers, just planes and boats which fill the sky and sea with action and flame, but never with the sense of a struggle between navies. The sea battles especially are so abstracted they become light shows, sensory experiences of dark boats on glistening water, moving with beauty and grace through the white shining explosions that burst around them, creating patterns of light against a black sky. The Japanese carriers go down in glorious fireworks, and the Americans who die in battle do so in silhouetted low angle against the fire-lit sky. The sea battles are beauty and light: it is in the hospital that death is a reality.

The corridor to the hospital is revealed through dark shadow passages that are strangely lit to create an expressionistic hell. Like the sea battles, the hospital is a highly stylized canvas of light and dark, but it reveals the other side of the battles. The hospital shows the people who deal with the results of the battles—the wounded men, the doctors, the nurses. It is no more "realistic" than the sea battles, but it is expressing an interior

Brick and Rusty leaving the island in defeat.

The war in *They Were Expendable:* an abstract light show of dark boats and glistening water; visual patterns against a black sky.

Death in battle: an abstract silhouette.

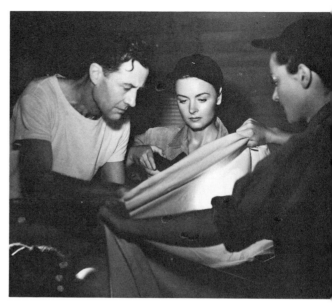

The reality of death in the hospital: Rusty watches an operation.

The hospital corridor: an underground link between the world of the living and the world of the dead.

darkness, filled with people and pain instead of illuminating the vast night with fire and action. The hospital is an enclosed, claustrophobic space as shot by Ford, not an open, limitless one like the sea, and the people who work in it are stylized by light like the boats at sea. In the operation which Rusty watches, the lights flicker, go out, are replaced by a flashlight, and finally return swaying over the operating table, with Sandy the only constant in the scene. Her face remains impassive, unchanging in the shifting light, and it is to this constancy that he responds. When the nurses walk out through the corridor, lit from behind, smoke swirling around them, they are silhouetted against the night like wraiths instead of women. The corridor seems an underground link between the world of the living and the world of the dead, and never more so than when the men visit Andy as he is dying. His bed is in the corridor itself, curtained off from the others. In the visit, the "small talk" sustains no one, and each man faces death alone in the person of Andy. Andy himself is not comforted by their chatter; indeed, he tries to comfort them but also fails.

Death here is a lonely experience, the final isolation. Ford does not try to romanticize it, but he does stylize it in a way that abstracts its full impact and allows for both the grim reality and the personal tragedy. The levels of Andy's larger representation for the unit and for the war, and his personal dimension to both the men and his family back home, are permitted through the visual style to exist simultaneously. It is Brick, in the isolation of his rank, who must face it even more alone than the others as Andy entrusts him with his final thoughts and letters to home. Only with Brick can Andy stop his comforting banter and confront his death with the honesty that could be of comfort to him, but only pain to Brick. He walks alone through the dark corridor to join the silhouetted figures of the rest of the men, isolated from them through light and composition as he was from Andy by the finality of facing his own death while having to go on living.

The funeral in the little Spanish church is another ritualized scene in which the structures of meaning and glory in burial are observed but fall short of their comforting possibilities. Rusty cannot even stay to observe the ceremony, but runs out to get a drink to sustain him as the religious service cannot. Neither the fullness of his bitterness nor the glory of the flag-wrapped ceremony overcomes the other.

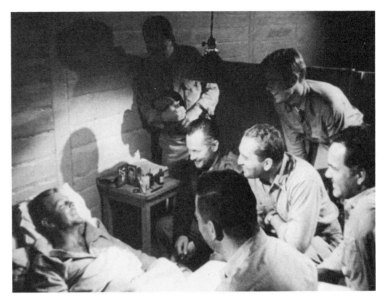

The personal experience of death is lonely and unromantic: Andy and his shipmates unsuccessfully try to comfort each other.

Andy entrusts Brick with his final thoughts and letters to home.

Like the absence of enemies in the film, the concept of home is abstracted, instead of conjured through flashback or misty memory. Home becomes a larger realm than simply "The States" in *They Were Expendable,* as does the military family. The men of the unit constitute a family, and their Torpedo Boat Squadron 3 makes up its home. They are even from the first displaced, having no specific role to play in the Navy's fight, and the first scene is of a rejection of their possible usefulness. They function as a smooth unit, and

115

The men of Torpedo Boat Squadron 3 constitute an artificial family.

Cookie remembers the "old *Arizona*," destroyed at Pearl Harbor.

the Admiral comments on their maneuverability, but he can see no place for them. Then comes the attack on the base, and their "home" is devastated. The squadron is continually leaving one island and going to another, until it is difficult to keep track of where they are. While it is true that in 1945 audiences had a closer knowledge of the battles of the Pacific, it seems that this constant upheaval has more to do with the impermanence of any kind of base for the men than with a disregard for details that may have been unnecessary when the picture was released. The family of men disintegrates as well, first with the loss of boats which frees two crews to go fight with the army. Men die, more boats are lost, until all that is really left is Brick, Rusty, and the small troop of men who will be left behind on the island, certain to be killed by the Japanese. The crew members we know best are the ones who die—Cookie, Slug, and Andy.

Home is more than a place in *They Were Ex-*

pendable—it is a condition that they are fighting for, and which they cannot maintain. This is the basis of the transcendent failure of meaning that underlies this picture: unlike other war films which depict men becoming a unit or family whose interests are greater than those of any individual or a physical America for which they are fighting, in this film the condition of "home" does not even exist structurally, and thus the sacrifices of war cannot affirm it. The war effort becomes a meaningless exercise, with the only possibility for creating meaning existing on an individual level. Rusty's eulogy over Slug and Cookie is ironic: "Home is the hunter, home from the hill, and the sailor home from the sea," for in no sense are the men, dead or living, home. Their only possibility for such a condition has been disintegrating since the picture began, and Rusty's bitterness is caused by the uselessness of their sacrifice. The concept of the team is all the men have. It runs through the picture from the first, when Brick asks Rusty if his ambition is to build a Navy career or to fight the war, to the end, when Brick again asks Rusty who he is fighting for. Rusty says the men were good men who did their jobs and did them well; that the job was one of "laying down the sacrifice" is less important than the fact that they did it well.

But Ford does not find the same value in professionalism that Howard Hawks does, and it cannot fully contain even limited meaning in his films. It is not the concept of professionals or patriots doing their job well that has meaning for Ford, but the social values created by the sacrifice. Rusty and Sandy try to conjure up a home that probably never existed when they talk of tall corn and apples, images tied to the primary drives for land and food. The dinner party attempts to reach for the feeling of community and home (Sandy's pathetic and touching attempts at femininity in a harsh, hellish world) but the real meaning of the party comes from its proximity to destruction and the maintenance of fragile if schematized normalcy in the face of it. Without the war, Ford suggests, the values represented by "home" would not have such meaning. Only in the face of loss and chaos can these values be even alluded to, though not realized. This is the dichotomy upon which Ford so often draws for depth in his films; life can be meaningful only because there have been *socially* required sacrifices for its continuance through rituals like religion and war, yet that sacrifice fails to return

meaning to those who must carry it out, and to whom the film gives the greatest attention and sympathy.

There is a self-conscious quality about the dinner in its extreme stylization (narratively as well as visually—Sandy's repeated, inadequate

Composition creates the fragile "normalcy" of the dinner party.

Soft light patterns across Sandy's face create a vision of the feminine beauty of home.

117

Rusty and Sandy: the sounds of war intrude on their memories of home.

The telephone is the only connection between Rusty and Sandy as the squadron pulls out to an unknown destination.

Dad (Russel Simpson) stays behind to face the advancing Japanese alone.

"swell") that is actualized in Sandy's breaking down when the men have gone and only Rusty remains: the show they have put on for each other only emphasizes their isolation from the hoped-for content of the forms they observed. Like the dance, in which soft light patterns conjure up an atmosphere of home with the softness, safety, and femininity of the setting, the proximity of the chaotic reality and the desired normalcy existing simultaneously at the party are more moving than either of them alone. Then tension between them keeps the scene on edge: the pure state is alluded to and the power of its nearness with the concomitant denial is bittersweet.

The telephone on which Rusty tries to tell Sandy goodbye represents the tenuous hold they have on each other, or on any permanence at all. Besides the lack of a permanent base, they have no real, dependable connection between each other. Their farewells are given under the worst circumstances, offering no foreseeable future together. The very fragility of their hold on their relationship and all it represents makes it achingly valuable: it is the acting out of the destruction of the bond that affirms the value of the bond. Yet it is not the sacrifice of some mythic patterns in which the suffering is payment for the social success: in *They Were Expendable* the required failure of their future offers no compensatory comfort.

Dad (Russell Simpson), the old man who runs the dry dock for the Navy, is the only character in the film who has a home for which he can fight. He prefers to die there rather than leave it, and the last shot of him, rifle in his lap and jug beside him, to strains of "Red River Valley," is one of the loneliest in the film. Its power comes from the many levels of the theme of home: he is displaced in the Philippines, so will die alone in an empty gesture. This tenuous hold on a commitment to "home" is still greater than the men's, and Dad's lonely, doomed figure sitting calmly waiting for certain death has a richness of meaning unapproached by the rest who have nothing to live or die for.

The smooth, graceful beauty of the PT boats performing at the beginning of the film has been reduced to nothing by the end, as the ordering chain of command has been broken beyond recognition. Brick and Rusty trudge through the dust and dirt in the unorganized disarray of the Army, Marine, and Navy men and equipment totally broken down and defeated. The smoke of the bat-

The stable, nearly geometric order of the first view of the PT boat squadron is completely destroyed by the end of the film.

The men left behind: the tragedy of their inevitable death is rendered beautiful in its visual abstraction.

tle provides a softening texture which contributes to the utter desolation of the chaotic mass of men without any chain of command or formal order, and expresses their inner breakdown. In the last shots the redeeming effects of formal abstract beauty are recruited to give a transcendent quality to the utterly despairing and hopeless ending of the men being left to die as Brick and Rusty bitterly fly off to "do their duty." The men are abstracted visually into an emotional entity, first the close up of Guns, then shots of two men we do not know, finally simply dark shapes on the beach as the plane flies into the distance. The men and the plane are moving to different destinies, but the beauty and stability of the compositions, along with the abstraction which takes the viewer's emotions out of the realm of response to specific individuals, informs the hopelessness of the film. It is in the visual expression of the film that the entire concept of value is contained. The dichotomy of the formal beauty and classical composition with soft, romantic lighting of the scenes which allude to home, contrasted to the unstable, harshly dark world of the hospital and the otherworldly character of the battles, is reconciled in the last scene of the men on the beach. No real point to the struggle is thematically offered in this last scene: the men have "laid down the sacrifice" for no reason that the film will give us; they are simply alone and cut off. The structures of the military family have broken down and all that remains are the dispersing men, who are removed from individuality through lighting. We feel the failure of the war on every level, with the loss of human contact and men left behind to die, and simultaneously feel the redeeming effects of the visual beauty. The despair of the film is not mitigated but rather intensified by the visual abstraction, because it generalizes the central theme of lack of meaning while leaving its specific representations intact.

Leaving Baatan in defeat.

THE LONG GRAY LINE

1955

CREDITS

Production company: Rota Productions–Columbia. *Director:* John Ford. *Producer:* Robert Arthur. *Scenarist:* Edward Hope, from autobiography, BRINGING UP THE BRASS, by Marty Maher with Nardi Reeder Campion. *Photography* (in Technicolor and CinemaScope): Charles Lawton, Jr. *Art director:* Robert Peterson. *Set decorator:* Frank Tuttle. *Music Director:* Morris Stoloff *Music adaptation:* George Duning. *Editor:* William Lyon. *Assistant directors:* Wingate Smith, Jack Corrick. 138 minutes. *Released:* February 9.

CAST

Tyrone Power (*Martin Maher*), Maureen O'Hara (*Mary O'Donnell*), Robert Francis (*James Sundstrom, Jr.*), Donald Crisp (*Old Martin*), Ward Bond (*Capt. Herman J. Koehler*), Betsy Palmer (*Kitty Carter*), Phil Carey (*Charles Dotson*), William Leslie (*Red Sundstrom*), Harry Carey, Jr. (*Dwight Eisenhower*), Patrick Wayne (*Cherub Overton*), Sean McClory (*Dinny Maher*), Peter Graves (*Capt. Rudolph Heinz*), Milburn Stone (*Capt. John Pershing*), Erin O'Brien-Moore (*Mrs. Koehler*), Walter D. Ehlers (*Mike Shannon*), Don Barclay (*Major Thomas*), Martin Milner (*Jim O'Carberry*), Chuck Courtney (*Whitey Larson*), Willis Bouchey (*doctor*), Jack Pennick (*sergeant*).

SYNOPSIS

A tragic-comic story of Martin Maher's life at West Point, encompassing fifty years of U.S. history.

> "I wouldn't know where else to go."
>
> Martin Maher to
> President Eisenhower

The genre categories of war film and military picture are not easy to distinguish. *The Long*

Filming *The Long Gray Line.*

Tyrone Power as Martin Maher and the Plebe Whitey—who will become President Eisenhower.

Irish immigrant Martin Maher fresh off the boat complete with name tag and work papers.

Marty and Mary O'Donnell (Maureen O'Hara): an Irish colleen.

Gray Line is definitely a military picture; war is never even seen, but is important. The film uses both World War I and World War II and "actual" Generals (Eisenhower, Bradley) as historical genre "objects." Its time period encompasses but is not limited to the wars; the military—both in peacetime and war—operates as a metaphor which includes cultural elements, family, and above all, tradition and its price.

Martin Maher (Tyrone Power) is Ford's outsider, but in a totally inverted dynamic. He carries out the integration process—first the movement from Ireland to the United States, then to the highly structured, family-like West Point Military Academy, then to marriage and the joining of his Irish family to West Point, then to a highly developed extension of his family to include the men of the corps, who march to do him honor after his audience with his old pleb Whitey, now President Eisenhower. It would seem that on every level—personal, family, professional, even national—he is fully integrated into his society by the end of his fifty years at West Point, with waves of family and friends returning even from the dead to honor him. But for precisely the reason that Andrew Sarris finds the ending reprise unsatisfying (". . . the ridiculous pomp and ceremony of a West Point graduation seems an inappropriate occasion for a visitation from the dear departed," *The John Ford Movie Mystery,* p. 137), Martin's life is not validated but rather mourned for over half the picture. The processes of integration have failed in every way, and all that is left at the end is an empty ritual, a formal structure whose intended meaning we know, but can't experience. The rituals are hollow and unfulfilling.

Ford's camera composes Marty as an outsider from the beginning: Eisenhower's unseen face gives him an impersonal quality, and Marty looks old and fragile in his presence. Once the long flashback that is the film begins, Martin is isolated by his movement in contrast to the rigidity of the cadets, his misunderstanding of their honor codes, and by the fact that as an enlisted man he is never one of them. The only other enlisted man we know at all is Rudy Heins (Peter Graves), and he does not appear often: once to court Mary O'-Donnell (Maureen O'Hara) and by doing so help push Marty into another enlistment, and later to go off to the war that Marty cannot join. Marty is never part of the military group—he cannot join the cadets as one of them and doesn't have his own group of men. Visually, he is shot alone or

Marty courts Mary in Colonel Koehler's kitchen.

Marty proposes—and is accepted.

framed to one side of a composition throughout the film. Marty's connection to West Point is an artificial one; it does not come from inside him as does Mary's and his father's. He is first induced to reenlist by Mary, and she—along with other family pressures—continues to bind him to the corps when he would leave. He feels an outsider when the first war begins, and again in the second: like Bill in *When Willie Comes Marching Home* he is refused overseas duty because he is doing a more important job at home. In his impotent rage at his own cadets dying in a battle he cannot fight, he can only throw silverware on the table and threaten not to reenlist again. Martin is in fact a loser—of all the sporting events he tries to teach (which become moments of comedy), of family, friends, surrogate family, and finally of all the roots his various ties to the academy ought to give him and the meaning they should give his life.

The interrelations between family, self, and the Point are very complex in this film. Marty comes in as an agent of chaos, breaking dishes, upsetting routine, visually moving in contrast to everyone's static postures. He remains such a force to some extent even to the end, going AWOL to see the President and breaking formation in the parade in his honor. But the process of the film is partially to confine him, and it begins with Mary. She will not even speak a word to him until he has proposed, and this has required a reenlistment.

123

Martin must stay behind to train the cadets when Col. Koehler (Ward Bond) leaves for the front.

Again, when their baby dies, she influences him to reenlist. Backs to the camera, in silhouette and soft light, Mary later asks him again to stay in the corps as they are framed as lovers in their own house. Mary brings his father and brother from Ireland and old Mr. Maher (Donald Crisp) increases the pressures to remain at the Point. He refuses to leave even when they do, and their last view of him is as they drive off. We have a privileged second view—a close-up of the lonely old man as he sits down to wait his death and be buried at the Point, preferring its rituals to those of his own family. Mary and Mr. Maher are the bearers of culture and tradition. Mary kneels and prays in the Irish, and only Marty is left alone and kneeling when the others rise. Mr. Maher has a family link to Mary that eludes Marty: it is he who tells his son about her pregnancy, and he who emerges triumphant from the delivery room to announce the birth of his grandson. But it is Marty who must receive the news of his child's death alone: we do not hear what the doctor says. Marty's face in full, direct close-up as he reacts is enough.

The child—long awaited and celebrated by the cadets, who have been surrogate sons and who make the baby one of their number by giving Marty a sabre and a West Point book for his name —unites all of the elements that have barely

Marty as the agent of chaos.

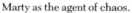

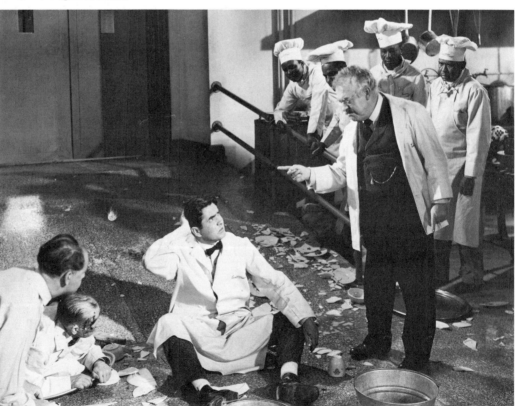

Old Mr. Maher (Donald Crisp) joins Mary to pressure Marty to stay at the point

Mary and Old Mr. Maher are bearers of Irish tradition and culture.

Old Mr. Maher is the center of attention in the hospital and the first to know when Marty's son is born.

The cadets honor the birth of Marty's son, designating him a future West Pointer.

In a stunning track in to his face, Marty breaks the saber, symbolizing his hopes for his infant son.

Christmas: Marty is surrounded by yet
another group of ever changing surrogate sons.

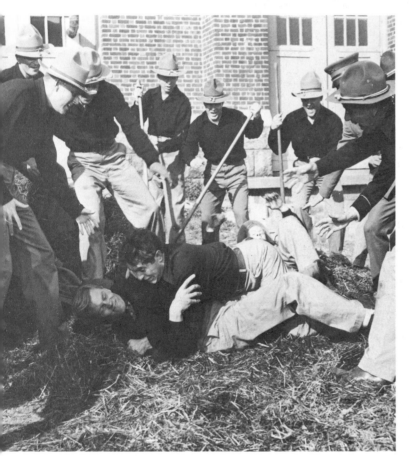

The young Marty impulsively attacks Rudy, thinking he and not their honor
code is responsible for the errant cadets marching punishment.

eluded Marty, and with his son's passing, he is
lost. He breaks the sabre, in a stunning camera
move from the close-up on his face to a medium
shot to see the action, and seems thus to have
broken a link that can never be reforged. Martin
Maher III is the bearer of the name and symbol of
Marty's link to the Academy via the cadets and
saber. His loss signifies the failure of all those
links—cultural, religious, family, and personal.
All subsequent attempts to make those contacts
are bitter and empty, even though their *form* is
sentimental and often beautiful. The conflict between the elaborate forms and empty content is
moving and disturbing.

The cadets become not only surrogate sons but
father figures as well, as when they find Marty off
limits and drinking after the boy has died and
fetch him back, then walk punishment for it the
next day. They come to see him at Christmas, and
the kindness they offer cannot mask the distance
and loneliness of the old man. Red Jr. (Robert
Francis) is the most direct surrogate son, especially for Mary. His letter of appointment to the
academy prompts Marty to defend the academy—
and Red Sr.'s death—against the angry widow,
and then to reenlist. At that moment, Ford cuts to
the baby crying, then to a now-grown Red taking
the oath. A funny moment and a disturbing one, a
relationship of repression is at least implied:
Marty is both a victim and is complicit in Red's

Marty in jail as the cadets try to explain their honor code: we share his disbelieving point of view.

unchosen career at West Point. This is carried out further when Red breaks the honor code and comes to Marty for absolution, which the father surrogate—now the tough military man—will not give. The irony is tinged with bitterness, for it was Marty in his exuberant early days who could not understand why anyone would turn himself in for an undetected act. The young Marty first makes Rudy an accomplice by insisting they did not see a cadet after hours, and then is sent to the guard house for fighting when he thinks Rudy turned them in. The camera is situated so that we are with Marty looking through the bars at the visiting cadets, thus implicating us in his puzzlement over their honor code. This is Marty's most lively and endearing characteristic, and later when he sternly enforces the code on his own "sons" even Mary threatens to shift her alliance. The loss is of Marty's rebellious, chaotic youth, repressed by the multiplicity of strictness.

Mary, the most important agent of Martin's attachment to the Point, is an odd combination of a strong, independent woman and a cultural agent that leaves her alone and unknown, even by Marty. She is always Mary O'Donnell even as she dies in his arms, their backs to the camera. But she is not always independent; she follows Col. Koehler's (Ward Bond) directive not to talk (to be repressed) until Marty proposes, and gets him to reenlist every time. Perhaps it was necessary for

Marty ridicules the rigidity of the long gray line.

After the death of their baby, Mary and Marty can have no more.

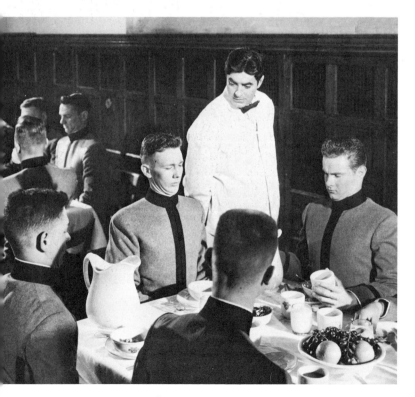

Marty watches in wonderment the harrassment of the plebs.

the child to die in order to focus both their attentions on the corps and not on themselves and their family. There is a visual link between the death of the child, announcement of no other children, and the cadets as they turn from an "interior scene" in the hospital room to the window overlooking the parade grounds. Mary chooses Red over the honor code, reversing their earlier positions vis-á-vis rules and people. And Mary is terribly alone—we cannot get too close to her since her function is to become a direct culture/West Point/family tradition line to Marty, and as such she remains removed from our direct identification. She ages more devastatingly than any character, and as her domain—the house—closes in (from the warm, bright, whole house with doors thrown open when old Mr. Maher arrives, to the dark corridor that confines Mary and Marty through the last third of the film) and hardens its edges, so does she. They are rarely together in the house at any time, always passing on the stairs or in the corridor. Mary is left unfinished, and with her last strength wants to go and watch the parade; her "sons."

When Mary first talks of bringing old Mr. Maher to West Point, Marty says, "Him that's lived free all his life? With all the rules and regulations?" yet it is only Marty himself who rebels against the rules, cannot understand them, and finally loses an important part of himself by embracing them. Mary asks him to accept the will of God in the death of their child and together they watch the cadets march, accepting them as surrogate sons. But all the tradition, honor codes, and even the "long gray line" seem only hollow rituals with no humanity to them by the end of the film. Marty is never fully realized as soldier, father, or husband, and is left in the end with only memories and the marching men to sustain him.

The visual look of the film is generally static or majestic low angle tracking shots of the long gray line. This was Ford's first CinemaScope film, and he minimized minor camera movements, rendering them very effective. Little tracks into an indi-

Marty as "Master of the Swim."

132

Marty transformed into a military man.

vidual or a couple, as when Mary and Marty are in the swing, or in on the singers when the baby is born, express a lovely tenderness. Brief follow shots have great impact, such as the one which follows Marty to the locker area to talk with Red. Transitions are very direct and comment on the previous scene, as when Marty remains on his knees when the others rise from prayer, then says "swimming" and Ford cuts to his new position as master of the swim. It is a very effective way to pass fifty years without becoming episodic.

In the first scene, Marty tells the unseen President Eisenhower he can't retire for various reasons which all come down to "I wouldn't know where else to go." This is what West Point has done for Martin—taken away his rebellious spirit, his options, and finally the freedom he prized so highly. All it has left him is a noisy crowd of ever-changing young men, and the formal rituals that Mary always loved so much. Marty laughed at the straight lines of cadets at the beginning, and stands receiving their tribute in the end. It is more than the story of a man who wasn't too distinguished and didn't go too far in life, it is a tragic picture of the molding of a man into something he didn't want to be. The forms are all that are left. Their meaning, which the young unregimented Marty questioned and tested, is not only missing —it is forgotten.

The old Martin: defender of the traditions of West Point.

134

The Long Gray Line.

THE WINGS OF EAGLES

1957

CREDITS

Production company: MGM. *Director:* John Ford. *Producer:* Charles Schnee. *Associate producer:* James E. Newcom. *Scenarists:* Frank Fenton, William Wiester Haines, based on life and writings of Commander Frank W. Wead, USN. *Photography* (in Metrocolor): Paul E. Vogel. *Art directors:* William A. Horning, Malcolm Brown. *Set decorators:* Edwin B. Willis, Keogh Gleason. *Costumes:* Walter Plunkett. *Music:* Jeff Alexander. *Editor:* Gene Ruggiero. *Aerial stunts:* Paul Mantz. *Assistant director:* Wingate Smith. 110 minutes. *Released:* February 22.

CAST

John Wayne (*Frank W. "Spig" Wead*), Maureen O'Hara (*Minnie Wead*), Dan Dailey (*Carson*), Ward Bond (*John Dodge*), Ken Curtis (*John Dale Price*), Edmund Lowe (*Admiral Moffett*), Kenneth Tobey (*Herbert Allen Hazard*), James Todd (*Jack Travis*), Barry Kelley (*Capt. Jock Clark*), Sig Rumann (*manager*), Henry O'Neill (*Capt. Spear*), Willis Bouchey (*Barton*), Dorothy Jordan (*Rose Brentmann*), Peter Ortiz (*Lt. Charles Dexter*), Louis Jean Heydt (*Dr. John Keye*), Tige Andrews (*"Arizona" Pincus*), Dan Borzage (*Pete*), William Tracy (*Air Force officer*), Harlan Warde (*Executive officer*), Jack Pennick (*Joe*), Bill Henry (*Naval Aide*), Alberto Morin (*second manager*), Mimi Gibson (*Lila Wead*), Evelyn Rudie (*Doris Wead*), Charles Trowbridge (*Admiral Crown*), Mae Marsh (*Nurse Crumley*), Janet Lake (*nurse*), Fred Graham (*officer in brawl*), Stuart Holmes (*producer*), Olive Carey (*Bridy O'Faolain*), Maj. Sam Harris (*patient*), May McEvoy (*nurse*), William Paul Lowery (*Wead's baby, "Commodore"*), Chuck Roberson (*officer*), Cliff Lyons, Veda Ann Borg, Christopher James.

SYNOPSIS

Spig Wead cannot unite his personal life as husband and father and his profession of career naval officer: he

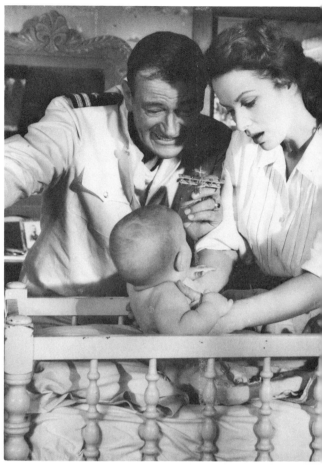

The family: John Wayne as Spig Wead and Maureen O'Hara as Minnie.

chooses the military. In spite of a crippling accident, he becomes a successful military man and playwright, but after a heart attack at sea during World War II, he thinks only of his wife and their lost life together.

> "If it's not a family, it's nothing."
>
> *Spig to Minnie*

In *The Wings of Eagles* the genre themes and narrative patterns of war films and Ford's deepest artistic commitments to his personal themes come together in a melodrama (but a "men's weepie" this time) that directly challenges not simply the underlying sensibilities of war, patriotism, and films about them, but the ideas and assumptions of the entire culture. *The Wings of Eagles* would seem to be about the life of an American hero, of a man of action who caroused with the boys, flew planes, fought wars, and lived the ideal of the masculine life to the fullest. Actually, this beautiful film protests that very ideal and is predicated on the failure of that life to satisfy Spig's most basic needs and his insistent denial of those needs.

The story is based on the life of Ford's close friend, Frank W. Wead, who wrote the screenplays of *Air Mail* and *They Were Expendable.* Ford says it is as biographically true as he could make it, including the slapstick comedy scenes. But in his choice of form for the story, Ford divorced *The Wings of Eagles* from any fidelity to a "reality" that art is both incapable of reproducing and would be committing itself to banality if it could. There is at least one other direct reference in this film: Ward Bond plays movie director John Dodge in fond parody of Ford himself. While this knowledge adds savor, like the film's proximity to Wead's life, it is merely coincidental and does not directly inform the themes of the film.

Along with his Ethan Edwards in *The Searchers,* John Wayne's Spig Wead is the actor's most difficult, subtle, complex, and fully realized role. Wayne gives the character exuberance, a firm belief in his country's cause, and profound sense of failure and loss while still remaining within the confines of the military man. Spig is one of the most profoundly moving heroes Ford has created. His need to act out the mythology of America that says a man fears nothing, finds pleasure in adolescent games with other men, and above all, has no emotional needs, especially with regard to women, is measured against the paralyzed, helpless Spig after the accident, who is then even less willing to admit need, and finally, to the reality of the broken old man suspended over the ocean between two ships. His pursuit of glory and action at the expense of family, love, and those softer aspects of his own personality leave him unbearably isolated from his wife and children, his dearest friends, and finally, from himself. It seems to be the special talent of Wayne to be capable of both embodying the ideal and exposing it at the same time. In *The Wings of Eagles* he does this with great skill, entering into the broadly directed silly games (fast motion fighting, slapstick cutting with cakes in faces) that mark the military throughout this picture, yet expressing the underlying loneliness of such escapades. His return home and the look on his face when he sees his children powerfully contradicts the value of the superficial, slapstick navy camaraderie.

Spig's ambivalent relationship to his family is apparent from the very first scenes of the film.

Slapstick comedy: Minnie at the airfield in the Stutz Bearcat.

Spig Wead: a broken old man suspended between two ships.

137

The Army-Navy race: Spig's team "triumphs" in this comic scene cut from the release print of the picture.

The congressmen: "fighting the voters every two years."

Coming home drunk with his pal Johnny (Ken Curtis), he brings Minnie (Maureen O'Hara) a little toy airplane, and finds it difficult to turn his attention from it to the sick child. When the baby dies later that night, the doctor tells Johnny that Spig could do Minnie some good, but they are separated by both the lighting and composition which divide the room into two separate planes. Spig will not go to her, for such motion would implicate him in the life of the family. The next scene is of Spig's graduation from pilot school, and Ford cuts from a long shot of the men to a low angle close-up of Minnie pinning the wings—like the toy—on her husband. This aspect of his life is already established as more important, compelling, exciting and self-validating than his personal life, and very soon he nearly totally gives up his family for his career. Their little boy's death seems a trade-off for the graduation and later advances in his career, which are also marked by sacrifices in his relationship to his family.

In Spig's ambitious, fast-rising life as a single-minded naval officer, the idiocy of the military is made abundantly clear. Ford's direction not only makes their antics broad self-parodies, but is still able to include some direct criticisms. In the encounter with the congressmen, the economics of both politics and war are startlingly clear, with the congressmen referring to "fighting the voters every two years" and generally referring to them as retarded but power-wielding adversaries. The congressmen agree to the army-navy race for its public relations value to the military, and because "we aren't trained to be losers." In this essentially comic scene, Ford is remarkably effective in criticizing an ethic which encourages war because its men were taught to value competition and need an arena in which to fight. The whole experience of the film performs a far-reaching critique on American attitudes toward strength and weakness. If Spig's life is an example of masculine strength, then real sustaining human value is shown to lie in feminine priorities of love and family. Spig is at his most compelling when he finally allows a little of his own need for love and gentleness to show. In San Francisco just after the attack on Pearl Harbor he tells Minne he needs her, and she tenderly kisses his head as he sits in her chair with his crutches beside him. As if sharing his pain with her, he finally allows another person to help him with the crutches. He tells her, "If it's not a family, it's nothing." The words come from bitter experience and desperate longing, but even that knowledge does not stop him from going back into the Navy when the war reaches America. Ford does not take lightly the ethic he is critiquing; even Spig's profound awareness of the failure of the values implicit in his military life is internalized, and he goes back to war. Ford has no illusions about the ability of people to act independently of the value systems of the cultures in which they live, and chooses to show the tragedy of the contradiction rather than a romantic individual transcending social priorities.

Spig's most basic failing with regard to his family is clearly demonstrated when he comes home to rejoin them. He feeds his daughters, cleans up the house, and waits for Minnie to return home from what has obviously been a date. In an amazingly mature and understanding scene, Spig accepts her story of a bridge party and she accepts his being there. He understands that she has unfulfilled needs and that his actions have been in part responsible for her behavior, which is definitely not easily permitted women of melodrama in 1957. He can accept her needs, but when he falls downstairs and is paralyzed, he refuses to let her accept his. He denies her first when the doctor wants his next of kin to approve the dangerous operation: Spig answers, "I'm my next of kin.

Let's go." When he winds up nearly totally paralyzed, he is so terrified of his own weakness and vulnerability that he sends her away, saying, "I had my turn. Now you take yours." He will not even let her kiss or touch him, and refuses to allow her to bring the little girls to see him. He cuts her off without any comfort or love, fearing that the "burden" he has become would be too great

Spig returns home to his family, but an accidental fall and resulting paralysis wrenches him away again.

Spig, now a hopeless cripple, rejects Minnie's love and help.

Spig and Carson (Dan Dailey).

for her. This macho gesture of self-sacrifice is in fact little more than immature fear—fear that he too is a needy person who must rely on others. Thus in what would seem like a gift to her, he lets her (and himself) down most completely. As Minnie leaves the hospital, the camera tracks in front of her: she walks steadily, not dissolved in tears (as we are), a woman of strength capable of giving the love he needs. We feel her pain and it is not for the loss of Spig, but for his rejection of her and of the self that he most desperately needs.

The sexual element of his fears of vulnerability is exposed when he accepts Carson (Dan Dailey) where he rejected Minnie. Carson becomes his steady companion, the person who knows how hopeless it is, who knows how badly off Spig is financially, and the person who makes no demands. Minnie sends flowers and continues to visit the hospital, but she does not infringe on the limits Spig has put on their relationship. It is only with Carson, continually joking, encouraging, sneaking whiskey, and above all, never requiring an emotional interaction, that Spig can be weak, discouraged, clumsy, and finally, begin to recover. Carson in many ways becomes a metaphorical wife to Spig, often putting him back in touch with Minnie (as after the successful opening of his play), and providing Spig's life with a continuity it would not otherwise have. In the final sequences, on the battleship at war, Carson suddenly and dramatically takes on greater and more threatening significance that frightens both men. When an enemy plane strafes the ship, Spig's paralyzed legs will not get him out of his very exposed position. Carson grabs him, protecting him with his own body. The climactic battle, which is visually separated and thus open to metaphorical connotations, surely has sexual implications which result in serious injuries to both men. Carson is wounded and Spig suffers a heart attack at Carson's hospital room threshold after his emotional attempt at thanks is refused by Carson's glib banter. In one of the most moving shots of the film, Carson watches from a porthole as Spig is being transferred from their ship to another after the heart attack. Carson stands and looks for a long, wistful moment in medium close-up framed by the oval window. They are both so very alone: Carson in his frame and Spig dangling over the Pacific. Carson turns away, and the words never said, feelings never exchanged between the two men shout out like thunder: a mute protest to their repression.

Spig's last thoughts before leaving his ship are of Minnie. He looks at the photographs of their life together, bringing the rest of the picture back to us in light of the new, fully developed critique. He smiles gently for the first time, realizing finally—now that it is lost—where the real value in his life always lay, and then goes out to receive the ritualized respect, gratitude and friendship of his fellow officers. As he walks to the side, the tears in his eyes seem more for her and all he has lost than for this life in which he has been so successful. As he goes over the side in a breeches buoy, the extreme long shot from above looks down on his tiny, helpless figure suspended between the two boats. He is indeed a lost soul. All the honor in the world cannot equal what he gave up so long ago, and even his physical representation is crippled and fragile.

The Wings of Eagles suggests the impossibility of making contact with another person, particularly when sexuality is involved, which requires dangerous vulnerability of intimacy. The Navy games are seen in retrospect as we gaze (with Spig) at the pictures of Minnie as evasions of that contact. The men act out adolescent rituals that keep them emotionally apart and safe rather than bringing them together. The military is a hollow, inadequate substitute family for Spig and the other men, like Carson, who cannot open themselves to the great intimacy (and greater love) of a real family. It is this possibility that Spig was repeatedly offered and he repeatedly rejected as exterior events (war, his accident) representing the forces of the culture which cannot be side-stepped prevented him from refusing the ethic even when he realized its inadequacy. The implications of this are even more far-reaching: the process involved in closing one's self off to love and intimacy is one of repression—repression of needs and desires, and finally, of aspects of one's self. Spig is fundamentally a wounded man, not because of his paralysis, from which he never fully recovers, but because he has refused expression to the gentle, loving, feminine aspects of his own personality. Even when he realizes his loss he cannot act upon it. When he can finally be vulnerable with Minnie, war overtakes the nation and Spig is not strong enough to refuse. His fear of vulnerability and the destructive power of his fear is acted out in the midst of war. When he gazes longingly at the photographs of himself and Minnie, they are frozen, undemanding, and they offer him only memories.

Like *They Were Expendable, The Wings of Eagles* protests the very existence of the military, war, and the ethic that make these things necessary. Instead of a glorification of war, these films mourn the repression that its culture requires and the hollow rewards only intensify the pain of that repression. *The Wings of Eagles* delves deeply into the human psyche, critiquing the denial and repression of love and sexuality. It exposes those forces which keep people alienated from each other and even from themselves, and protests that alienation in a radical way that both mourns and protests the repression, yet refuses to co-opt its own critique by using characters who transcend it. *The Wings of Eagles* is radical for the very reason that it roots its characters firmly in their culture, and makes us *feel* the pain that begins with the values of the culture and insists on both its specific expression in the lives of the characters and its all-pervasive, generalized existence in all our lives.

The final result of his life of war and glory: Spig is crippled, doomed to die in a matter of weeks, and lost, suspended alone over the ocean.

THE
IRISH FILMS

The Plough and the Stars: Irish genre pictures are often set in an Irish rebellion locale.

INTRODUCTION

As a genre category within Ford's oeuvre, the Irish pictures constitute a structure as clearly delineated and mappable as the Westerns. With the exception of *How Green Was My Valley,* they are set in Ireland, generally use a rebellion as a historical backdrop, and deal with values of patriotism, family, love and responsibility. These narrative themes are then used to construct larger mythologies by which the recruited ideologies of an imagined Ireland become fundamental precepts in Ford's contribution to the shaping of our popular culture. The Irish element runs through virtually all of his films, from the Irish names of the cavalry films—Quincannon appearing with humorous regularity—to the displaced, nostalgic Irish sensibility of *The Last Hurrah* and *The Long Gray Line.* The traditions of family go back generations. Sean is accepted by the men of the pub in *The Quiet Man* only after establishing his lineage—both symbolic through the shared name "Sean" and biological through his grandfather who emigrated to Australia. They sing "Wild Colonial Boy" for both the rebel emigrant grandfather and the returned Irish son. The age-old folk music becomes another link in the rich association of culture and tradition. The family itself is self-contained, providing humor, drama, and above all, *meaning* to the larger society of these films. In *How Green Was My Valley* the idealized memory of the destroyed family is the only heritage the boy takes with him from the valley. These rich, unknowable, but deeply powerful and evocative associations of home, family, music and country weave a dense and comforting fabric of wholeness that Ford creates and recruits directly in the Irish films. It is extended past its specific Irishness to touch the longing for such wholeness and depth in our own cultural mythology, and thus informs that dimension in the modern American context. A mythical Irish conscious-

The Long Gray Line: Maureen O'Hara as an Irish immigrant fresh off the boat.

Young Cassidy: Music—especially singing in pubs—is a genre element.

147

ness functions in the same way as a mythical American West for Ford. It is a time of greater wholeness, greater heroes, and a reference point for a present which cannot sustain its dreams.

But unlike the Westerns, the Irish pictures do not constitute a genre category outside of Ford's work. It would be possible to assemble a number of films set in Ireland, but they would not share narrative themes, patterns, and use of the country's ideology as do Westerns, war films, musicals, and other identifiable genres. Thus in this category the intersection of genre and auteur is not simply determining, as it is in the Americana films, but concentric, with the entirety of the genre inside the auteur category. The critical hypotheses drawn from these films have a narrower viability for film theory than might insights made from a genre shared by many directors. Ford's Irish films as a genre are important only with reference to his career, not to all of American narrative film, but the genre constructs inform nearly all of his films and certainly all of his artistic preoccupations.

Sean Aloysius O'Feeney was born in Maine of Irish immigrant parents. He took the name Ford from his brother who was already working in pictures when John went to California in 1913. Ford never let go of his Irish heritage; indeed, in his work he celebrated it and made it a metaphor for some of his broadest concepts. This additional, personal dimension to Ford's Irish pictures which already have a definite set of narrative patterns and traditional associations makes the genre as conventionalized as the Westerns, with motifs

How Green Was My Valley: The family is a theme of the genre.

148

running through them that build on their use in previous films.

The myths and traditions of the Irish function both within the constructs of the individual films and as metaphors for similar constructs in Ford's total artistic vision. The family in *How Green Was My Valley* mirrors the little Welsh mining town, which itself carries out the breakdown of tradition that marks the economic and moral decline of the nation. The boy who is the outsider is like the Western heroes who stand outside their culture, and whose backward-looking view of those cultures is nostalgic and yearning. The traditions associated with the Irish—drinking, the authoritarian father, the prominence of religion, the propensity to rebellion, the importance of music—constitute the genre structures. The weight of other associations is carried in these traditions from film to film: the IRA from *The Informer,* in which it is romantic, necessary and nearly holy, to *The Plough and the Stars,* in which it is heroic but impotent, to *The Quiet Man,* in which it is a fond, humorous reference indicative of character rather than rebellion.

Irish history itself, like the history of the American West in the Westerns, functions prominently in the Irish pictures. Ford uses specific rebellions in *The Informer, Young Cassidy, The Plough and the Stars* and *The Rising of the Moon.* The view of

Sean Aloysius O'Feeney: John Ford circa 1930.

Ford used stock Irish characters and actors: *The Plough and the Stars*

The Informer: Brawling as an Irish character trait.

The Quiet Man: John Wayne and Victor McLaglen exchange insults and blows.

this history changes from film to film, as it does in the Westerns, and it becomes a genre element subject to ideological weighting. History is used as a myth and as backdrop for a personal story, and the relationship between individuals and their history or social context is presented by the films as dialectical. In *Young Cassidy,* the myth of the artist who outgrows his home is played out with very direct formulations of his development by family, nation, and class background. In *How Green Was My Valley,* the relation between the breakdown of the family and the collapse of the town is clearly an economic one which informs both aspects. Although this film is set in Wales, its themes of family, the past as a time of innocence, music, and beauty which is destroyed from the outside root it firmly in the Irish picture genre. Like *The Rising of the Moon,* the past is referred to and mourned even while it is presented as a myth.

The genre constructs are history, family and tradition, the elements include music, ritual, rebellion; and the values are those of the innocent, mythical past of Ford's vision: heroism, patriotism, national and family wholeness. These myths play a more direct role in the Irish pictures than they do in most of his films, and thus the films become highly ritualized and conventionalized. But they are less accessible because they are so much more personal, created as they are from Ford alone and not from a large body of films drawing from an entire popular culture. Myth is critiqued even while it is celebrated in all his pictures, but in the Irish films the celebration is always stronger than the critique.

The Quiet Man: the formation of a new family.

How Green Was My Valley: the community of the Welsh mining town is defined by class.

150

The three women in black shawls dominate the foreground as agents of fate.

THE INFORMER
1935

Production company: RKO Radio. *Director:* John Ford. *Associate producer:* Cliff Reid, *Scenarist:* Dudley Nichols; from the novel by Liam O'Flaherty. *Photographer:* Joseph H. August. *Art directors:* Van Nest Polglase, Charles Kirk. *Set decorator:* Julia Heron. *Costumes:* Walter Plunkett. *Music:* Max Steiner. *Sound:* Hugh McDowell. *Editor:* George Hively. 91 minutes. *Released:* May 1.

CAST

Victor McLaglen (*Gypo Nolan*), Heather Angel (*Mary McPhillip*), Preston Foster (*Dan Gallagher*), Margot Grahame (*Katie Madden*), Wallace Ford (*Frankie McPhillip*), Una O'Connor (*Mrs. McPhillip*), J. M. Kerrigan (*Terry*), Joseph Sawyer (*Bartely Mulholland*), Neil Fitzgerald (*Tommy Connor*), Donald Meek (*Pat Mulligan*), D'Arcy Corrigan (*blindman*), Leo McCabe (*Donahue*), Gaylord Pendelton (*Daley*), Francis Ford ("*Judge*" *Flynn*), May Boley (*Mrs. Betty*), Grizelda Harvey (*an obedient girl*), Dennis O'Dea (*street singer*), Jack Mulhall (*lookout*), Robert Parrish (*soldier*), Clyde Cook, Barlowe Borland, Frank Moran, Arthur McLaglen.

SYNOPSIS

Gypo Nolan informs on his friend, IRA leader Frankie McPhillip, for twenty pounds, which he then spends on everyone in the street. Sentenced to death by the IRA as an informer, Gypo escapes, is wounded but struggles to a church, where he dies in the shadow of the cross after Frankie's mother forgives him.

The *Informer* is one of Ford's most critically honored films, winning Oscars for McLaglen as Best Actor, Dudley Nichols for Best Adaptation, Max Steiner for Best Musical Score, and Best Director for Ford. He also received the New York Critics Best Director Award. Like another much-awarded Ford film, *Stagecoach,* The *Informer* is

Victor McLaglen as Gypo in *The Informer:* one of Ford's most theatrical films.

The nearly expressionistic visual style premonishes the fate that dooms Gypo.

Gypo and Frankie in the pub.

153

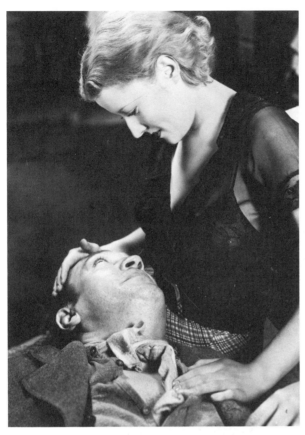

Katie and Gypo.

The IRA

not actually one of his best achievements. The theatrical structure and devices of the film are easily discernible, making elements which can be rooted deep within character and mise-en-scene very accessible and stripped of ambiguity. The beautiful, nearly German Expressionist street film photography of Joseph August, with shadow, fog and low-key lighting, dooms Gypo (Victor McLaglen) and Frankie (Wallace Ford) from our first view of them. The poster blowing against Gypo's legs for the rest of the film and the blind man who "sees" Gypo's actions demonstrate the forces of fate. As Gypo stares at Frankie in the Durby House, Ford dissolves through to the "Twenty Pounds Reward" on the poster. Later as Gypo gazes longingly at the "America—Ten Pounds" sign, Ford dissolves to his fantasy of Katie (Margot Grahame) and himself, married and on their way to the promised land. This visual directness lacks the complexity and subtlety with which Ford usually surrounds his characters, and the nearly silent character of the film (the first dialogue is spoken ten minutes into the film) contributes to the often iconographic characterization of the characters.

Katie is first seen silhouetted in moody, low-key light. With her shawl over her head, she is a Madonna figure. Then a man, a customer, comes to her and she becomes a "street angel." She retains this iconic and dichotomized characterization through the film—driven by poverty and life to prostitution, but somehow pure underneath. Dan Gallagher (Preston Foster) is a kind-but-tough, pipe-smoking leader of the IRA whose dedication is to its cause and whose love is for the virginal Mary (Heather Angel), Frankie's sister. In creating these immediately recognizable, iconographic figures, Ford and Dudley Nichols not only made it possible to make a nearly dialogue-free film in 1935, but completely transformed the intention of Liam O'Flaherty's book from which the film was made. The characters in the book are not beautiful if miserable icons—they are the scum of a poor city upon whom O'Flaherty forces the reader to gaze so closely that one can be nothing but repulsed. The intimate point of view is maintained so religiously, with long descriptions of people's horrible faces and the unromantic, starkly dehumanizing environment, that lofty ideas of revolution, dignity under hardship, and purity through suffering become meaningless. They are not a part of the book. The vision of the film is completely transformed—it is a tragic ro-

Gypo is driven to his ignominy by forces beyond his control.

Katie and Gypo: doomed by fate.

155

Gypo in expressionistic angle and lighting which emphasize
his inability to control the forces that will destroy him.

mance. Ford adds understandable motives and a romantic notion of fate contained in the expressionistic visual style of the film. It is visually very clear that Gypo wants the twenty pounds to take Katie to America where they can live a good life, and that Frankie is on the verge of death anyway. The film's characters are much more attractive: Dan Gallagher in the book is a cold, scheming, ugly man, and Mary is neurotically, masochistically attracted to him. These changes not only make the whole piece more palatable, but give it meaning.

Gypo can be seen as a demented Christ figure who carries all humanity on his back and is crushed by it, fated to die on the cross and be forgiven by the mother. He is also very similar to many of Ford's favorite characters, the innocents who are driven to a life of moral failure through forces beyond their control. The fate that blows the poster against Gypo's legs and brings Frankie to him when he has just dreamed of saving Katie from her degradation is much more powerful than he is, and his childlike ignorance leaves him une-

qual to resist it. He asks Gallagher, "Can't someone tell me why I did it?", and later talks to Katie about the fog in his mind. The exterior controls people exercise over their lives are unavailable to him—he cannot get work, he lives in the poorest, toughest section of Dublin. He cannot even be a revolutionary, as he lacks the necessary discipline. Gypo is raw strength and power, and there is not enough love in his world to shape and control him. After being shot, he is "undead" until he is forgiven by the person he has hurt most—Frankie's mother. "You didn't know what you were doing," she tells him, and he dies on the cross in church. He is not merely the Judas premonished in the opening title, but a sacrificial character for all of Dublin. His life and death are given a dignity they did not have in O'Flaherty's book, and the unsparing criticism of the book is not included in the film.

Frankie also takes on an "epic" character he did not have in the book. Ford and Nichols removed the father who hounded him and dominated him so that Frankie becomes the man of the house,

Ten pounds to America: Gypo is obsessed by the dream.

158

Gypo spills his "blood money" at Frankie's wake.

The malevolent crowd separates Gypo from his friend, his money, and, finally, his life.

and thus the most important person for both Mary and his mother. All the characters in the film, except for the "Tans"—the English police—and the upper class and probably English patrons of the last pub Gypo and his mob visit, are given dignity by the film. Ford is characteristically generous to his characters, rarely leaving a major character without reasons for his/her mistakes or failures. It seems the supreme achievement of this skill to make Gypo Nolan a character we mourn. The crowd in both film and novel, however, share the malevolence that makes Gypo its natural prey. They readily crown him king and spend his money—thereby exposing his guilt—until it runs out; then they leave him to die.

The transformation from an ugly, realistic novel of degradation and treachery into a film of dignity and transcendence is accomplished first at the visual level, with the elements of fate romantically and beautifully expressed in the tracking shots and shadow, and second at the level of character, with the people of the film turned into rec-

ognizable icons whose inability to escape their wretchedness takes on dignity.

The film treats the historical subject—the 1922 Sinn Fein Rebellion—as a mythic setting, visually abstracting the characters, situations, and ideological issues from the realistic base the novel insisted upon. It thus becomes the Christian and pagan myth of sin and redemption through suffering which is acted out by one member of a community for the benefit of the entire community. The elements of ritual and fate—the blind man, the entrapping shadows, the blowing poster—mark the progress of the myth which fate has determined and signaled from the opening shot. This operation of fate is radically different from the one of social process in the book. It leaves no room for critique or protest, the hallmark of Ford's best works, and makes *The Informer* an easily accessible but fundamentally uncomplicated retelling—and reinforcing—of an old myth.

Gypo informs on his best friend for twenty pounds.

THE PLOUGH AND THE STARS
1936

CREDITS

Production company: RKO Radio. *Director:* John Ford. *Associate producers:* Cliff Reid, Robert Sisk. *Scenarist:* Dudley Nichols, from the play by Sean O'Casey. *Photography:* Joseph H. August. *Art director:* Van Nest Polglase. *Music:* Nathaniel Shilkret, Roy Webb. *Editor:* George Hively. 72 Minutes. *Released:* December 26.

CAST

Barbara Stanwyck (*Nora Clitheroe*), Preston Foster (*Jack Clitheroe*), Barry Fitzgerald (*Fluther Good*), Dennis O'Dea (*The Young Covey*), Eileen Crowe (*Bessie Burgess*), Arthur Shields (*Padraic Pearse*), Erin O'Brien Moore (*Rosie Redmond*), Brandon Hurst (*Sgt. Tinley*), F. J. McCormick (*Capt. Brennan*), Una O'Connor (*Maggie Corgan*), Moroni Olsen (*Gen. Connolly*), J. M. Kerrigan (*Peter Flynn*), Neil Fitzgerald (*Lt. Kangon*), Bonita Granville (*Mollser Gogan*), Cyril McLaglen (*Corporal Stoddart*), Robert Homans (*barman*), Mary Gordon (*first woman*), Mary Quinn (*second woman*), Lionel Pape (*the Englishman*), Michael Fitzmaurice (*ICA*), Gaylord Pendleton (*ICA*), Doris Lloyd, D'Arcy Corrigan, Wesley Barry, Irish Abbey Players.

SYNOPSIS

During the failed Irish Rebellion of Easter Week, 1916, a man leaves his wife to assume leadership of the rebel forces.

Set in the Irish rebellion of Easter Week, 1916, *The Plough and The Stars* falls far short of Ford's standard. Despite some beautiful photography, it suffers from miscasting of both principals, Barbara Stanwyck as Nora and Preston Foster as Jack (although the minor characters are excellent), and

Barbara Stanwyck as Nora and Preston Foster as Jack.

The Plough and the Stars: set in the Irish rebellion of Easter Week, 1916.

The film often looks like a stage drama: the rebels plan their strategy.

163

Ford wanted the film to focus on a man and his wife: Jack and Nora.

Nora and the dying girl who dreams of a family.

structurally from the addition of documentary footage (presumably) of the rebellion itself. This is intercut with the story and matches neither the photographic style nor the narrative story of a man and his wife separated by the demands of country. *The Plough and the Stars* is one of the only two or three films Ford made in his entire career that simply does not work on any level.

Adapted from a play by Sean O'Casey, the film often looks too much like a stage drama, and conversely, during the sequences using documentary footage, looks too little like a structured dramatic work. The credits are run over scenes from the picture, rather like a preview. Once the film begins, we see sequences, but there is little continuity between them: the play seems in search of an underlying thematic structure. According to Ford, this structure was subverted by the studio cut of the picture: his version is not in existence in this country today, and focuses on a man and his wife.

The most interesting element of the film is this tension: the conflicting pulls of wife and country on a man who cannot reconcile them. He takes the job of leader of the rebels, saying that "Ireland is greater than mother or wife," but in leading this ill-fated (and, it is implied, ill-planned and executed) uprising, risks losing both wife and country. Ford, who in so many other films equates family and country, using one as a metaphor for the other, shows us what Jack can't see: Ireland *is* wife and mother, not an abstract concept, and she requires both devotion and sacrifice.

In the most beautiful and moving scene in the film, Nora talks to the lovely, doomed young girl who will die of consumption before the film's close. She tells Nora of her desire for a family, a

164

Nora searching for Jack.

The ill-timed uprising is doomed to failure.

The film is from Nora's point of
view as she tries to keep Jack
out of the fight.

Battle scenes are dominated by chaos and looting.

The most heroic act is Nora's search for her husband in the midst of battle.

husband to take care of, but despairs her strength ever to do so. Nora, tormented that Jack has gone to the IRA despite her pleas that he stay with her, replies that life is difficult because it is woman's nature to love and man's nature to fight. In Ford's world, the ability to love is far superior to that of fighting, and the total loss of the battle certainly underscores this. In the end when Jack says this defeat is only the beginning, Nora asks him, "The beginning of what?" In spite of the narration over documentary footage of the free Ireland that is won a few years later, our feelings are with Nora and her question. The men will go on fighting, Jack tells her, and she responds, "Then we'll go on weeping."

The point of view throughout the film is Nora's, from the opening when she sees the call to meeting and smiles to herself, thinking she has perhaps kept her husband out of it this time, to the end when we search with her for the point to all the suffering and dying. Although this viewpoint is a little unusual for Ford, who usually tells his stories from the point of view of a male lead (even when the point of the film is a man's loss of his feminine aspect), it is not the last time he will use it. *Drums Along the Mohawk* uses a similar point

of view, and is a fully successful film. Whatever success there is in *Plough and the Stars* comes entirely from Nora, created by her feelings and our response to them.

The focus on Nora is not the only indication that Ford's sympathies are more with the women of the film than with the rebels. In spite of the glory of the lines of armed men, the fiery speeches, and the scene of the signing of the proclamation that creates the free Ireland, the scenes of war in the picture are of looters and of disjointed battle scenes in which no objectives are established so no gains or heroic losses can be measured. We are not sure of the progress of the fighting in relation to other action, and the clearest heroic act is Nora's search for her husband. She is so alienated from him that she believes him to be dead more than once. Her faith in the cause and his sacrifice to it are models for our own. When Jack does come home from his sniper's post on the rooftop (which even the narration tells us is useless and only gets innocent people hurt) it is the women who save him. Most ironically, the little girl who so envied Nora's family (which we have seen to be almost nonexistent, the only efforts towards building a life together coming

167

The dead girl saves the rebels: they hide weapons in her coffin.

from Nora's efforts alone) ends up giving Jack the refuge he needs to save his life: they hide his weapons in her coffin.

It is not difficult to imagine the possibilities of *The Plough and the Stars.* There is some beautiful

Nora and the dying girl: the visual style refers to the dreams that will never be fulfilled.

(*Opposite page*) Nora: beautiful expressionistic photography.

expressionistic photography, primarily of Nora. With her eyes lit from below and soft shadows around her, Ford creates a lovely Madonna image. This visual treatment separates her from Jack even in the beginning when he vows he will not leave. When the men sign the independence proclamation, the lighting throws huge, pretentious shadows on the wall behind them. The outdoor scenes of Nora and the young girl are filled with the shadows of dreams that can never be for the child, and are lost to Nora because of her husband's insensitivity. The unearthly quality to this late-night scene could relate to other elements in the film if handled differently. The theme of a man torn between the country he loves and the woman he loves, trying to do his duty to both without losing either, is a very personal one for Ford, used in *The Wings of Eagles* most successfully. Because of the studio recut, as well as real problems in the material itself and in the direction, the possibilities of *The Plough and the Stars* did not materialize, and it remains an interesting but deeply flawed film, one of Ford's poorest.

HOW GREEN
WAS MY VALLEY
1941

The military family of *She Wore a Yellow Ribbon.*

CREDITS

Production company: Twentieth Century-Fox. *Director:* John Ford. *Producer:* Darryl F. Zanuck. *Scenarist:* Philip Dunne; from the novel by Richard Llewellyn. *Photography:* Arthur Miller. *Art directors:* Richard Day, Nathan Juran. *Make-up:* Guy Peirce *Set decorator:* Thomas Little. *Costumes:* Gwen Wakeling. *Music:* Alfred Newman. *Choral effects:* Eisteddfod Singers of Wales. *Sound:* Eugene Crossman, Roger Heman. *Editor:* James B. Clark. *Narrator:* Rhys Williams. 118 minutes. *Released:* December.

CAST

Walter Pidgeon (*Mr. Gruffydd*), Maureen O'Hara (*Angharad Morgan*), Donald Crisp (*Mr. Morgan*), Anna Lee (*Bronwen Morgan*), Roddy McDowall (*Huw Morgan*), John Loder (*Ianto Morgan*), Sara Allgood (*Beth Morgan*), Barry Fitzgerald (*Cyfartha*), Patrick Knowles (*Ivor Morgan*), The Welsh Singers (*singers*) Morton Lowery (*Mr. Jonas*) Arthur Shields (*Mr. Parry*), Ann Todd (*Ceiwen*), Frederick Worlock (*Dr. Richards*), Richard Fraser (*Davy Morgan*), Evan S. Evans (*Gwinlyn*), James Monks (*Owen Morgan*), Rhys Williams (*Dai Bando*), Lionel Pape (*Old Evans*), Ethel Griffies (*Mrs. Nicholas*), Marten Lamont (*Jestyn Evans*), Mae Marsh (*miner's wife*), Louis Jean Heydt (*miner*), Denis Hoey (*Motschell*), Tudor Williams (*singer*), Clifford Severn, Eve March.

SYNOPSIS

Leaving the Welsh mining town of his childhood, Huw Morgan remembers when the valley was green and the town healthy. In dreamlike flashback, the disintegration of the valley and the Morgan family is chronicled as sons die and others are forced to leave the valley because of economic changes at the mine. Finally Mr. Morgan is killed in a mining cave-in, marking the last

The Cheyenne Nation constitute a family in *Cheyenne Autumn.*

The family of *How Green Was My Valley* has personal, national, and mythic dimensions.

stage in the economic, physical, and moral breakdown of the valley and its people.

The breakdown of the family—whether a personal family, an extended one (as in the Cavalry and other military pictures), or a national family which loses touch with its tradition (the Cheyenne tribe and the Irish nation)—is John Ford's most anguished theme. Through it he expresses personal alienation as well as socioeconomic disintegration: the family functions as a flexible metaphor for an entire range of artistic/mythic preoccupations. In *How Green Was My Valley* the family has both the personal and national dimensions: the destruction of the Morgan family parallels the socioeconomic life of the town, and Huw's passage into an impoverished present.

The present of *How Green Was My Valley* is Ford's idealized past, seen through the memory of the boy who lost it before he was to possess it. His past is his family, with brothers and sister grown and able to function as full members of that wonderful life from which he is always apart. And his past is the valley itself, metaphorically defining in space a quality of life and a myth. It is his point of view that permits the film such an idealized depiction of the Morgans. We are con-

The grown man who remembers the past of the valley is faceless.

The old woman of the past: a static, frozen composition.

series of moving pictures with no sound of their own except those sounds which belong to memory, such as the church bells and the calling of his sister. The sequence of his father and brothers coming home, washing the coal dirt from their bodies, and then sitting down for dinner, has no natural sound, only effects and the voice-over. Thus traditions of the family are set up as *already* existing in the past. Their relationships are clearly defined, first by the line past the paymaster in which each receives an amount according to his position in the family (a relationship based on economics), then in the washing and dining. They all stand before the table in a momentarily frozen tableau remembered by the child. This form reoccurs throughout *How Green Was My Valley* to indicate their position in the child-man's mind. When he first sees Bronwen (Anna Lee), when his brother Ivor (Patrick Knowles) and later his father are brought up out of the mine

Huw and his father in the valley of the past: open and unbounded.

stantly reminded that this is Huw's (Roddy Mc-Dowall) memory and not an attempt at any other kind of reality. His voice-over begins the film, telling us that the valley and his family are doomed even from this point and that he is leaving the valley which is so unlike the one in his memory. The camera pans from the faceless man to the window in the little room and tracks through it, opening up the frame spacially while moving in a right-left direction, which is backwards, into the past. The film cuts gradually (first a long shot, then a medium shot, and finally a close-up) to an old woman in a static, frozen composition. Her expression is backward-looking, rapt with memory. From this shot the film dissolves to an unbounded, moving long shot of the valley of memory—identified by the voice-over narration. The movement of Huw and his father (Donald Crisp) and of the sheep lend the scene a sense of awakening movement, indicating that the life lies in the past, in contrast to the dead present. Thus the flashbacks begin with Huw's voice-over narrating, introducing the family in a

172

dead, the picture freezes in a balanced and finished composition. In the last such composition, Mr. Gruffydd (Walter Pidgeon) stands on the platform over Huw and his dead father like a comforting angel, and for the first time Huw is a part of the tableau instead of simply observing the rest of his family as they form this moment in his memory. Combined with unnatural sound, this visual construction abstracts the moment from the narrative reality, slowing it down and momentarily stopping the dynamic of the story. It continually reminds us with each reoccurrence that it is Huw's point of view that we are watching. The sound, like the clinking of the coin his father tosses in Huw's bowl when he distributes money to the family, is exaggerated and also functions to situate the sequence in memory, not historical reality. The voice-over represents the man stepping in to tell us about the boy's story, both reminding us that it is his story and providing in-

The men washing: there is no natural sound to make the idealized picture "real."

173

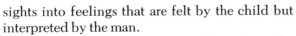
The family relationships are defined at the pay window.

sights into feelings that are felt by the child but interpreted by the man.

This point of view is a doomed one from the beginning. The past it will interpret is already gone and thus its players are predestined to tragedy by the bleakness of the very first sequence and the sadness of the narrator. As in *The Man Who Shot Liberty Valance,* the hero is dead before the story ever begins. In the Western, however,

The frozen tableau is a fixed memory:
The family

Ivor's death

Bronwen

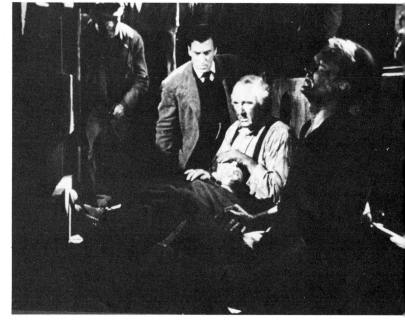

Ivor's death

there is the positive aspect of the larger story: the civilizing of the West for which its greatest son was required to die. The form of the genre itself is a distancing device, placing the film in the world of myth and allowing the expression of feelings that would not be tolerable if experienced more directly. In *How Green Was My Valley,* however, Ford must construct his own distancing devices to protect against too directly confronting the

Mr. Morgan's death

The lines of composition oppress the workers at the mine.

The triangular composition defines the hierarchical relations of the family and at the mine.

Freudian implications (the death of the father which frees the son and finally allows him a place in the visual world of the film) and stark tragedy of the breakdown of the nation and family. Thus the flashback structure and voice-over are devices which maintain a specific point of view and function as distancing devices in a form which does not automatically provide them as does the Western. This function is provided stylistically in *How Green Was My Valley* instead of generically as in the Westerns.

The frame of the film is enclosed even in exte-

riors by light and compostion. The line of houses on the right side of the frame looking up at the mine always bounds that side of the frame. We never know what is on the other side of the houses, and within a shot it functions to limit and cut off the little town. The mine with its smoke towers and the church with its bell tower define the upward limits of the frame of the town. When Ford cuts to either of them it is an announcement of a new scene or perspective. In the first view we (and Huw) have of Bronwen as she comes to visit the Morgans, the village is enclosed on the other side by the steps that she comes down. These structures are composed to constantly appear at the edge of the frame, limiting and defining a boundary. Inside, low ceilings, dark foreground objects, and dark areas confine and limit the frame. Rarely, except in close-ups, does a scene take place without dark objects dominating the frame, or a low ceiling providing an upper limit for the action. Low angles emphasize this, and characters are often pressed against the ceiling or skyline by an extreme low angle. The effect of these enclosed frames is not one of claustrophobia, but rather that of defining the world of the film within the memory of the boy. The enclosure is more cozy than threatening. Even the darkness which figures so prominently in the compositions is warm and friendly until the last part of the film. It is always fraught with emotion and meaning, as

176

when Bronwen has her baby upstairs in the dark-
ened Morgan house where her husband lies dead.
When the house itself is threatened by the poison
which spreads over the landscape and into the
hearts of the people, the quality of light in the
house becomes cold and crisp and the angles become longer, diminishing the family in the house
and emphasizing the space between them.

The film grows visually and thematically darker as the family disintegrates. The traditions
which the boy remembers as safe and warm are
set up in the light: the washing, returning home,
dining, walking with his father on the sunlit hill.
Later, these very traditions are broken down in
darkly threatening scenes, as the one at the dinner
table which culminates in the four older boys
leaving the house to take lodgings in the town.
Early in this sequence there is a shift in the relationship between the father and sons which is
indicated by composition. He occupies no greater
power position than any one of the sons, unlike
earlier compositions in which he is the apex of a
triangular, hierarchical construction. The lighting
is unstable, coming from below the characters in
contrast to the warm soft light of previous scenes.
The union's threatened strike sets off the change
in the family structure, but the film makes clear
that this is only the surface issue. In fact, the split

Low ceilings and dark foregrounds confine and limit the
frame.

In one long take during Ivor's wake, his brother leads the
camera from the mourners, to the father, and to the stair, above
which Ivor's baby has just been born.

The foreground is dominated by the lantern, indicating the fragility of the scene.

Huw and his father: the warm, safe, balanced and well-lighted scenes of the early picture give way to darker scenes. The grown sons leave home in the night.

In the labor struggle the power relations in the family shift, and the father no longer occupies center frame.

between labor and management has been forced by *outside* conditions—general recession, unemployment which increases management power—and the father who has been the balancing factor as leader of the workers must choose sides. This process of polarization or heightened contradiction is illustrated visually—first by Mr. Morgan working in the rain as a management sign of power over the workers (an unbalanced composition indicating order undermined) and then by the dinner sequence in which the father cannot keep the home isolated from the economic tensions of the mine. In a high, off-angle shot (contrasted to the eye-level shots of the opening, remembered dining scenes which were head-on or profile), Ivor first rises, overbalancing his father. Then Ianto (John Loder) in close-up visually challenges his father's authority, and finally in long shot all the grown sons stand as their parents and Huw remain seated. The polarities are defined as the sons leave the shot, crippling the composition and isolating the father. He is shot from across the long, empty table, emphasizing his aloneness. Only Huw, not yet grown with a place in the family, is with him. The breakdown process has been represented economically, with the heightening contractions and loss of balance beginning at work and spreading to infect the home.

Economic tensions interrupt the ordered visual balance of the dinner table.

Ianto is visually given authority and strength as he challenges his father.

Once the grown sons leave the table, the long shot emphasizes the father's aloneness. Only Huw impotently remains.

Traditions expressed visually: the old couple and the new.

It is not the unworthiness of the sons or the meaninglessness of tradition, but the demands of time which destroy the old ways. This is Ford's bittersweet nostalgia: the old ways must go, not because they are not good or strong or because the new ways can push them out, but simply because the times change and the requirements of coping with those times change. The old ways always seem the most beautiful: this film is a testament to that fact. But we respond as much to their destruction as we do to their beauty, and by acting out the conflict with understanding for both aspects of change, the film serves a mythic function in relieving the tensions of irreconcilable desires. When Ianto stands up at the table, composed in low angle against the ceiling, and, protesting his father's ill treatment at the mine, insists that if manners prevent his speaking out against injustice he will be without manners, we understand the necessity. Ford sets up a dichotomy: the old respect and tradition must go for the men to live, but he mourns the passing as does the boy who remembers. Unlike other pictures (*She Wore a Yellow Ribbon, The Last Hurrah*) in which the past becomes doubly attractive because the young men of the present do not seem able to measure up to the old men, in *How Green Was My Valley* the sons are as strong of character as is old Mr. Morgan. The compositions of the film structure Huw's brothers as symbolically large as his father. Indeed, Ianto always seems to be about to burst out of the confines of the frame. Only the narration (and early in the film his center frame position, which he loses later to Mr. Gruffydd) gives the father a place greater than theirs.

How Green was My Valley is structured to hang carefully between happiness and tragedy, with the sadness gradually taking over a larger and larger portion of the film until there is no happiness left, except of the bittersweet kind when Huw says good-bye to Mr. Gruffydd. From Ivor and Bronwen's wedding, with Angharad (Maureen O'Hara) and Mr. Gruffydd laughing, the film cuts to a sign announcing the pay reduction at the mine. From there it never quite recovers the uncomplicated happiness of the wedding party, although the shifts in mood continue to partially relieve the deepening sadness of the film. Dark sequences are also laced with jokes and laughter. When the first two boys must leave home because there are no longer enough jobs at the mine after the strike, Beth Morgan (Sara Allgood) is asked by

181

Ivor and Bronwen's wedding party: the camera tracks in to isolate Angharad and Mr. Gryffith.

Huw why she ever had babies, and she replies "To keep my hands in water and my face in the fire, perhaps," and the family laughs with her. Immediately following this moment comes the telegram to sing before the Queen. The great honor, laced with tradition and ritual, mitigates the loss of the two sons as it visually affirms the family and community through the beautiful and stable image of the men singing at night. From that the camera tracks to follow the two sons leaving home, ending with a close-up of Beth, Angharad, and Bronwen. Unlike the earlier unbalanced shot of Beth outside the house when the others go back inside, leaving her alone, this last three-shot is comforting in its satisfying composition and lighting, implying acceptance of values that encompass but transcend sadness.

Huw's schooling outside the valley is one such sequence which lightens the tragedy after this point, but it is perhaps the least satisfying of the film. As *How Green Was My Valley* is seen through the eyes of a boy who remembers it, it follows that the heroes of his drama (Mr. Gruf-

The men sing for the Queen in a dark, stable composition while the first two sons leave home in a shot that ends with the women.

Beth is left alone outside the house in an unbalanced shot, when her sons are forced to leave home.

184

fydd, his father and his brothers) should be larger than life and have the dimensions of an adult world seen by a child anxious to grow up and take his place in it. That it is no longer as it was when he is grown is also consistent, giving the memory a bittersweet sense of loss. The villain of the story, however, also takes on a larger-than-life dimension which is not mitigated by any real truth that carries it beyond the demands of reality within the context of the story. Both the schoolteacher, Mr. Jonas (Morton Lowery), and the elder (Barry Fitzgerald) who obstructs Mr. Gruffydd whenever he can, therefore emerge as one-dimentional comic-bad foils to the emotional content of the story. Mrs. Nicholas (Ethel Griffies) is a similar character. All their sequences act as in a Shakespearean play to relieve tension when it is necessary to build it further later, but none are satisfying in themselves. In a film that is so generous in its understanding of all characters who play an important part, these characters seem jarring and out of place.

Huw's moments of triumph, in which he is on the verge of becoming a full member of the family in his own right, are always snatched from out of

Huw is isolated by focus from the rest of the children in school.

The men of the family are larger than life in low angle: Huw's memory.

his grasp and the attention shifted to someone else. When he comes home with his Latin report, his parents fuss over him for a moment, but then Bronwen "upstages" him with her visual position in the frame and her talk of her loneliness since Ivor's death. Later, when Huw has gone down into the pit and received his first pay, he takes it to his father who exclaims over him; then his brothers, just discharged, enter the frame in very low angle, upstaging him again and shifting the attention of their father and of the audience from Huw. There seems nothing he can do to truly become part of the world he watches, and he remains an outsider until the moment of his father's death. Then he seems to take his father's place, and in the untold time between the death of old Mr. Morgan and the beginning of the film (by which time Beth has died, releasing Huw to leave the valley) he remains alone, the last son, with his mother.

Huw's moments of attention and triumph are snatched from him by tragedy: Bronwen's sadness. Ianto and Davy's termination at the mine.

Huw is always the watcher of the adult world.

By the time Ianto and Davy (Richard Fraser) leave home, there is nothing but sorrow left and no lightness to remove the sting of their leave-taking. Indeed, the Bible reading as they leave is bitterly ironic: just as they close the door for the last time, Mr. Morgan reads the last line of "The Lord is my shepherd"; "My cup runneth over," he says in lonely close-up. Angharad's unhappiness and Mr. Morgan's death follow with increasing blackness as the life of the valley itself deteriorates, with nothing except the mitigating distance of the backward-looking point of view to make it bearable.

Angharad and Mr. Gruffydd's tragedy stands out even in the dark backdrop of death, at the mining accident. In Ford's world, the greatest loss a man can suffer is the loss of the feminine side of his psyche, symbolically represented by a woman. This is poignant in *The Wings of Eagles,* but perhaps its most simple, clear depiction comes in *How Green Was My Valley.* Mr. Gruffydd denies Angharad in a gesture of self-sacrifice, telling her, "I have a duty to you. Please let me do it." In this act Mr. Gruffydd, a man of great wisdom and tolerance, chooses the false values of materialism and comfort over the real one of love, and like so many Fordian heroes, dooms himself

With all his brothers gone, Huw is the only son left at home with his mother.

Ianto and Davy leaving home: "My cup runneth over."

and Angharad to lives as emotional cripples. Huw, the observer in the film, sees their similar pain and its effects.

Throughout the film, Ford is acutely sensitive to social oppression of sexuality. An unwed mother is accused in a public church meeting of sin, and only the fiendishly evil elder takes any satisfaction in her humiliation. Angharad's reaction to the incident, which is to affirm her love for Mr. Gruffydd in the face of society's condemnation, is represented as a better way of relating to life than his own. And as in so many Ford films (most notably *The Sun Shines Bright*), the woman who has sinned and suffered for it becomes the most innocent and justified character, perhaps because she has risked everything for love and lost.

The failing in Mr. Gruffydd which makes him sacrifice Angharad's and his own happiness is essential: heroes can never be whole, well-balanced characters and still be effective in their roles. And it is significant that what is missing in Ford's masculine heroes who must remain alone is sexual. The myth requires that their hero status be gained at some cost, and in a Ford film that is generally in the form of requiring those heroes to be outsiders. They can never fully become part of the community they serve. In spite of Mr. Gruffydd's ability to drink beer at Ivor's wedding party and even to join in the economic struggles of his people (aspects of the people's lives former

Angharad and Mr. Gruffydd.

Angharad: unhappy new wife in the Evan's house.

Ford puts the audience in the accused unwed mother's point of view in the church.

Angharad falls in love with Mr. Gruffydd at first sight.

Mr. Gruffydd and Angharad are visually separated when the rich Evan's son courts her.

ministers did not involve themselves in), he remains alone in the community. At Angharad's wedding he stands in silhouette under a tree as the bride and groom are sent off in a bleak parody of the earlier wedding. In the first wedding, the camera is inside the church and the people rock with music and joy when the married couple comes out. In Angharad's, the music is forced, and we simply see her appear, glassy-eyed, to join her new husband.

Mr. Gruffydd failed in his personal life in the village by refusing Angharad. His failure in his professional life is demonstrated by his leaving the church. There is a casual relationship which is more than suggested: he leaves because the community is going to censure Angharad, whereas the only crime has been his, and it was against their love. His inability to bring his kind of religion to the community is irrevocably tied to the deterioration of the town, which begins with

Mr. Gruffydd is a silhouetted observer at Angharad's wedding; she is glassy-eyed and nearly catatonic.

Angharad and Mr. Gruffydd meet again only at the tragedy of the mine explosion.

Mr. Gruffydd points an accusing finger at the elders of the church.

The idealized memory in the reprise: Huw's brothers.

the pay cut, the firing of the men, the boys leaving home because they cannot get work, and ends with the darker, nasty natures of the people surfacing to poison the valley emotionally as the mine has physically. Mr. Gruffydd might have succeeded, but his denial of Angharad (and therefore part of himself) foreshadows the tearing apart of the village that will follow. When their eyes meet over the tragedy of her father and the destruction of that night, a relationship of cause is implied. That cause is a complex and multileveled mixture of Marxist and Freudian concepts that Ford seems uniquely able to combine in a full, satisfying work of art. In *How Green Was My Valley* there is a dialectical relationship between the Oedipal motif and the economic analysis of the relations of production and of the family and community. It is through both processes, which are marked in their deterioration by the refusal of love and sexuality between Mr. Gruffydd and Angharad, that the family of the Morgans and the economic stability of the mining town are destroyed forever.

We experience the film through the memory and perception of the now-grown Huw, distancing us from the disillusion born of hope, yet rendering the experience intensely personal as we share his point of view throughout, yearning to participate in the glorious past which ceases to exist as soon as he becomes part of it. Thus the myth is validated even as its underlying structure is destroyed.

Huw and his father.

Angharad

The women in classical composition at the moment of Mr.
Morgan's death.

THE QUIET MAN
1952

John Wayne and Maureen O'Hara in *The Quiet Man*.

CREDITS

Production company: Argosy Pictures-Republic. *Director:* John Ford. *Producers:* John Ford, Merian C. Cooper. *Scenarist:* Frank S. Nugent; from a story by Maurice Walsh. *Photography* (in Technicolor): Winton C. Hoch, Archie Stout (second unit). *Art director:* Frank Hotaling. *Set decorators:* John McCarthy, Jr., Charles Thompson. *Music:* Victor Young. Songs, "The Isle of Innisfree," by Richard Farrelly; "Galway Bay," by Dr. Arthur Colahan and Michael Donovan; "The Humour Is On Me Now," by Richard Hayward; "The Young May Moon," by Thomas Moore; and "The Wild Colonial Boy," "Mush-Mush-Mush." *Editor:* Jack Murray. *Assistant Editor:* Barbara Ford. *Second-unit directors* (uncredited): John Wayne, Patrick Ford. *Assistant director:* Andrew McLaglen. Exteriors filmed in Ireland. 129 minutes. *Released:* Sep. 14.

CAST

John Wayne (*Sean Thornton*), Maureen O'Hara (*Mary Kate Danaher*), Barry Fitzgerald (*Michaeleen Oge Flynn*), Ward Bond (*Father Peter Lonergan*), Victor McLaglen (*Red Will Danaher*), Mildred Natwick (*Mrs. Sarah Tillane*), Francis Ford (*Dan Tobin*), Eileen Crowe (*Mrs. Elizabeth Playfair*), May Craig (*woman at railroad station*), Arthur Shields (*Reverend Cyril Playfair*), Charles FitzSimmons (*Forbes*), Sean McClory (*Owen Glynn*), James Lilburn (*Father Paul*), Jack McGowran (*Feeney*), Ken Curtis (*Dermot Fahy*), Mae Marsh (*Father Paul's mother*), Harry Tenbrook (*policeman*), Maj. Sam Harris (*general*), Joseph O'Dea (*guard*), Eric Gorman (*railroad conductor*), Kevin Lawless (*fireman*), Paddy O'Donnell (*porter*), Webb Overlander (*railroad station chief*), Hank Worden (*trainer in flashback*), Patrick Wayne, Elizabeth Jones, Antonia Wayne, Melinda Wayne.

SYNOPSIS

Sean Thornton (John Wayne), retired from boxing after killing a man in the ring, leaves America to find his roots and peace in Ireland. He immediately runs up against fighting Red Will Danaher (Victor McLaglen), first when Sean buys his ancestral home of Innisfree, and again when he falls in love with Mary Kate Danaher (Maureen O'Hara), who needs her brother's permission to marry. Danaher is tricked by both the Catholic and Protestant ministers into letting Sean and Mary Kate marry, but this is only the first step. In order to really be a wife, Mary Kate needs "her fortune" and the traditions behind it, which Danaher refuses to give her until Sean demands it. This results in a mammoth, cathartic fight between Sean and Danaher in which the entire village participates and is restored to health as the Thornton–Danaher family becomes whole.

That John Ford called *The Quiet Man* his "first love story" cannot be taken literally, since nearly every film from *Straight Shooting* in 1917 to *What Price Glory* in 1952 is really a love story. The action of Ford's best films is a metaphor for the progress of the love story, and when the problem —be it the joining of the transcontinental railroad or the winning of World War II—is resolved, so is the love story. But *The Quiet Man* is the first of Ford's films in which the situation is reversed; the love between Sean Thornton (John Wayne) and Mary Kate Danaher (Maureen O'Hara) is the center of the film and its resolution is the force by which the rest of the problems and imbalances of

The visually impressionistic flashback to Sean as a fighter in America.

Michaeleen Flynn (Barry Fitzgerald) is the "chorus" of the film.

the film are righted. Thus Ford's usual manner of using exterior action to describe a character or a relationship (i.e., the Indians appearing just when Mrs. York arrives at the post in *Rio Grande*) is turned on its head and it is the emotional content of each scene and relationship that determines the action.

Like so much great art, and so many of Ford's films, *The Quiet Man* is a movement to emotional (and thereby physical) health and stability through the journey into Sean Thornton's physical and mythological past, which results in a restoration of balance to the past as well as to the present of the characters. It is a magnificently *complete* work, with all elements of the visual and dramatic unified on the emotional level.

Like *How Green Was My Valley* (but with totally different effect), *The Quiet Man* is provided with a flashback structure through voice-over narration. In the earlier picture, the increasing darkness and tragedy of the Morgan family is rendered even more complete because we know the end from the beginning: the family is split up and the valley is ruined. In *The Quiet Man,* however, a similar structure provides instead a kind of comfort and ease which is part of the lightness and comedy of the film. Since the story exists in the past, there is no need to fear its problems will not all work themselves out satisfactorily.

Michaeleen Flynn (Barry Fitzgerald) is both narrator and catalyst in the movement of the film, guiding Sean's journey into his own past and commenting on it. Michaeleen is the chorus, the dramatic device by which the movement is initiated, remaining somewhat outside the action himself in order to interpret it. In this highly classical and structured context, Ford creates one of the most revolutionary films of the American cinema.

The journey into the past begins with the first images of the film. The visual steps in Sean's passage into another time use movement in the direction of the past (*in,* toward the back of the frame) and are marked by barriers which are passed through. The first shot of the film is the train pulling into the station, blocking off one side of the frame. Sean is seen through the window, looking through its frame at the quiet village. He passes through this, and once off the train, Michaeleen takes his bags, and without so much as a by-your-leave, guides him to his next step. A pony cart (in contrast to the modernness of the train) is framed through another window. It is like looking at a picture of the past and then walking into it as

Sean's first look over the bridge at his ancestral home of Innisfree.

Sean passes through the window. The next step is one of direction and sound juxtaposition: Michaeleen drives him into town, past his ancestral home of Innisfree (the name itself represents the freedom from an oppressive present into a past innocence than Sean is seeking) which he sees over the bridge. He gets out of the cart and is framed with the bridge and Innisfree before him, and his mother's voice is cut in to represent the direction of his goal—to a past (in the R. D. Laing sense of returning to the past in order to continue into a future) that is filled with personal and mythological significance. The bridge itself, and the wind which seems to blow continually around the idyllic little cottage, convey the "extra-worldly" connotations of Innisfree, and these are linked with sexuality through their connection with Mary Kate Danaher.

Sean's next glimpse into the real and imaginary past he is seeking comes in his vision of Mary Kate, which is shot through a frame of trees and woods, from Sean's point of view, with "otherworldly" lighting and wind whipping around her. He asks, "Is that real?", meaning not simply

the woman but the scene and its context. It is his first look at the world of the past and future, the sensual world that will put him back in contact with himself and his natural past. Whenever he sees her from then on it is in a rich visual context of sensual reds and blues, warm lighting on her, and energy in the form of wind and storm all around them. His first close-up view of his home (once he buys it from the Widow Tillane) is one of mystery, with long shots cut with close-ups building tension, until Sean and Mary Kate crash together with the violence and passion of the storm around them.

The barriers to their union are the dramatic excuse for the rest of the steps in Sean's (and Mary Kate's, and the rest of the village's) return to maturity through integration. The most revolutionary element of his journey is its economic foundation: it requires him to give up romantic illusions and understand the economic basis of Mary Kate's (and thereby his) relation to herself, her environment, and her husband. It is the most difficult step for him to take and is dramatically represented by the comic fight that covers the emo-

197

Sean's "vision" of Mary Kate.

Sean and Mary Kate meet in the violence of the storm.

Instant rivals: Sean and Squire Danaher.

Sean brings the threat of disruption to the Squire's household in courting Mary Kate.

tional and physical space between Sean and Mary Kate's brother, Red Will Danaher (Victor McLaglen).

This economic base is represented by Mary Kate's dowry. First, the only barrier Sean can understand to their marriage is the Squire's refusal to allow the marriage and Mary Kate's refusal to go against her brother's order and flaunt *tradition* —which is the basis of the stability that Sean must be reintroduced to in order to regain his own health. The Squire's refusal is his own internal fear of maturity, for while Mary Kate is in his house the Widow Tillane (Mildred Natwick) will not marry him and bring order to his life, which is clearly lacking in the visual representation of his home through unbalanced shots and chaotic art direction. This barrier is overcome largely through the intercession of Michaeleen, and by Sean's working out of his own unhealthy desire to oppose tradition in this sexual matter, which is represented by the black hunter he rides violently over the moor. The horse race is the final step in this sequence, and Sean, with the help of the Protestant and Catholic ministers—Rev. Playfair (Arthur Shields) and Father Lonergan (Ward Bond)—wins partially by dispossessing Mary Kate of her due in the retrieval of hats. The support of the deception by the church—both denominations—mirrors the ministers' roles in Sean's and Mary Kate's marriage; later Sean goes to Rev. Playfair and Mary Kate goes to Father Lonergan when they need to reveal themselves and their problems, and are helped to come back together.

The last step in Sean's journey to health is an internal one—he must realize the economic base of his marriage and rid himself of the guilt of killing a man in the ring. These are linked by money because Sean blames his own greed for the man's death and initially accuses Mary Kate of similar motives when she insists on her "fortune." Squire Danaher refuses to give her the money when he realizes he has been tricked; the Widow Tillane will not automatically marry him when Mary Kate is gone from the Danaher house. Sean must be made to realize the dowry's importance to her. It is her Innisfree—when she first meets him she makes clear her place by seeing him in the parlor, where the things are hers, in spite of the house belonging to her brother. Sean must respect her independence and her need for identity before she will come to him. When she speaks of "having my things around me" he calls

Father Lonergan and Michaeleen Flynn.

Mary Kate's fortune.

her materialistic and feels she doesn't love him enough, but indeed, he hasn't yet come to respect her as a person with a traditional past she needs just as he needs his. Without her furniture and dowry, she tells him, she will be a wife in name only, but really a servant just as she has always been. Only through the recovery of her past—as for him—can she be a whole person for him. She is partially restored when Michaeleen convinces the Squire to give her her furniture, and there is a beautiful love scene between Sean and Mary Kate when he comes home to find her barefoot by the fire. The sequence of shots brings them closer together and encloses them in a tighter and tighter space until they are embracing in his chair. But the promise cannot be fulfilled until he recognizes her need for the carrying out of her traditions and comes to terms with his own feelings about money, and she forces the issue by leaving him the next morning. This leads to the confrontation with the Squire, in which both Sean's and Mary Kate's needs are filled. When the Squire gives the "fortune," Sean goes to burn it, but is joined in the movement in the frame visually by Mary Kate, who becomes his partner in destroying the money and all it means to Sean. Having demanded it from the Squire restored her sense of self and dignity; the money meant nothing to her. His guilt that he fought for money which resulted in the accidental death of the man he was fighting is exorcised by the burning of the money, and

Without her fortune, Mary Kate is a wife in name only.

Sean has to learn to respect tradition.

they are together able to accept each other on their own terms. In one of the most comic, touching and at once mature shots of the film, Mary Kate, having occupied a balanced, powerful angle shot with Sean in the burning of the money, walks off alone. Ford cuts to a shot of her by herself; she is now a wife in more than name, and can be on her own with no need to gain power or identity from either her brother or her husband in the frame with her. The fight is the physical joining of the Squire and Sean as "brothers." It brings them home to Mary Kate, whose house is finally her own, and unites the three as a family—the most stable and healthy configuration in Ford's world.

The village itself is brought together through Sean's journey as well: the Squire and the Widow are courting, the dying old man is "brought to life" in a comic manifestation of restored health, and the entire village is united in the aid of the Protestant minister who might otherwise be re-

moved from the village because he does not have enough people in his parish. Even Father Lonergan turns his collar around and cheers for the minister. It is at this point that the voice-over narration by Michaeleen Flynn, which has determined the flashback structure, returns us to the present: the journey is over and the elements of the drama are complete and whole. The end is finally signaled by Sean and Mary Kate walking away from the camera into their house hand in hand; their unity is accomplished through their love and their journey through time and space, to come together as equals in a traditional present.

Sean and Danaher are joined in a cathartic fight which involves the entire village.

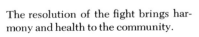
The resolution of the fight brings harmony and health to the community.

Mary Kate and Sean Thornton.

THE RISING OF THE MOON

1957

CREDITS

Production company: Four Province Productions–Warner Bros. *Director:* John Ford. *Producer:* Michael Killanin. *Scenarist:* Frank S. Nugent; from the story, "THE MAJESTY OF THE LAW," by Frank O'Connor, and the plays, A MINUTE'S WAIT, by Michael J. McHugh, THE RISING OF THE MOON, by Lady Gregory. *Photography:* Robert Krasker. *Art director:* Ray Sim. *Costumes:* Jimmy Bourke. *Music:* Eamonn O'Gallagher. *Sound:* Basil Fenton-Smith, Len Shilton. *Editor:* Michael Gordon. Filmed in Ireland. 81 minutes. *Released:* August 10.

CAST

(Introduction): Tyrone Power; (THE MAJESTY OF THE LAW): Noel Purcell (*Dan O'Flaherty*), Cyril Cusack (*Inspector Michael Dillon*), Jack MacGowran (*Mickey J.*), Eric Gorman (*neighbor*), Paul Farrell (*neighbor*), John Cowley (*The Gombeen Man*); (A MINUTE'S WAIT): Jimmy O'Dea (*porter*), Tony Quinn (*railroad station chief*), Paul Farrell (*chauffeur*), J.G. Devlin (*guard*), Michael Trubshawe (*Col. Frobisher*), Anita Sharp Bolster (*Mrs. Frobisher*), Maureen Potter (*barmaid*), Godfrey Quigley (*Christy*), Harold Goldblatt (*Christy's father*), Maureen O'Connell (*May Ann McMahon*), May Craig (*May's aunt*), Michael O'Duffy (*singer*), Ann Dalton (*fisherman's wife*); "1921": Dennis O'Dea (*Police Sergeant*), Eileen Crowe (*his wife*), Maurice Good (*P.C. O'Grady*), Frank Lawton (*Major*), Edward Lexy (*R.Q.M.S.*), Donal Donnelly (*Sean Curran*), Joseph O'Dea (*chief of guards*), Dennis Brennan, David Marlowe (*English officers*), Doreen Madden, Maureen Cusack (*false nuns*), Maureen Delaney (*old woman*), and members of the Abbey Theater company.

SYNOPSIS

Three Irish tales: "The Majesty of the Law," in which old Dan O'Flaherty mourns the passing of the "old

Noel Purcell as Dan O'Flaherty, eulogizing the "lost secrets" of whiskey making.

ways" and goes to prison for assaulting a brewer of inferior moonshine, "One Minute's Wait," about the havoc wreaked on a train's schedule by its passengers and engineers, and "1921," in which a rebel leader is rescued from the British gallows by the Abbey Theater Players.

Nearly all of the elements of narrative and character in addition to locale and history that distinguish the Irish film genre find abundant and exaggerated representation in *The Rising of the Moon.* Andrew Sarris called it "institutionally Irish with a vengeance" (*The John Ford Movie Mystery,* p. 138), and it does rigorously cover every proud or parodied "Irish trait" that was either developed in earlier Irish films or drawn from the stereotyped image of the Irish people. From the dignified, if unreasonably stubborn, pride of Dan O'Flaherty, who is summoned to jail after refusing to pay a fine for assaulting an incompetent moonshiner, to the sharp-tongued wife whose harassment of her policeman husband allows a condemned rebel leader to escape, the "impossible but lovable" nature of the idiosyncratic Irish is parodied, mocked, and ultimately affirmed in the three tales that comprise *The Rising of the Moon.*

All of the elements are here, including the funeral jokes—a man drops dead at a rolllicking wake, thereby spoiling the fun for everyone—and the near canonization of drunkenness, but the failure of the film is that they remain mere ele-

205

Dan and the inspector (Cyril Cusack) who must serve a warrant on him.

The Inspector walks into a misty, mythical setting that evokes the past when he calls on Dan.

Dan's victim—assaulted for selling bad whiskey—offers to pay his fine.

ments of comedy. The value, the tradition, the meaning that these components refer to in previous films is missing. The film becomes a performance in which the forms do not refer to another realm of meaning. Indeed, most of the actors are not film actors at all, but Abby Theater regulars. The last sequence is self-consciously set in and around the Abbey Theater itself, with its artifices becoming the means by which the condemned revolutionary is saved. Rather than a recruitment of generic elements which creates metaphors for emotion through the action of the film, *The Rising of the Moon* is about its own borrowed metaphors. The drunkenness, the pride, and the songs which indicate the "old ways" should be an unreachable but deeply *felt* repository of real value, but are instead merely forms which refer only to their own presence. References to previous Ford films abound: *The Quiet Man* is remembered in the use of the train of "One Minute's Wait," *The Informer* is practically quoted in "1921," Tyrone Power as narrator conjures *The Long Gray Line,* and nearly every character has points of reference to earlier Irish genre films or Irish characters in other Ford films. But these references do not function as an enriching second expression (as *The Sun Shines Bright* is a deepening expression of the Will Rogers Trilogy in the Americana films). Although *The Rising of the Moon* is a virtual summing up of the elements of the Irish genre, it does not deepen and universalize Ford's Irish sensibility, but rather impoverishes it.

The three episodes of the film are related only by a common heritage, and each one is less concerned with the working out of a narrative problem than it is with the creation of a relentlessly Irish mood. "The Majesty of the Law" mourns the passing of the old ways in the person of old Dan O'Flaherty (Noel Purcell), who mourns the "lost secrets" of whiskey making. His juxtaposition to the inspector (Cyril Cusack) indicates the modern direction that Ireland is taking. The first shots of the inspector *walking* (he would not take the car to serve the warrant on Dan) into a misty, nearly mythical setting, beautifully evokes the past. In spite of this and Dan's great dignity, especially in the moving scene in which he painfully kneels to uncover his hidden money which *could* pay his fine if he wished, the past is ultimately trivialized by the inconsequentiality of the issues. Similarly, the second episode, titled "A Minute's Wait," is about the havoc wreaked on a train's schedule by both the engineers of the train and

In the village pub of "A Minute's Wait."

the local populace. In a round of vignettes that returns to each component every time another delay has been announced, a match is made and a ghost story is told in stages. An English couple is played for all the stereotyped humor of their "Britishness": when a hurling team joins the train, the woman remarks upon seeing a wounded man, "Is this another of their rebellions, Charles?" They want only a quiet cup of tea as the rest of the train's members guzzle brew, and finally they are the only ones to be left behind when the train does leave, hours late. The humor and self-conscious quaintness of these episodes is without reference except to the most superficial stereotyped images of the boisterous Irish. No meaning, value, or even unit of action and purpose is introduced, and the effect is one of tedium (not comedy), as another "one minute's wait" is called.

The final sequence, "1921" is set in "the troubles," the time of the black-and-tans. The most serious episode, it comes closest to actually developing a narrative dynamic: the escape of rebel leader Sean Curran (Donal Donnelly) from the gallows the British have raised. But the plot machinations have more to do with the foibles of the Irish, as the Abbey Theater players engineer an escape which depends on the distraction of a slow-witted policeman by his wife. The most pervasive impression is that all Irish are actors and players. Their songs, antics and routines can be recruited for various uses, but they remain play and form rather than becoming means to revolu-

The British couple is removed from their first class compartment in favor of a goat.

Another minute's wait: for lobster.

Station master and conductor nearly come to blows over the mangled schedule.

Rebel leader Sean Curran (Donal Donnelly) poses as a folksinger to get past British troops.

tion, independence, and sovereignty for the Irish nation.

The Rising of the Moon is, finally, the least in Ford's Irish genre films, not the greatest, as indicated by the determined "Irishness" of its conception. The forms, the jokes, the fond racial associations are reproduced without including the richness behind them. Families, the traditional repository of this richness in the greatest of the films of the genre—*The Quiet Man* and *How Green Was My Valley*—are totally missing in this film. Their substitute social forms—the theater players, the village folk on the train, the illegal whiskey fraternity—are presented for superficial comedy rather than depth of involvement. Instead of the warmly human characters that people the other films, we know only a series of lovable, stubborn, irritating, but always uniquely Irish personality traits that form a comic-book sketch. This is primarily because the relations between people are based on such inconsequential concerns. We are offered the process of acting out, not the substance or goal of the process. The depth of emotion, of tradition, and of connections between generations and individuals that is created in other films is nearly completely missing, leaving *The Rising of the Moon* a play of manners instead of a work of art capable of "speaking" of and to the deepest and most inarticulable needs and values of a people.

Dan O'Flaherty on his way to prison: his dignity triumphs over the law.

YOUNG CASSIDY
1965

CREDITS

Production company: Sextant Films–MGM. *Directors:* Jack Cardiff, John Ford (official credit: "A John Ford Film"). *Producers:* Robert D. Graff, Robert Emmett Ginna. *Associate producer:* Michael Killanin. *Scenarist:* John Whiting, from autobiography, MIRROR IN MY HOUSE, by Sean O'Casey. *Photography* (in Metro color): Ted Scife. *Art director:* Michael Stringer. *Costumes:* Margaret Furse. *Music:* Sean O'Riada. *Editor:* Anne Coates. Filmed in Ireland. 110 minutes. *Released:* March.

CAST

Rod Taylor (*Sean Cassidy*), Maggie Smith (*Nora*), Julie Christie (*Daisy Battles*), Flora Robson (*Mrs. Cassidy*), Sian Phillips (*Ella*), Michael Redgrave (*William Butler Yeats*), Dame Edith Evans (*Lady Gregory*), Jack MacGowran (*Archie*), T. P. McKenna (*Tom*), Julie Ross (*Sara*), Robin Sumner (*Michael*), Philip O'Flynn (*Mick Mullen*), Pauline Delaney (*Bessie Ballynoy*), Arthur O'Sullivan (*foreman*), Tom Irwin (*constable*), John Cowley (*barman*), William Foley (*publisher's clerk*), John Franklyn (*bank teller*), Harry Brogan (*Murphy*), James Fitzgerald (*Charlie Ballynoy*), Donal Donnelly (*undertaker's man*), Harold Goldblatt (*Director of Abbey Theatre*), Ronald Ibbs (*theatre employee*). May Craig, May Cluskey (*women in the hall*), Tom Irwin, Shivaun O'Casey, and members of the Abbey Theatre.

Daisy Battles: the "little tart."

SYNOPSIS

Sean O'Casey's autobiographical account of the young artist molded by his class, the women in his life, the political struggles of his people, and his own exuberance for learning, love, and his art.

The credits on *Young Cassidy* read, "A John Ford Film," and "Directed by Jack Cardiff." Although Ford actually shot only a few days of the picture, he prepared the production and Cardiff followed his concepts. The ending Ford would have preferred (and the producers promised to respect when Ford became ill and left the production) makes bittersweet the young playwright's departure. Its omission was described to Peter Bogdanovich by Ford: "I wanted Julie Christie, by now a streetwalker, to come over to him and say, 'Oh Sean, I loved it—it was wonderful—you ought to be very proud of yourself. God bless you.' It took this poor little tart to appreciate what he had done. And she walks away, disappears in the rain, leaving him there." This is pure Ford— Johnny's passion for life, politics, and learning is only directly touched by the "little tart" whom he finds laughing and alive in the riot, and who wants his body as much as he wants hers. He cannot take her home, much less with him to fame and success, but the leaving behind of the one person who could touch his deepest source of life and love—his passion—would have made the leaving much richer. In many other ways, however, Ford's direction is evident and his shaping of this picture so like his others that, while questions of authorship become too confused to be worth the asking, *Young Cassidy* can be illuminating in a consideration of Ford's career.

Johnny is first and last a man of strong, uncontrolled, and most surprisingly, united feelings

209

Rod Taylor as Johnny Cassidy: the artist is marked by his exuberant lust for life.

Johnny is warned to "control your personal feelings."

about life. In the first few minutes of the film he is told by a political friend to "try to control your personal feelings." But Johnny intuitively knows that the poverty of his own home, his growing interest in politics, and his writing are all part and parcel of his personal feelings. He cannot separate anything, and must therefore succeed or die. He cannot be compromised. The violence of the riot, the injustice of it, and the woman virtually

The riot.

delivered into his arms by the crowd, Daisy Battles (Julie Christie), are all in the same category for Johnny. The bookstore and his eventual love for Nora, its proprietress (Maggie Smith), belong there as well: the same need and energy informs them all, and each is pursued with the same fervor.

Only two figures—both "mothers" to him—can draw out one aspect of him and repress others.

With Lady Gregory (Dame Edith Evans) Johnny must control his speech and physical energy. His politics and exuberance are repressed in favor of his intellectual, playwright side. She becomes the "only person he is comfortable around" once his own mother dies, making the connection even clearer. Lady Gregory's faith, money, and encouragement are essential to Johnny's success, but they repress the class roots which are the source

Johnny and Lady Gregory.

A class difference: Johnny has never seen a check before

Johnny Cassidy:
the artist as a visionary young writer.

of his art. His mother liberates these, as well as providing love, comfort (such as poverty can) and a sense of his own class background in the most material of ways. However, she represses the rebel in him, arguing the conservative line of safety traditionally belonging to women, especially in this genre. It takes first the death of his sister, made sad and hard by poverty, and finally the beautiful, terrifying death of his mother to free him for real success. The choice between "beauty and the head" which his sister makes in favor of beauty and Johnny refuses to make at all, is constantly posed at home. Politics and writing are the liberating elements, and with his mother's death Johnny is free to combine them. She counseled him to "suffer it" if a law is unfair, and she valued peace over justice. "Aye, for the dead," he answers. Life is movement to him, and when his mother dies, he shocks Nora by getting drunk, brawling and laughing to comfort himself. She is a difficult anchor to let go, but Johnny's development requires the loss of her repressive influence.

Nora is another profoundly liberating influence on Johnny which must be left behind because of the attendant repressive elements she recognizes but he does not. It is she who sends him books after first chiding him for attempting to steal them: her class is a bit higher and more respecta-

214

ble than his own. She brings out the intellectual side of him, but in her inability or unwillingness to "match his passion" physically, she recognizes she would hold him back and he must go off alone.

Young Cassidy deals centrally with class. Johnny becomes a bit more refined with Lady Gregory and, to a lesser extent, with Nora, but he insists on his class roots in both his personal life and in his work. His own people reject the lusty, common characters of his plays, but it is they who make him great. It requires the approval of the upper-class British—in the person of Lady Gregory and the director of the Abbey Theatre (Harold Goldblath)—to validate his Irish lower class roots and the brilliance of his art. While this certainly undercuts the value of his class—since it *becomes* valuable only when recognized by the upper class—they are all in art which, according to the myth, transcends class lines. Thus the film first validates, then co-opts Cassidy's background.

It is perhaps too comfortable, too romantic, and too mystifying a vision of the artist and his devel-

Rebellion is part and parcel of Johnny's life and his art.

Fighting in the streets of Ireland.

Nora and Johnny.

Daisy and Johnny.

opment that we experience in *Young Cassidy*. His genius springs from within, and although it must be fed by many muses—mostly women—they must all be abandoned once they have given all they can as he faces his future unencumbered. "Can't I take *anything* with me?" Johnny pleads with Nora, and she replies firmly, "No!" Not only must she recognize and accept the romantic necessity of her own abandonment, she must enforce it as well. Johnny backs up the aisle of the empty theater, the camera tracking with him, leaving her behind, leaving her alone in the theater. They yell "I love you" to each other, and then the credits roll as the film dissolves to Johnny boarding the ship that will take him from Ireland. It is the same direction as the movement out of the theater, away from Nora, and becomes thus through the dissolve and the direction of movement part of the same movement. She, like the rest of the women in his life, is both implicated and sacrificed in his journey. His mother must die for his development, the "little tart" must answer his passion, the upper-class women must encourage the art his own people reject, the revolution must provide him with fire and a cause, the intellectual woman must touch his mind and speak his feelings, and then he stands alone—fired by them all, accepting their sacrifice for his art. It is a common myth—the chosen hero who is first *born* a hero, then infused with knowledge—in the broadest sense—by others and thus is above the responsibility of mere mortals.

The deep humanism of both the film and of the Sean O'Casey autobiography from which the story was taken give the film warmth and life. But this overlays a very invidious basic view of the artist as a privileged, overvalued, and isolated member of society. The links are stronger in *Young Cassidy* because of the Irish quality of the culture and of O'Casey, but he is still leaving at the end—on a boat away from his country and his people. His removal is an essential element in his growth (even his own class of people do not understand his work) and an accurate portrayal of O'Casey's life, but both its inclusion and manner of depiction weight it in favor of the ancient myth, not the actual life. In his personal life Johnny remains the brawler, lacking not only the mores of respectability in Nora's neighborhood, but even the lower-class taboos and respect of the dead. All this he takes with him, but the detachment from love, physical roots, and political struggle serves the myth of the artist's necessary isolation and attendant isolated completeness.

The Director of the Abbey Theater validates Johnny's talent.

The artist: necessarily isolated visually and emotionally from his community.

219

THE
ACTION FILMS

John Ford in 1931, on the deck of the world's biggest submarine, the U.S.S. *V-4*, for the filming of *The Seas Beneath*.

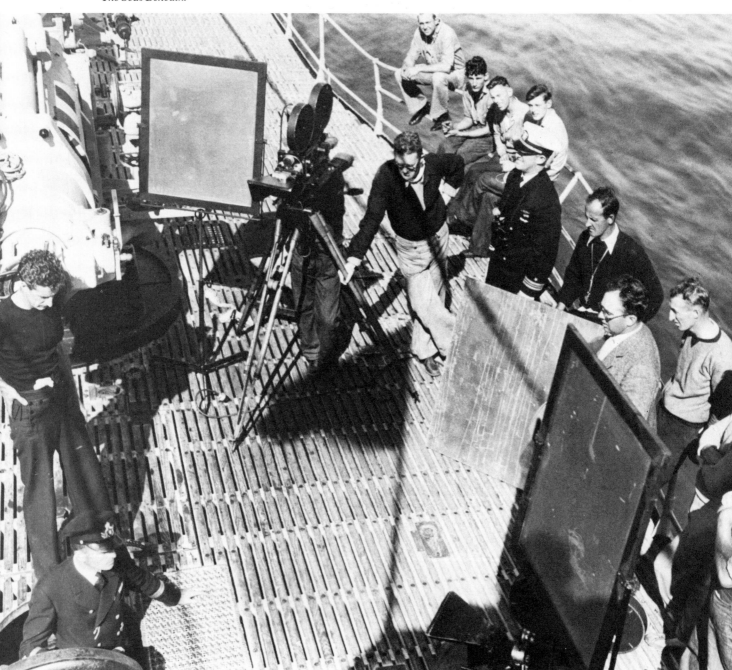

INTRODUCTION

In standard genre classification, the crime or detective film, the thriller, the sports picture and the revenge-quest film are identifiable categories. There are virtually none of these genres in Ford's oeuvre, although elements of their themes run through many of his films, especially the Westerns. The five films that comprise this chapter, then, do not constitute a genre but are rather grouped here because they do have some similarity and, more important, do not belong in any other genre.

Because he was working in a cinema which made wide and enduring use of action genres, the nearly complete lack of such films in Ford's oeuvre is surprising. Ford is regarded as a superb director of action, as demonstrated in many Westerns, but in fact the distinguishing skill in thrillers is not action but plot. These films tend to involve intricate narrative plot machinations whose denouement is the key to the meaning of the film. Ford not only did not locate his more constant and enduring themes in the narrative, but often paid it little serious attention. The narrative action of *She Wore a Yellow Ribbon* makes no sense at all, but since very little of import goes on in the plot, it is rarely noticed. In Ford's films, the psychological and emotional dimension of the characters tends to determine the action, even when that requires it to go against dramatic logic. This is at least a major reason that films which rely heavily on narrative intricacy are relatively few in his career.

The lack of such psychological dimension accounts for the abject failure of one film of this "action" category, *Four Men and a Prayer,* and the unengaging quality of another—*Gideon of Scotland Yard.* In both these films the characters have little or no internal conflict to be acted out in the narrative: one is a quest for revenge, the other a day-in-the-life of a detective, and Ford did not

Action in *Gideon of Scotland Yard.*

make the action of either film compelling enough to supply this necessary tension. *Up the River* does indeed act out the problems of the film to a successful end, and the two vital characteristics of his Westerns give this film its depth: the solving of the narrative problem to bring the lovers together, and the incredibly engaging "outsider" (played by Spencer Tracy) who makes it all possible. *Flesh* takes the love story as its *only* concern, and is more like a melodrama than a boxing picture in its priorities. *Air Mail* assumes the love story and probably comes the closest—along with *Up the River*—to expressing its real concerns in the narrative action of the film.

Among Ford's silent pictures, there are many of the action film variety which are as successful as these last two. Next to Westerns, action films comprise a majority of the silents. Perhaps the necessary simple narrative structure—though not necessarily simple psychological and emotional makeup—of silent film interested him more than the complex plot possibilities in talkies. Perhaps having worked extensively in this genre, he found it not to be his favorite. In any case, even in the silents, the human qualities of kindness, love, and emotion were the realm of meaning, not the exterior action of the plot. This is not, of course, to say that these elements are missing from thrillers by other directors, only that Ford's talents for expressing them did not lie in this area. Thus the

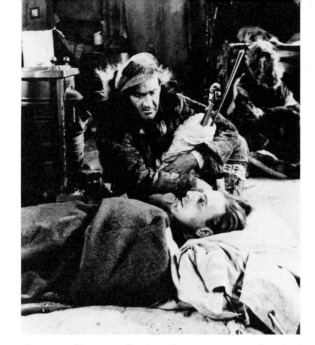

films of this chapter do not share consistent genre themes and recurrent patterns: their similarity comes from their auteur conformity rather than their narrative. The most successful among them have more in common with totally different genres: *Up the River* with the Westerns and *Flesh* with melodrama.

Early action films: *North of Hudson Bay,* 1923; *The Black Watch,* 1929; *The Seas Beneath,* 1931

John Ford and Duke Kahanamoku in Hawaii, after Ford sailed his yacht *The Araner* from Los Angeles in 1935.

UP THE RIVER
1930

Spencer Tracy as St. Louis and Warren Hymer as Dannemora Dan in the prison variety show.

CREDITS

Production company: Fox. *Director:* John Ford. *Writer:* Maurine Watkins (*and uncredited:* John Ford, William Collier, Sr.). *Photographer:* Joseph H. August. *Sound Engineer:* W. W. Lindsay, Jr. *Editor:* Frank E. Hull. 92 minutes. *Released:* October 12.

CAST

Spencer Tracy (*St. Louis*), Warren Hymer (*Dannemora Dan*), Humphrey Bogart (*Steve*), Claire Luce (*Judy*), Joan Lawes (*Jean*), Sharon Lynn (*Edith La Verne*), George McFarlane (*Jessup*), Gaylord Pendleton (*Morris*), Morgan Wallace (*Frosby*), William Collier, Sr. (*Pop*), Robert E. O'Connor (*guard*), Louise MacIntosh (*Mrs. Massey*), Edythe Chapmen (*Mrs. Jordan*), Johnny Walker (*Happy*), Noel Francis (*Sophie*), Mildred Vincent (*Annie*), Mack Clark (*Whitelay*), Goodee Montgomery (*Kit*), Althea Henley (*Cynthia*), Carol Wines (*Daisy Elmore*), Adele Windsor (*Minnie*), Richard Keene (*Dick*), Elizabeth and Helen Keating (*May and June*), Robert Burns (*Slim*), John Swor (*Clem*), Pat Somerset (*Beauchamp*), Joe Brown (*Deputy Warden*), Harvey Clark (*Nash*), Black and Blue (*Slim and Klem*), Robert Parrish.

SYNOPSIS

A genial, family-like prison is the site of Steve and Judy's love affair. St. Louis, gangster boss of the yard, engineers the lovers' union and reunion outside prison by protecting Steve's very proper New England family from his shame. St. Louis then returns to his real home in prison.

Spencer Tracy and Humphrey Bogart enact Ford's favorite narrative motif in this lovely, funny, beautifully balanced "crime" film. St. Louis (Tracy) is from one world—that of gangsters, power, and men. Steve (Bogart) is from another—a rich New England family whose genu-

ine respectability would be outraged if his mother and sister knew of his prison term. The film validates the normal world of family, small-town virtues, and romantic love, but it is St. Louis who performs the validation. As in many other Ford films in which the outsider must sacrifice himself for the society to flourish—the three outlaws of *Three Bad Men* who literally sacrifice themselves for the little family which can't protect itself, or Tom Doniphon who gives up power, future and love for a society which denies him in *The Man Who Shot Liberty Valance*—St. Louis is the architect of both Steve's romance and his escape from a life of crime. In *Up the River*, however, the sacrifice is not depicted as a very costly one for St. Louis. The "family" of the prison in which he is a hero prevents him from being Ford's typical outsider. In fact, his world seems infinitely more interesting and exciting even as the film validates that of normalcy. This balance—and potentially subversive appeal of the gangster world—might seem to reflect an early optimism in Ford's career, and this may be true to some extent, but *Three Bad Men*, made three years prior to *Up the River*, is nearly as dark as Ford's final work in its portrayal of the valued members of a society dying for its continuance.

St. Louis and Dan escape from prison together.

St. Louis and Dan start a fight that lands them back in prison.

Value in the present and the future is generally determined by value in the past in a Ford film. Of St. Louis's past we know only his escape from prison with Dannemora Dan (Warren Hymer) in the sequence which begins the film. After tricking Dan out of the car and abandoning him during the escape, St. Louis lands them both back in jail years later when he finds Dan preaching with a Salvation Army band. Rich and surrounded by beautiful girls, St. Louis taunts Dan with "Crime doesn't pay!" until a brawl starts. The two remain a team throughout the film, Dan always a comic foil for St. Louis. Steve, however, has a past that is built from the first moment we see him. His family must not know where he is—there is something at stake. Its cornerstone is of course his mother. This is demonstrated not only in her archetypical "mother" presentation, but by the convicts' show, during which a sentimental tenor sings "M-O-T-H-E-R" as the tough prisoners brush tears from their eyes. Steve's class background is another element in his value presentation: by Judy (Claire Luce), the woman he falls in love with in prison, and the men regard his rich, solid family as intrinsically of greater worth than any of their own. And his family is feminine: he is the only male member. Both mother and sister constitute those elements of culture which must be preserved even by the outsiders behind bars. It is not so much what Steve is but where he comes from that determines his role. He will be the one for which the others act.

But the men of the prison are not Ford's outcasts. In this comedy, the "family" structure of the prison is pretty complete, with "Pop" coaching the baseball team, the warden's little girl playing with the men in the yard, and the men and women prisoners finding ways to get messages back and forth to each other. St. Louis can even play matchmaker for Steve and Judy, and in a beautiful piece of well-timed comedy, gets Steve engaged with the complicity of the entire yard, all of whom know about it before Steve does. This structure, easy to escape from and comfortable to be in, is a fairly reasonable alternative to the family of the middle class. In fact, although Dan and St. Louis escape to get Steve out of trouble (which is no more than the possibility of his family finding out he was in prison) the world of the convicts is more attractive. Ford minimizes the action itself by spending more time on hayrides and interaction between the characters than on the actual theft that will release Steve from danger. St. Louis and Dan are never really comfortable in Steve's house, although St. Louis is always graceful and Dan charmingly impressed, and when they arrive back at the prison—breaking *in*—to the crucial play in the baseball game, they are cheered like returning heroes. The final scenes of the film are of the convicts. After St. Louis has again convinced Judy to go to Steve, his last act in the construction of their new family, Ford returns to the game and fades out on a two-shot of Dan and St. Louis. Thus in spite of the ostensible validation of the ideal of the bourgeois family, the multiplicity of effort that St. Louis goes to in order to construct and maintain Steve's future, and the valued past that goes along with that future, the film actually gives more sympathy, and ultimately, excitement and fun to the outer world. Without roots, without social meaning except that which it mourns in absence, it is much more alive and vibrant. Ford usually generates more love for his outsiders, but rarely do they fare as well as in this film. Usually the required sacrifice leaves the outsiders without freedom, friends, and often, their lives. In *Up the River,* St. Louis loses nothing in his efforts to sustain Steve and is even more powerful afterwards. The validation of the action of the film is for the bourgeois family, but the film itself validates the freer, less structured, exciting world of the prison.

Dan and St. Louis backstage at the prison variety show.

AIR MAIL
1932

John Ford and Gloria Stuart on the set of *Air Mail*.

CREDITS

Production company: Universal. *Director:* John Ford. *Producer:* Carl Laemmle, Jr. *Scenarists:* Dale Van Every, Lt. Commander Frank W. Weak, from story by Wead. *Photographer:* Karl Freund. *Special effects:* John P. Fulton. *Aerial stunts:* Paul Mantz. 83 minutes. *Released:* November 3.

CAST

Pat O'Brien (*Duke Talbot*), Ralph Bellamy (*Mike Miller*), Gloria Stuart (*Ruth Barnes*), Lillian Bond (*Irene Wilkins*), Russell Hopton (*"Dizzy" Wilkins*), Slim Summerville (*"Slim" McCune*), Frank Albertson (*Tommy Bogan*), Leslie Fenton (*Tony Dressel*), David Landau (*"Pop"*), Tom Corrigan (*"Sleepy" Collins*), William Daly (*"Tex" Lane*), Hans Furberg (*"Heinie" Kramer*), Lew Kelly (*drunkard*), Frank Beal, Francis Ford, James Donlan, Louise MacIntosh, Katherine Perry (*passengers*), Beth Milton (*plane attendant*), Edmund Burns (*radio announcer*), Charles de la Montte, Lt. Pat Davis (*passenger plane pilots*), Jim Thorpe (*Indian*), Enrico Caruso, Jr., Billy Thorpe, Alene Carroll, Jack Pennick, Lew Kelly, James Donlan.

SYNOPSIS

In a postal airmail station, Mike Miller oversees the dangerous flights in poor weather conditions that "get the mail through." When two of his flyers quit, Mike is forced to hire ace flyer Duke Talbot, a daredevil notorious for his flashy and often reckless flying. Duke and the wife of another pilot run away together and Mike is forced to fly the most dangerous mission himself. He crashes on a desolate mountain slope, and only Duke has the skill necessary to rescue him. The plane, however, is seriously damaged, and after forcing Mike to parachute, Duke crashes in a nearly fatal landing. Duke's pompous bravura never fails, and his only concern as they rush him to the hospital is, "How do I look?"

It is impossible to see Ford's *Air Mail* without thinking of Howard Hawks's *Only Angels Have Wings* (1939). Both were written by Frank W. (Spig) Wead, about whom Ford made *The Wings of Eagles* twenty-five years later. The plots of the two films are similar and the characters and their conflicts are nearly identical. Women play somewhat different roles: Bonnie (Jean Arthur) is the central disruptive force in the later film and Ruth (Gloria Stuart) is much more integrated and thus less powerful in the early film. The love story is already essentially over when *Air Mail* begins, with Mike (Ralph Bellamy) and Ruth clearly a couple with an "understanding," and the love story is at the heart of *Only Angels Have Wings*. But both are redemptive films in which the male character becomes vulnerable, redeeming himself as well as others.

The groups are very different in the two films despite their similar roles, narrative dynamic, and nicknames. There are fewer rituals and "insider" codes in Ford's film, less suppression of personal feelings. When Joe is killed in *Air Mail*, the mourning can be expressed, in sharp contrast to the elaborate suppression of feeling in *Only Angels Have Wings*. The sexual tension of *Air Mail* is embodied by Irene (Lillian Bond), Dizzy's (Russell Horton) wife and eventually Duke Talbot's (Pat O'Brien) mistress, and it is expressed in action: she and Duke run off. The lack of suppression of erotic energy (male/female and male/male in the Hawks film) changes the central problem, which is acted out between Duke Talbot and Mike Miller. Duke is the ace flyer with no responsibility—to his fellow flyers, to the profession, even to the specific job. Arrogant, a womanizer, he offers no point of sympathy. Mike is paternal, takes risks he won't ask others to take, and is dedicated to his job. Through their initial hatred and eventual heroism, the two are both redeemed. Mike is unexpectedly criticized when he wants to take the most difficult flight: Ruth tries to stop him (but not with a gun as in the later film), "Pop" tells him he just wants to be a big shot, that Duke is a better flyer. When Mike takes off anyway, he crashes, and only Duke is good enough to rescue him. Mike's conservatism is shown in its worst light: he whines to Duke that they will never get off the ground, points out every new tear or break in the plane with a weary, resigned shake of his head, and finally has to be dumped out of the crashing plane. When Duke tells him, "Mike, you're always wrong," we agree. Duke lives through the crash, and to relieve his dangerous mission of its nobility, he remains the pompous, conceited dandy as he asks, "How do I look?"

Air Mail is a surprisingly "silent" film—airplane noise covers much of the track and even the group scenes are done with much gesture and pantomime, or with camera positions that dictate that no dialogue could be heard. While generalized statements based on one or two films always do more violence than justice to the films, *Air Mail* and *Only Angels Have Wings* do offer interesting contrasts in two director's treatment of very similar material.

Pat O'Brien as Duke Talbot and Lillian Bond as Irene Wilkins.

Ralph Bellamy as Mike Miller, "father" of the air mail station.

229

FLESH
1932

CREDITS

Production company: MGM. *Director:* John Ford. *Scenarists:* Leonard Praskins, Edgar Allen Woolf: from a story by Edmund Goulding. *Dialogue:* Moss Hart. *Photographer:* Arthur Edeson. *Editor:* William S. Gray. 95 minutes. *Released:* December 9.

CAST

Wallace Beery (*Polakai*), Karen Morely (*Lora*), Ricardo Cortez (*Nicky*), Jean Hersholt (*Mr. Herman*), John Miljan (*Joe Willard*), Vince Barnett (*waiter*), Herman Bing (*Pepi*), Greta Meyer (*Mrs. Herman*), Ed Brophy (*Dolan*), Ward Bond, Nat Pendleton.

SYNOPSIS

Polakai, an incredibly good-natured and powerful wrestler, falls in love with Lora after her release from prison in Germany. She still loves fellow inmate Nicky, and Polakai helps arrange the release of "her brother." When Nicky learns that Lora is pregnant, he walks out on her, and she marries ever-faithful Polakai. Polakai becomes a championship wrestler in America, and Nicky manages to attach himself to them as Polakai's manager because Lora still loves him. Nicky arranges for Polakai to "throw" matches, causing the idealistic Polakai to become a heavy drinker. When Nicky hits Lora angrily, Polakai kills him. Polakai is sent to prison, where Lora visits him and affirms that finally she loves only him.

The love story in *Flesh* resembles the transcendent love stories of Frank Borzage (*Seventh Heaven, I've Always loved You, Little Man, What Now?*) and Alfred Hitchcock (*North by Northwest, Notorious*) in that through suffering and testing, love is affirmed and the conditions of suffering transcended. Polakai (Wallace Beery) is the

John Ford, Wallace Beery, Vince Barnett and wrestlers on the set of *Flesh.*

innocent, the "pure" sensualist (his native German both provides a reason for his inarticulateness and gives some distance on him—necessary for such unmediated innocence) who loves without expecting or needing anything in return to sustain his love, who can be betrayed over and over (with Nicky, in the wrestling ring, by Lora nearly each day) and not be swayed by it as he waits for the moment his love will be returned. Without the rich complexity of the Lora character (Karen Morley) and the comedy of the entire picture *Flesh* would be unremittingly sentimental, but Ford provides a fully sustaining backdrop for this story of "souls made great through love and adversity," as Fred Camper described Borzage's characters.

Lora is the tough-but-tender, wisecracking, worldly counterpart to Polakai's innocence. When we first see her in the credit sequence of the film, she is in prison, walking endlessly around in a circle with other women in high angle. The angle expresses their hopelessness, and when Lora is released in the next sequence the scene of freedom is a sensual one for us as well. She is really the main character of the film (unusual for Ford): she is the outsider, the person who has constructed—out of need—such defenses against the world that she is caught in an outwardly capable, fast-thinking, alienated incarnation which is actually neurotic and from which she must be liberated. The movement of the film—like so many of Ford's—is to emotional health for Lora. Both she and Polakai must suffer to achieve it.

Lora is immediately caught between two forces, one healthy and one destructive. She contacts Nicky (Ricardo Cortez) as soon as she is freed, and when Polakai takes her in she convinces him to pay for "her brother's" release. But it is evident even in these first scenes when Polakai appears painfully shy and bumbling—breaking the door of her bedroom to get out—that he is the one who can and will take care of her, and indeed, Nicky walks out the moment he learns she is pregnant. Polakai's love must destroy Nicky's hold on her emotions, and, seeming to know this, he endures all the humiliation Nicky has to give out until Lora herself rejects Nicky.

Nicky is defined both narratively and iconographically as a reprehensible character. He leaves Lora when she needs him most, virtually pimps her to Polakai, and then returns when Lora and Polakai, the new German wrestling champion, are married and in America. Polakai wins the title on the same night as the birth of Lora's (and Nicky's) baby, and would seem to be a turning point for the newly married couple, but Lora stills plans to leave Polakai for Nicky. The trip to America is the only way to exorcise Nicky's hold on her, and when he learns their fortunes are looking up, he immediately joins them as Polakai's manager. He then tries to pimp Polakai, calling him "that big hunk of flesh" and forcing him to throw matches. But Polakai remains indestructible emotionally, morally, and physically, and when he sees Nicky hit Lora Polakai rises to protect her. Indeed, Nicky is probably the primary weakness in the film—he has to be as despicable as he is to provide the narrative rationale for the trials Lora and Polakai must go through, but this renders him so unsympathetic that no audience can easily understand Lora's obsession with him.

Without the rich humor and ethnic German quality which removes us a little from Polakai, he would be *too* kind and uncomplicated to draw Lora finally away from the corrupt and neurotic influence of Nicky. Even as it is, his charms—his unfailing ability to protect Lora from poverty, arrest, and injury, and his gentleness and humor—lack a sexual dimension that Nicky (at least when Lora is passionately embracing him) incorporates. This dimension is never introduced into the Lora–Polakai relationship, and leaves it perhaps a little too "pure" to be really compelling. It is the spiritual content of the last scenes that is an indication of the final resolution and health of their love.

After killing Nicky, Polakai goes on to rid himself of the attempted corruption by winning a wrestling match he was supposed to throw. He is immediately arrested for murder. In the very last shots of the film, Lora goes to see him in jail, and Ford cuts from each one's point of view to the other, thus placing each equally behind bars. They affirm their love for each other, and Ford fades out on his point-of-view shot of her, with their fingers touching through the bars. They have come through all their trials of corruption, both internal and external, and triumphed over them in their love.

Flesh is exactly counter to the usual "redeemed through love" stories, which are generally made by male directors. It is generally the woman who gives without question, is betrayed without protest, accepts her lover back again gratefully, and is finally rewarded with his love. It is a process of integration: the love she offers integrates him—the outsider who cannot settle—into his world, and into his own personality. But in *Flesh* the pattern is reversed, and it is interesting to see how Ford makes it possible for a man to provide this function for a woman, as unrequited love without protest is generally seen as a weakness. For a man to give all and ask nothing in return he must be balanced by his own extreme strength (Polakai is champion of all Germany, and capable of flattening anyone in America as well) and equilibrium, which cannot be undermined by the most severe of threats. The distance on Polakai also is important, because too much "goodness" in a man still looks like weakness in a culture based on men repressing needs and always "winning." Like so many of Ford's later films, *Flesh* is subtly subversive in that it challenges attitudes and themes that its audiences are accustomed to seeing.

FOUR MEN AND A PRAYER
1938

CREDITS

Production company: 20th, Century Fox. *Director:* John Ford. *Producer:* Darryl F. Zanuck. *Associate producer:* Kenneth Macgowan. *Scenarists:* Richard Sherman, Sonya Levien, Walter Ferris; from novel by David Garth. *Photography:* Ernest Palmer. *Art directors:* Bernard Herzbrun, Rudolph Sternad. *Set decorator:* Thomas Little. *Music:* Louis Silvers, Ernst Toch. *Editor:* Louis R. Loeffler. 85 minutes. *Released:* April 29.

CAST

Loretta Young (*Lynn Cherrington*), Richard Greene (*Jeffrey Leigh*), George Sanders (*Wyatt Leigh*), David Niven (*Christopher Leigh*), William Henry (*Rodney Leigh*), C. Aubrey Smith (*Col. Loring Leigh*), J. Edward Bromberg (*General Torres*), Alan Hale (*Famoy*), John Carradine (*Gen. Adolfo Arturo Sebastian*), Reginald Denny (*Douglas Loveland*), Berton Churchill (*Martin Cherrington*), Claude King (*Gen. Bryce*), John Sutton (*Capt. Drake*), Barry Fitzgerald (*Mulcahy*), Cecil Cunningham (*Pyer*), Frank Baker (*defense attorney*), Frank Dawson (*Mullins*), Lina Basquette (*Ah-Nee*), William Stack (*prosecuting attorney*), Harry Hayden (*Cherrington's secretary*), Winter Hall (*judge*), Will Stanton (*Cockney*), John Spacey, C. Montague Shaw (*lawyers*), Lionel Pape (*coroner*), Brandon Hurst (*jury foreman*), Eddie Abdo (*sheik*), Frank Lackteen, Nobel Johnson (*natives*).

SYNOPSIS

After the mysterious death of their father, a colonel in the British service in India, his four sons set out to discover the truth. They uncover the murder and restore honor to the family.

Ford was interested in courtroom drama, falsely accused men, and the pursuit of truth,

Richard Greene, William Henry, David Niven, and George Sanders as four sons planning to clear their father's name.

throughout his career. If *Sergeant Rutledge* (1969) is the best of these and *Prisoner of Shark Island* (1936) nearly as good, *Four Men and a Prayer* is surely the worst. *Sergeant Rutledge* has a deep psychological dimension to it which includes racism, sexuality, and patriotism. The earlier film has the Lincoln myth, the personal theme of family, and Southern history to enrich it, but *Four Men and a Prayer* lacks any deeper levels of articulation as well as the suspense of a routine whodunit. The British restraint of the family of historic honor degenerates into parody as the sons line up for their father's inspection, roughhouse on the docks of Alexandria, and generally treat each other according to their stock character roles. Little warmth or family feeling that could give their quest to avenge their dead father some significance is exhibited among them. Rodney (William Henry), the youngest, is at Oxford; Wyatt (George Sanders), the eldest, is a lawyer; Chris (David Niven) a playboy; and Geoff (Richard Greene), the earnest beloved of the Girl (Loretta Young). Their money is never explained, and we can't help but wonder, how does a British officer in India, however honorable, get to be that rich? Their English banter and their unrelentingly observed "forms" render them the least likable group of Ford characters outside his later demonic villains. Their reverence for their mother's portrait (in a shot to be repeated exactly in *The*

Last Hurrah) which hangs over the fireplace takes on elements of parody when nothing seems to exist inside such formalities. The old colonel dies like later beloved Ford characters, with the camera position behind him as his arm falls gently to indicate his passing. Mary O'Donnell in *The Long Gray Line* and Lincoln in *Prisoner of Shark Island* signal their deaths with this gesture, but the sad beauty is lost in this film. The forms of the Leigh family and its eventual restoration of both honor—a medal awarded posthumously to the Color by "His Majesty"—and of a woman—Lynn (Loretta Young) joins their line to walk off in the last shot—are not informed by human values of love or a darker element of tension, sexuality or sacrifice. Without the inner drama of nearly any other film in Ford's oeuvre, *Four Men and a Prayer* ranks high as his least satisfying.

Christopher and Jeffrey Leigh arrive in Alexandria.

The lovers: Loretta Young and Richard Greene as Lynn and Jeffrey.

Lynn and the successful "detectives."

233

GIDEON OF SCOTLAND YARD
1959

CREDITS

Production company: British Productions–Columbia. *Director:* John Ford. *Producer:* Michael Killanin. *Associate producer:* Wingate Smith. *Scenarist:* T.E.B. Clarke, from the novel Gideon's Day by J.J. Marric (pseudonym for John Creasey). *Photography* (in color, but released in black and white): Frederick A. Young. *Art director:* Ken Adam. *Music:* Douglas Gamley. *Music Director:* Muir Mathieson. *Editor:* Raymond Poulton. *Assistant director:* Tom Pevsner. Filmed in London. 91 minutes. *Released:* February.

CAST

Jack Hawkins (*Inspector George Gideon*), Dianne Foster (*Joanna Delafield*), Anna Massey (*Sally Gideon*), Cyril Cusack (*Herbert "Birdie" Sparrow*), Andrew Ray (*P.C. Simon Farnaby O'Green*), James Hayter (*Mason*), Ronald Howard (*Paul Delafield*), Howard Marion-Crawford (*Chief of Scotland Yard*), Laurence Naismith (*Arthur Sayer*), Derek Bond (*Det. Sgt. Eric Kirby*), Griselda Harvey (*Mrs. Kirby*), Frank Lawton (*Det. Sgt. Liggott*), Anna Lee (*Mrs. Kate Gideon*), John Loder (*Ponsford, "The Duke"*), Doreen Madden (*Miss Courtney*), Miles Malleson (*Judge at Old Bailey*), Marjorie Rhodes (*Mrs. Saparelli*), Michael Shepley (*Sir Rupert Bellamy*), Michael Trubshawe (*Sgt. Golightly*), Jack Watling (*Rev. Julian Small*), Hermione Bell (*Dolly Saparelli*), Donald Donnelly (*Feeney*), Billie Whitelaw (*Christine*), Malcolm Ranson (*Ronnie Gideon*), Mavis Ranson (*Jane Gideon*), Francis Crowdy (*Fitzhubert*), David Aylmer (*Manners*), Brian Smith (*White-Douglas*), Barry Keegan (*Riley, chauffeur*), Maureen Potter (*Ethel Sparrow*), Henry Longhurst (*Rev. Mr. Courtney*), Charles Maunsell (*Walker*), Stuart Saunders (*Chancery Lane policeman*), Dervis Ward (*Simmo*), Joan Ingram (*Lady Bellamy*), Nigel Fitzgerald (*Insp. Cameron*), Robert Raglan (*Dawson*), John Warwick (*Insp. Gillick*), John Le Mesurier (*prosecuting attorney*), Peter Godsell (*Jimmy*), Robert Bruce (*defending attorney*), Alan Rolfe, (*C.I.D. man at hospital*), Derek Prentice (*1st employee*), Alastair Hunter (*2nd employee*), Helen Goss (*woman employee*), Susan Richmond (*Aunt May*), Raymond Rollett (*Uncle Dick*), Lucy Griffiths (*cashier*), Mary Donevan (*usherette*), O'Donovan Shiell, Hart Allison, Michael O'Duffy (*policeman*), Diana Chesney (*barmaid*), David Storm (*court clerk*), Gordon Harris (*C.I.D. man*).

John Ford, Dianne Foster, and Jack Hawkins on the set of *Gideon of Scotland Yard.*

SYNOPSIS

Inspector Gideon deals with murder, an overeager young patrolman who gives him traffic tickets but winds up as his son-in-law, graft inside his organization, and a comic, constantly interrupted dinner party.

In any artist's career there are bound to be not only failures, but works which are simply anomalies for that artist. They just don't seem to fit, either in his/her oeuvre, or in his/her development at the time they were made. *The Whole Town's Talking,* (1935), *Mogambo* in 1953, and *Gideon of Scotland Yard* are three such pictures. They are not the failures that *The Plough and the Stars* (1936) and *Four Men and a Prayer* (1938) are; they simply are out of step with Ford's usual artistic concerns, especially at that point in his career. It is easier to imagine almost any other director associated with the films. This poses many difficulties for a consideration of these films in a study of John Ford, where it is assumed that

Gideon is exasperated by his family,

is given two traffic tickets by a young patrolman,

the director's authorship insures a commonality of theme and visual style which can be informed by his other films. If this is not the case, the rather negative project of discussing how the film is unlike the rest of Ford's oeuvre seems the only course. It should be the case that the anomalies illuminate the rest of the films as well as vice versa, and this is clearly true of many films which are not in the mainstream of Ford's work, like *Arrowsmith, Wee Willie Winkie,* and *Mary of Scotland.* But it is not true of *Gideon.* Only some visual elements that Ford generally uses mark the director's hand, and even then they do not refer clearly to their use in other films.

It is extremely difficult to rely on anything Ford says about his films. From what we learn from interviews, he must have been a totally intuitive artist with very little consciousness about the profound implications of his films. Yet he was interviewed countless times, loved the tough-man image, and was often ironic to an extent that an interviewer did not catch. When asked why he made so many Westerns, he said he liked to camp out in Monument Valley. Therefore his comment to Peter Bogdanovich about this film, "I wanted to get away for a while, so I said I'd like to do a Scotland Yard thing and we went over and did it,"

probably cannot be taken as an accurate reading of his interest in *Gideon,* but the film certainly indicates a low level. It is structured by a "day in the life" framework, held together by Gideon's (Jack Hawkins) voice narration and running between the comedy of his family life (complete with young patrolman who gives Inspector Gideon two traffic tickets and then turns out to be his

and prevents a murder, all in the course of a day's work.

All conflict is external instead of being reflective of inner forces of the characters and their relations.

future son-in-law), the action/drama of his professional life (complete with inter-Scotland Yard crime), crazy people, and a murderer. His two lives interrupt each other as he remembers he must buy fish in the middle of a case, and a crime takes him away from a dinner party. The mixture of comedy and action, and occasional heavy drama, are held together by voice-over narration. Ford even uses two flashbacks for the audience to witness an event we could not possibly have seen.

All this works pretty well; the problem with the film—both as a Ford film and as a piece of drama —is that there is no tension or conflict within the central characters. Plenty comes from his job, but Gideon himself becomes less and less compelling in spite of the comedy and the action, because all conflict is external and is in no way reflective of inner forces as action generally is in Ford's films. We identify with Gideon both dramatically and structurally because he narrates the film, and the level of identification is the same as in a routine action picture. We lack any psychological involvement which might resonate in our own lives. Thus the essential function of art in this culture, which is to liberate through emotions and sensual experience, is completely lost in this film. Ford's art, especially, is marked by its ability to reach out and touch the viewer in a profound way. As a light comedy *Gideon of Scotland Yard* is an adequate film, but in Ford's oeuvre it is totally inadequate.

Gideon attempts to deal with diplomats and an angry wife on the phone at the same time.

236

Gideon and his future son-in-law, receiving yet another traffic citation.

John Ford shooting *Gideon of Scotland Yard*.

THE "FOREIGN" FILMS

The Fugitive: set in a fantasy version of an actual place.

240

INTRODUCTION

John Ford directed a group of films which do not constitute a broad genre category outside his ouevre, and do not even represent a genre within his work as do the Irish films. But these films share such important themes that their grouping adds a dimension of understanding to all. They are the films that are set away from Ford's own current or historic social context (that is, America of the Westerns, Americana, or war films) and further, away from his—and our—shared familiarity with the mythic Ireland of the Irish pictures. Their settings are uncompromising fantasy—*The Hurricane, Donovan's Reef* (a fantasy version of an actual place), *Arrowsmith, Wee Willie Winkie, Mogambo, The Long Voyage Home, The Fugitive, Seven Women*—or, in the case of *Mary of Scotland,* a retreat into history. Like the Western genre, this removal of the setting from any directly knowable milieu releases the director from expectations of conformity to some recognizable version of an audience's reality. The director is free to create structures of parable or myth which are generally less complex constructions than those more closely tied to a social reality.

In the last part of Ford's career, from 1959 through *Seven Women* (1966), his last film, he chose only projects which would either take him into the "foreign" fantasy world of *Donovan's Reef, Gideon of Scotland Yard,* and *Seven Women,* or Westerns which would similarly give him a setting of simpler, mythic dimensions. These films thus tend to have a more direct expression of the mythic content of Ford's work, and indeed, some are so abstracted from any social reality that their issues seem unattached to anything. In *The Long Voyage Home* the fog, the storm, and the sea are the only expressive elements of the long conversations of death. This process of abstraction can function in different ways. In *Seven Women,* the obviously "unreal"

John Ford and Ava Gardner on the set of *Mogambo.*

Mary of Scotland: a retreat into fantasy.

The Long Voyage Home is abstracted by its setting at sea and its visual style.

Dr. Cartwright in *Seven Women:* Ford's consummate outsider, who gives her life for a less valuable community.

Primitive forces of sensuality, violence and fear are unleashed at sea in *The Long Voyage Home.*

China of studio sets and primitive, powerful savages succeeds beautifully in making the complete alienation of the heroine poignant, since there is no substantial society to receive her sacrifice. She becomes Ford's consummate character—the most valued member of a society who gives her own life to save that society in spite of its total inadequacy.

In this detached setting, Ford is able to leave certain elements out and exaggerate others. The complexities of social process, legal process, and ongoing struggle are not included in the mythic structure which is permitted by the fantasy setting, but the archetypal forces can be much more directly expressed. The primitive forces of violence, love, sensuality, fear are all freed to threaten or liberate the omnipresent Western hero. In *Wee Willie Winkie* the little girl, child of the sophisticated European culture but in touch with the primitive drives of India, can save the day. A remembering doctor wistfully tells the story of the lovers for whom freedom was more compelling than life, and how the forces of nature itself rose up to rescue them in *The Hurricane. Mogambo* unleashes sexual energies in the excesses of Africa, where the primitive forces of violence and libido are paramount, not those of social process. This makes for an element of racism which, though not directed at any one group, is invidious in its very romanticism. Racism is clearest in *The Hurricane's* depiction of the happy, simple, childlike natives. In *The Long Voyage Home* they are the sensual native women who bring the rum that causes a fight. In *Arrowsmith* they are the frightened natives who are edited with raging fire and superstitious fears to express the terror of the plague. They are the ultimate forces of chaos and destruction in *Seven Women.* Generally, the natives in these pictures are attractive, in touch with direct experience, love, sensuality, fear, and become sort of noble innocents. In *The Fugitive* they are beautiful in low-key lighting and shimmering candles, but in all they remain children in the adult world of the film. Even when viewed fondly, the racism is powerful.

The primitive society of the native people is an unrestricted arena in which the whites function. It is also an implicit comparison for their unseen culture. *The Hurricane's* repressive governor, *Donovan's Reef's* fear of censure from the Boston society, *Seven Women's* repressive European reli-

Mogambo: The lush setting of Africa releases repressed sexual energies.

gious orders; all contain an implied criticism of the oppressive culture of the whites. Like science fiction, which is generally not about the future at all but only a criticism of the present, these films do not pursue their racism vigorously. Their presentation of the primitive values of the native cultures is meant not as a critique of their lack of sophistication, but rather an indictment of our own repressive hierarchical structures.

As Ford needed to abstract and alienate his heroes and heroines from their inadequate social context to a greater and greater extent, this physical removal from the social processes of his own culture became crucial. In the early films, heroes went from a native society back to their own (*Arrowsmith, The Long Voyage Home*). In the later films they remained exiles—either happy, fantasy ones as in *Donovan's Reef* or chillingly alone and forsaken like Dr. Cartwright in *Seven Women*. In all films of these "foreign" settings, the individual is examined more closely and required to supply his/her own validation because the social context will not.

The Chinese in *Seven Women* are clearly unreal and not racial types.

The Long Voyage Home: All the men of the *Glencairn* are exiles from the land of the living.

The Fugitive: The natives are beautiful in religious conviction or cruel in revolutionary zeal, while the priest remains chillingly alone.

John Ford on the set of *Seven Women,* his last film.

ARROWSMITH
1931

CREDITS

Production company: Goldwyn–United Artists. *Director:* John Ford. *Producer:* Samuel Goldwyn. *Scenarist:* Sidney Howard; from the novel by Sinclair Lewis. *Photographer:* Ray June. *Art director:* Richard Day. *Music:* Alfred Newman. *Recording Engineer:* Jack Noyes. *Editor:* Hugh Bennett. 108 minutes. *Released:* December 1.

CAST

Ronald Colman (*Dr. Martin Arrowsmith*), Helen Hayes (*Leora*), A. C. Anson (*Prof. Gottlieb*), Richard Bennett (*Sondelius*), Claude King (*Dr. Tubbs*), Beulah Bondi (*Mrs. Tozer*), Myrna Loy (*Joyce Lanyon*), Russell Hopton (*Terry Wickett*), De Witt Jennings (*Mr. Tozer*), John Qualen (*Henry Novak*), Adele Watson (*Mrs. Novak*), Lumsden Hare (*Sir Robert Fairland*), Bert Roach (*Bert Tozer*), Charlotte Henry (*a young girl*), Clarence Brooks (*Oliver Marchand*), Walter Downing (*City Clerk*), David Landau, James Marcus, Alec B. Francis, Sidney McGrey, Florence Britton, Bobby Watson.

SYNOPSIS

An idealistic young doctor must choose between humanistic medicine and research science when plague breaks out in the tropics. His wife dies during the epidemic. He responds by giving his serum to the entire native population, thus ruining the conditions of his research experiment. In a transcendent love story ending, he renounces pure science and is emotionally reunited with his wife.

Medicine and the doctors who practice it are strong and mysteriously powerful figures in the popular culture of America. Medical themes are important recurring elements in American films, generally signifying moral disease and healing as well as physical illness. In Ford's Americana film *Dr. Bull,* the doctor (played by Will Rogers) is the

Ronald Colman as Dr. Martin Arrowsmith.

Stagecoach: Thomas Mitchell as the drunken doctor.

244

most powerful moral figure, capable of performing near miracles, both physical and spiritual. Ford starred doctors in *Dr. Bull, Arrowsmith, Prisoner of Shark Island,* and *The Horse Soldiers.* He used the drunken doctor motif in many Westerns. Their repeated use constitutes conventions of sacrifice, nobility, dedication, and the justified subservience of all other character and plot elements to the medical.

Unlike the general pattern of this motif, Ford does not affirm the dedication and selflessness of Martin Arrowsmith (Ronald Colman). His absorption in his work often looks more like selfishness from the point of view of his wife or family. Like *The Wings of Eagles, Arrowsmith* reveals the darker aspects of that single-minded dedication fairly early in the film. They are expressed through the wife and family: Leora (Helen Hayes) is a small-town girl of independence and spirit, which is increasingly dissipated in her marriage. When Martin gives up being a doctor to become a more noble but less well paid research scientist, they must move to New York. There he will work in a laboratory on the thirtieth floor of an imposing, inhuman skyscraper. It seems miles high as they look up at it; they are shot from high angle and the building from low angle to increase its oppressiveness. Inside, the huge doors, long corridors, and statues emphasize the oppressive sterility. Leora, identified with her small town and its values, refuses to go above the twenty-fifth floor, and is thus symbolically as well as emotionally excluded from the most important part of Martin's life.

Dr. Gottlieb (A.C. Anson) is the stereotypical pure scientist who encourages Martin's dedication to science rather than to people. He tells Martin he will be a great scientist: the potential must be born in a man, and Martin has it. Gottlieb's pronouncement becomes a threat of doom as the film continues and finds Martin carrying out a destructively inhuman, cruel experiment. In it the values he must choose between are made explicit, as is the price he pays for choosing wrongly. Far away from his own culture, Martin attempts to minister to a plague-infested island and continue research on his new serum at the same time. Gottlieb advises Martin to give half of the people serum and to withhold it from the rest. Only under such "laboratory" conditions can the test be effective. An interesting, complex comment on racism—or recruitment of it—is also a part of the experiment. When the white inhabitants of the

Helen Hayes as Leora, a girl of spirit and independence.

Martin as the research scientist.

Martin and Dr. Gottlieb.

Plague in the West Indies provides the laboratory for a medical "experiment."

Leora is left to die alone.

island, to whom the serum is "naturally" first offered, refuse the conditions, Marchand (Clarence Brooks), a black doctor, offers his people. Martin accepts, and a hellish montage of fire, shadows, rats, and fleeing black bodies follows. The choice is between science and people. When Martin insists on leaving Leora behind to die in the untreated but "safer" white sector of the island, the choice becomes even clearer. His racist treatment of the natives as laboratory specimens is directly implicated in Leora's death.

There is a central ambiguity in *Arrowsmith* that is lacking in *The Wings of Eagles*. Martin loses Leora, realizes then how wrong he has been, returns to New York and Gottlieb dies in his arms. Martin walks out of the "monument to pure science," leaving in a burst of understanding and with a bright expression to join his friend Terry (Russell Hopton) in a less sterile, but presumably just as "pure" form of research science. Unintentionally ironic, he calls to Terry, "Wait, Leora and I are coming." His loss of her—and his criminal implication in that loss—is thus mediated to the extent that it becomes noble as he and Terry go off to their mission in the uncorrupt back woods of Vermont. Science and medicine itself are only ambiguously criticized, unlike Ford's unremitting critique of the military in *The Wings of Eagles.* Medicine in *Arrowsmith* is either noble or diabolical according to its use. The early scenes of Martin as a doctor, even a "bad" doctor as he accuses himself, are full of the fun and gentle charm that mark Ford's Americana pictures with Will Rogers. Yet the ascetic appeal of pure science in pure nature is certainly antihuman. The experience of the film resembles that of a melodrama by Frank Borzage in which love transcends tragedy and loss. After causing Leora's death and accepting that guilt, Martin rejects the city woman who was instrumental in preventing him from returning to his wife in time to save her. Once he repudiates his former mentor's ideals, Martin's departure from the McGurk Institute seems to imply a similar kind of formal redemption. He bursts through the crowd that has gathered to congratulate him on the success of his experiment (all but Terry offering condolence for Leora only after the congratulations) into a spatial freedom. The medium close-up with the background out of focus behind him suddenly becomes a freeze frame. It is an image of freedom and transcendence, and his evocation of Leora indicates a reunion on a spiritual level.

MARY OF SCOTLAND
1936

CREDITS

Production company: RKO Radio. *Director:* John Ford. *Producer:* Pandro S. Berman. *Scenarist:* Dudley Nichols: from the play by Maxwell Anderson. *Photography:* Joseph H. August. *Art Directors:* Van Nest Polglase, Carroll Clark. *Set decorator:* Darrell Silvera. *Costumes:* Walter Plunkett. *Music:* Max Steiner. *Musical director:* Nathaniel Shilkret. *Editor:* Jane Loring. *Assistant editor:* Robert Parrish. *Special effects:* Vernon L. Walker. 123 minutes. *Released:* July 24.

CAST

Katherine Hepburn (*Mary Stuart*), Fredric March (*Bothwell*), Florence Eldridge (*Elizabeth*), Douglas Walton (*Darnley*), John Carradine (*David Rizzio*), Monte Blue (*messenger*), Jean Fenwick (*Mary Seton*), Robert Barrat (*Morton*), Gavin Muir (*Leicester*), Ian Keith (*James Stuart Moray*), Moroni Olsen (*John Knox*), Donald Crisp (*Huntley*), William Stack (*Ruthven*), Molly Lamont (*Mary Livingston*), Walter Byron (*Sir Francis Walsingham*), Ralph Forbes (*Randolph*), Alan Mowbray (*Throckmorton*), Frieda Inescort (*Mary Beaton*), David Torrance (*Lindsay*), Anita Colby (*Mary Fleming*), Lionel Belmore (*English fisherman*), Doris Lloyd (*his wife*), Bobby Watson (*his son*), Lionel Pape (*Burghley*), Ivan Simpson, Murray Kinnell, Lawrence Grant, Nigel De Brulier, Barlowe Borland (*judges*), Alec Craig (*Donal*), Mary Gordon (*nurse*), Wilfred Lucas (*Lexington*), Leonard Mudie (*Maitland*), Brandon Hurst (*Arian*), D'Arcy Corrigan (*Kirkcaldy*), Frank Baker (*Douglas*), Cyril McLaglen (*Faudoncide*), Robert Warwick (*Sir Francis Knellys*), Earle Foxe (*Duke of Kent*), Wyndham Standing (*sergeant*), Gaston Glass (*Chatelard*), Neil Fitzgerald (*nobleman*), Paul McAllister (*Du Croche*).

SYNOPSIS

Exiled from England by her usurper cousin Elizabeth, Mary falls in love with Lord Bothwell. For political

On the set of *Mary of Scotland.*

reasons, she is betrothed to Lord Darnley, who is jealous of Bothwell and conspires with other Scottish lords against his wife and her lover. Too late, Mary renounces her bid for the throne. She is captured at Bothwell's castle, imprisoned, and eventually executed by Elizabeth. Although Mary is martyred, her son will eventually rule England.

In spite of Ford's reputation as a director of Westerns, war films, and action drama, the concept of prevailing through submission is a constant one in his work. In *Prisoner of Shark Island* (1936) Sam Mudd wins his freedom by first submitting to humiliation, torture, and finally by ministering to his tormentors. His victory is not won by superior strength or cunning, but by adherence to his own medical principles, which requires the acceptance of his oppressors. The priest in *The Fugitive* (1947) gains his own salvation by submitting himself to the people who will kill him. To underscore the point, Ford's camera tilts up to the heavens with the shots that signal his death. Ashby Corwin in *The Sun Shines Bright* signifies his return to the community by praying on his knees in front of everyone, and is only shamed when he defends Lucy's honor by whipping her cruel tormentor Buck Ramsey. In Ford's last film, *Seven Women*, Dr. Cartwright saves the rest of the women and the baby she brought into the world by submitting to the nightmarish Tunga Khan—a fate worse than death. Indeed, she kills herself and him rather than live

Katharine Hepburn as Mary of Scotland.

Mary exiled in France.

Mary: isolated from her country and her people.

through it. In a more subtle way, this submission, or its failure, marks the success and failure of countless other Ford characters. In *Rio Grande*, both husband and wife must give up some of their own pride to come together and be complete. Both lovers in *The Quiet Man* must put aside their own prejudices and give in to the other to a greater extent than either foresaw. The failure of such submission in *The Wings of Eagles* and in *How Green Was My Valley* is directly responsible for the tragedy which besets the lovers of those films.

This idea is most clearly expressed in *Mary of Scotland* but is schematized in its very directness and thus loses the complexity of interrelation of the later films. Mary (Katharine Hepburn) and Elizabeth (Florence Eldridge) are posed as opposites: Mary is beautiful and sensual, always associated with fireplaces and warm light. Close-ups and intimate lighting convey her warmth and integrity. Elizabeth is associated with medium shots or long shots, jealousy and harshness. She is a conniving opportunist who revealed her superficial commitment to her religion by changing it to be queen. The music differentiates them; Mary's is always softer, warmer, and more intimate than Elizabeth's. Mary is exiled in France, away from her home and her roots in England. This setting is rendered even more "foreign" by Ford's visual style. Isolating compositions frame her high on a platform or regally distanced in long shot from her supporters. Emerging alone from the fog in the opening shots of the film, she is separated from her people both geographically and visually. Because she is a queen and derives identity and structure from that relationship to her country, her forced exile is even more determining in this film than in the other "foreign" films. The process of abstraction of the themes from any grounding in the character's culture becomes proportionally exaggerated. Mary is the ostensible loser in the story—she is unsuccessful at her bid for the throne, she loses her lover Bothwell (Frederic March) and by the end she loses her life to the jealousy of Elizabeth. But as they meet for the last time, Elizabeth says, "I am a queen," and Mary answers, "I am a woman." It is through her insistent expression of the woman in her that she has loved, borne a son who will win the throne, and like the priest in *The Fugitive,* by visual intimation won her salvation as well.

Mary's integrity never wavers even when her judgement and power do. Her commitment to her religion, to her love for Bothwell, and to her country is left intact. Elizabeth's is compromised and exposed at every step; Mary is seen to be the true patriot, Elizabeth simply acts out of self-interest. *Mary of Scotland* is a religious film only in the broadest sense: through submitting to her fate Mary wins all even at the moment she loses all. Critic John Baxter (*The Cinema of John Ford,* 1971) sees the religious theme of martyrdom to her fate as Mary's triumph, with her "weakness. . . linked with her human failings, her femininity. . . ." While the influence of Catholicism that lurks behind many of Ford's characters—especially the Irish—is invoked more often here than in nearly any other of his films, it is not a generating principle, but rather a symptomatic one. Mary is true to her beliefs—including religion—not in spite of her femininity, but because of it. This personal commitment to the *woman,* not the queen in her, is the source of the strength she calls upon to face her death and redemption. She is photographed using the iconography of martyrdom; the beautiful soft light and high angles in the court scene, the close-ups held just a fraction too long. But she is martyred to her own womanness, not to politics or to Catholicism, and it is clear that Ford values the woman over the queen.

In exile and in defeat, Mary remains a queen.

The men in Mary's personal and political life: John Carradine as David Rizzio, Douglas Walton as Darnley, Fredric March as Bothwell.

Katharine Hepburn and John Ford on the set of *Mary of Scotland.*

WEE WILLIE WINKIE

1937

Shirley Temple and Victor McLaglen on the set of *Wee Willie Winkie.*

Shirley Temple

CREDITS

Production company: 20th Century-Fox. *Director:* John Ford. *Producer:* Darryl F. Zanuck. *Associate producer:* Gene Markey. *Scenarist:* Ernest Pascal, Julian Josephson, from story by Rudyard Kipling. *Photography:* Arthur Miller. *Set decorator:* Thomas Little. *Costumes:* Gwen Wakeling. *Music:* Louis Silvers. *Sound:* Eugene Grossman, Roger Heman. *Editor:* Walter Thompson. 99 minutes. *Released* (with tinted sequences): July 30.

CAST

Shirley Temple (*Prisicilla Williams*), Victor McLaglen (*St. MacDuff*), C. Aubrey Smith (*Col. Williams*), June Lange (*Joyce Williams*), Michael Whalen (*Lt. "Coppy" Brandes*), Cesar Romero (*Khoda Khan*), Constance Collier (*Mrs. Allardyce*), Douglas Scott (*Mott*), Gavin Muir (*Capt. Bibberbeigh*), Willie Fung (*Mohammed Dihn*), Brandon Hurst (*Bagby*), Lionel Pape (*Major Allardyce*), Clyde Cook (*Pipe Major Sneath*), Lauri Beatty (*Elsi Allardyce*), Lionel Braham (*Major Gen. Hammond*), Mary Forbes (*Mrs. MacMonachie*), Cyril McLaglen (*Corporal Tummel*), Pat Somerset (*officer*), Hector Sarno (*conductor*).

SYNOPSIS

In the British colony of India, a small girl becomes the heroine of a British regiment by persuading an Indian rebel to return to jail. Adapted from a story by Rudyard Kipling.

In spite of its foreign setting—India of 1897—which might require a development of cultural characteristics endemic to its locale or at least an ideal of "otherness" with which to contrast American mores and ideology (as in *The Hurricane* and

250

Donovan's Reef), Wee Willie Winkie is deter-
minedly reflective of thirties Americana genre
values. The problems it poses at the beginning of
the film that will be worked out are the restoration
of the family—marriage for the widowed mother
and unbending of the Colonel to become a grandfather—first, and the bringing of peace to India
only a poor second. The nearly androgynous
child, Priscilla, or Wee Willie Winkie, is played
by Shirley Temple, whose incredibly popular star
persona speaks to the child worship in films of
that time and this genre generally. Through the
purity of her kindness, through the naïveté of
childhood, she alone can perform all these miracles. The character's power—and make no mistake, its functioning in this and other films is a
nearly totalitarian power—comes from her innocence and her "natural" unrepressed impulsive-
ness. Through an elaborate suppression of process which is not unique to this film, her lack of
experience in the world gives her more direct ac-
cess to the sources of power and intuition than
does the years of military service of her grandfather or her mother's years of living. The basic
notion—common ideology in the Americana genre—is that experience is corrupting—especially
sexual experience, which is the primary reason
Wee Willie Winkie (and Shirley Temple in many
other roles) is a "tomboy," or indistinguishable
boy/girl figure. In order to permit maximum physical contact to emphasize emotional issues, she
must be a girl, but in order to be the "imp of
action" she must be like a boy. In her purity of
youth, she sees straight to the correct heart of
things, and complex matters of British imperial-
ism and Indian rebellion become even simpler
than the restoration of the family, which she also
accomplishes in the suppression of social process
that is necessary in such a construct.

Wee Willie Winkie is a force of happy, healthy
chaos in the world of over-rigid military structure. She reduces rank barriers to nicknames
("Coppy" for the Lieutenant she immediately
chooses for her mother), touches her grandfather,
the gruff, distanced Colonel who cannot even approach his own daughter, and runs under physical barriers (such as a fence) meant to structure
physical space. Her attempts to win her grandfather's affection necessarily mean assuming
greater order herself—hence, she dons a uniform
and becomes Private Winkie. But her truer in-
stincts know better and she forces the Colonel to
demonstrate his affection and love by risking his

C. Aubrey Smith as Col. Williams and June Lange as his daughter Joyce.

Victor McLaglen as the Sergeant: the most valued adult who is
not a member of the family.

life when she runs away to ask the Indian rebel to come back to prison. Out of this childish act of disobedience comes the bloodless peace treaty, indicating that her impulsive action and faith in everyone's goodwill are truer than the complex machinations of the adults. Thus the social processes which allow society to function through oppressive order are devalued in the film and the chaotic, impulsive, "natural" unschooled intuition of innocence valorized. This is the common

Wee Willie Winkie and Afghan leader Kohda Khan.

The rigidity of the military: Col. Williams and the Sergeant.

operation of myth: through an acting out of a defiance to the established order, the tensions caused by its necessarily repressive nature are reduced and eased by the symbolic presentation. This leaves the ideology itself firmly intact; the ultimate process of the work of art is to reestablish the myth.

This is done in two operations; first is through the death of the most valued adult, who is significantly not a member of the family. The Sergeant (Victor McLaglen), who is both friend to Wee Willie Winkie and military man, bridges the gap between strict order and chaos with power—not with weakness as does the mother—and is thus the eventually unnecessary (because the gap is healed) and beloved sacrifice to the restoration of benevolent order. The child is chastised and suffers through his death, mitigating her "unfailing" insight. Thus punished, she is able to carry out the rest of her chaotic mission. The second operation is that of co-opting the healing chaos that she brings. It is not the end of opppressive, rigid order that she will accomplish, but rather its humanizing. She will not challenge her grandfather's military and patriarchal leadership, but rather soften it and affirm it in the face of the earlier challenge, which doubly valorizes it. Thus the ideological operation is the common one of myth: the oppressive social structure is challenged, social process suppressed, and the unchanged structure reaffirmed through an ineffectual reform and eventual reconciliation.

Sarris notes that *Wee Willie Winkie* was a peculiar assignment for Ford, both as a "man's man" directing the sugarness of America's sweetheart and as an Irish patriot reaffirming the imperalism of British rule in India. In spite of the generally pleasing—and commercially successful—result, it is this profound difference between the concerns of the narrative and Ford's own artistic concerns that makes the ideological operation of the film so drastically standard. In other situations Ford has demonstrated the working of the ideology through the visual style of the film, but in *Wee Willie Winkie* this does not occur. As it is best accomplished when his own contradictory themes can be deeply expressed at many levels, and since this project offered little opportunity for such complexity, Ford did not even attempt such a critique. *Wee Willie Winkie* is thus a fascinating ideological study of the working of a myth in the films of the thirties.

THE HURRICANE
1937

The nature/culture dichotomy is the primary source of dramatic tension in *The Hurricane*.

CREDITS

Production company: Goldwyn–United Artists. *Director:* John Ford. *Producer:* Samuel Goldwyn. *Associate producer:* Merritt Hulburd. *Scenarist:* Dudley Nichols; from the novel by Charles Nordhoff, James Norman Hall, adapted by Oliver H.P. Garrett. *Associate director:* Stuart Heisler. *Hurricane sequence:* James Basevi. *Photography:* Bert Glennon, Archie Stout (second unit). *Art directors:* Richard Day, Alex Golitzen. *Set decorator:* Julia Heron. *Costumes:* Omar Kiam. *Music:* Alfred Newman. *Editor:* Lloyd Nosler. *Sound recording:* Thomas Moulton. *Assistant director:* Wingate Smith. Exterior locations at Samoa. 102 minutes. *Released:* December 24.

CAST

Dorothy Lamour (*Marama*), Jon Hall (*Terangi*), Mary Astor (*Mrs. DeLaage*), C. Aubrey Smith (*Father Paul*), Thomas Mitchell (*Dr. Kersaint),* Raymond Massey (*Mr. DeLaage),* John Carradine (*guard),* Jerome Cowan (*Captain Nagle*), Al Kikume (*Chief Meheir*), Kuulei De-Clercq (*Tita*), Layne Tom, Jr. (*Mako*), Mamo Clark (*Hitia*), Movita Castenada (*Arai*), Reri (*Reri*), Francis Kaai (*Tavi*), Pauline Steele (*Mata*), Flora Hayes (*Mama Rua*), Mary Shaw (*Marunga*), Spencer Charters (*judge*), Roger Drake (*captain of the guards*), Inez Courtney (*girl on boat*), Paul Strader.

SYNOPSIS

Terangi, a native of a beautiful Polynesian island, goes to Tahiti and buys a present for his new bride Marama. There he is insulted by a white man and imprisoned in spite of his innocence. DeLaage, governor of his island, refuses to intercede to free him, and the desperate Terangi makes repeated escapes until his sentence is life. As Terangi makes a last effort to rejoin Marama, a hurricane hits the island and almost destroys it. The governor responds to the godlike wrath of the hurricane by freeing Terangi.

The tensions that create rich and complex characters and relationships between characters in later Ford films are external structuring determinants in *The Hurricane*. They take the form of a basic nature/culture dichotomy, with the natives, sexuality, passion, freedom and beauty opposed to law, prison, repression, duty and honor. The film performs essentially the same ideological function as most of the "South Seas" genre; it valorizes the natives for their "noncultural" virtues and sets them against the corruption of "civilized" virtues. The actual interworkings of the forces of nature and culture are thus externalized and romanticized and the critique of the white presence in the South Seas is rendered gutless. It is rather at the level of myth or parable that *The Hurricane* finds its expression. It performs the usual function of mediation and reintegration with great beauty and emotional satisfaction, if not with Ford's usual power of ideological critique.

Like all myths, *The Hurricane* has a narrative past inscribed in its structure, as well as a narrator whose relationship to the myth is both privileged because he was there and distanced because his involvement was primarily as observer and mediator, not agent of action. The film opens as a ship in the South Seas passes a desolate island upon which the wrath of god seems to have been

253

The wedding of Marama (Dorothy Lamour) and Terangi (Jon Hall).

Mary Astor as European Governor De Laage's wife.

Terangi in the prison of Tahiti.

visited. Dr. Kersaint (Thomas Mitchell) begins his role as narrator, telling the others that it was once the most beautiful island in the Pacific. The essential movement of the film has already been described: how did the island become scorched earth? A dissolve into the past immediately sketches the tensions which will conflict to produce the answer: the European governor, Mr. De-Laage (Raymond Massey) represents "the law" in his white coat and uncompromising posture. He is contrasted to the natives, Marama (Dorothy Lamour) and Terangi (Jon Hall), whose wedding is being celebrated. The couple is identified with smooth freedom of movement, passion, and the trees and flowers of nature, as they run out of the church. Terangi is immediately linked with birds, an imagery which continues through the film. In the next of the building series of oppositions, De-Laage's wife (Mary Astor) arrives by ship. She is kinder and less stiff than her husband primarily because women in the archetype are always closer to the nature side of the opposition, regardless of

their primary identification. Likewise Marama is closer to nature than Terangi; his wish to wear a uniform cap and be "just like a white man" is the seed of their tragedy. Their reserve is contrasted with the sensuality of the newly married couple; further, DeLaage inhibits not only the natives but his own wife as well.

Once this is set up, Terangi sails off to Tahiti, already nearly fully corrupted by the European influence, leaving Marama behind. The best in Terangi will destroy him in this corrupt place, not the worst. His imprisonment (building on his earlier bird imagery) is determined from tensions set up in the first sequence. Terangi's passionate nature, which cannot be suppressed, leads to a fight with a white man who insults a present he bought for Marama. The injustice which makes this a serious crime begins with the relation of the governor to the native population. The governor as the agent of the law thus becomes his jailer, and the structural opposition is concretized.

Terangi, with more libido than logic, *cannot* be

The mythical, virginal Polynesian island before the hurricane.

Terangi escapes, accidentally killing a sadistic guard.

Like the wrath of God, a hurricane hits the island.

The aftermath: DeLaage and his wife are reunited.

confined. The visual depiction of the jail is dark, claustrophobic, with shadows, chains, and a sadistic guard (John Carradine). Terangi escapes over and over, each time enduring savage beatings and lengthening his sentence. DeLaage, who has more sense of honor and duty to the law than to his subjects, continues to carry out the cruelly mechanistic increase of the sentence, in spite of the counsel of both his wife and our narrator. As a doctor, somewhat morally weak, Kersaint is closer to the European woman and to the natives than to DeLaage. The source of Terangi's need is clear in the bird imagery and through a montage of dissolves between Marama and Terangi: his life and its sustenance is tied to his sensuality and to nature. He cannot do otherwise than to try to escape even as they systematically beat him down. The level of opposition and of injustice increases until Terangi escapes again, accidentally killing the sadistic guard. Upon hearing of the escape, the governor swears he will lock Terangi up again, but as the exhausted Terangi paddles his canoe to the island, he brings with him not the logic of escape, but the wrath of God. A hurricane hits the island; one of its first acts is to sweep the legal papers off DeLaage's desk. The hurricane destroys everything on the island in one of the most impressive storm sequences on film. In a convulsion of the forces of nature, a baby is born and Dr. Kersaint's role as mediator is best illustrated. He is able to give aid because he has not been acting on the side of the anti-nature forces. When the storm finally abates, many people are left alive, but no trees or buildings. In her wrath, nature has wiped out the site of European cruelty, but the governor still has the power of the legal system he represents behind him. He has to give some sign of learning before the tension of the established opposition can relax. This is achieved, in accordance with the archetype, through his wife. Thinking her dead, he is so overjoyed when a canoe brings her to him that he runs into the water to greet her, and having been touched by it and by her, says he will not pursue Marama and Terangi, who have given her back to him.

The romantic notion that Polynesians (like Blacks) are closer to nature, simpler, more childlike, more sensual (and musical!) is probably the least attractive aspect of *The Hurricane*. The abundance of destructive stereotypes in the film (the governor, the sadistic guard, and the unbelievably evil corruption of Tahiti) points up the archetypal level of the narrative, rendering it perhaps dangerous, but no less savory. It is still the Europeans who can learn. They can take on some of the characteristics of the natives without losing their sophistication. But the natives, who cannot learn and retain their sensuality, are destroyed by the contact with the cultural reality, and not vice versa. A European has the role of narrator/mediator who can somehow be in touch with both poles. Further, as a doctor he is the agent of the life born of the storm. These are not likable aspects of the film; neither do they contain the lasting relevance that is the great and unusual hallmark of even Ford's early films. But at the level of myth, *The Hurricane* describes its task and carries it out with amazing clarity, satisfaction, and grace. Despite the simplicity of the binary oppositions, Ford fills the space between with life and emotional color, and the film is richly successful on that level. The primary criticism is that it is not the depth one can generally expect of John Ford.

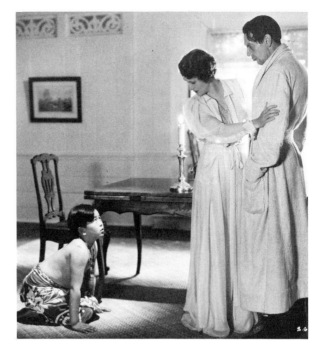

The romantic racial attitudes of the film are its least appealing aspect: the native population is simple, pure, and childlike.

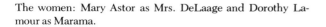
The women: Mary Astor as Mrs. DeLaage and Dorothy Lamour as Marama.

The Europeans bring their corrupting culture and ideology to the island in their very presence.

THE LONG VOYAGE HOME

1940

The plot is tangential: the visual mood carries more meaning than the killing.

CREDITS

Production company: Wanger–United Artists. *Director:* John Ford. *Producer:* Walter Wanger. *Scenarist:* Dudley Nichols; from one-act plays, THE MOON OF THE CARIBBEES, IN THE ZONE, BOUND EAST FOR CARDIFF, THE LONG VOYAGE HOME, by Eugene O'Neill. *Photography:* Gregg Toland. *Art director:* James Basevi. *Set decorator:* Julia Heron. *Music:* Richard Hageman. *Music director:* Edward Paul. *Editor:* Sherman Todd. *Sound editor:* Robert Parrish. *Special Effects:* Ray Binger, R.T. Layton. 105 minutes. *Released:* October 8.

CAST

Thomas Mitchell (*Aloysius Driscoll*), John Wayne (*Ole Olsen*), Ian Hunter (*Thomas Fenwick, "Smitty"*), Barry Fitzgerald (*Cocky*), Wilfred Lawson (*Captain*), Mildred Natwick (*Freda*), John Qualen (*Axel Swanson*), Ward Bond (*Yank*), Joe Sawyer (*Davis*), Arthur Shields (*Donkeyman*), J.M. Kerrigan (*Crimp*), David Hughes (*Scotty*), Billy Bevan (*Joe*), Cyril McLaglen (*Mate*), Robert E. Perry (*Paddy*), Jack Pennick (*Johnny Bergman*), Constantine Frenke (*Narvey*), Constantin Romanoff (*Big Frank*), Dan Borzage (*Tim*), Harry Tenbrook (*Max*), Douglas Walton (*Second Lieutenant*), Raphaela Ottiano (*Daughter of the Tropics*), Carmen Morales, Carmen d'Antonio (*girls in canoe*), Harry Woods (*the Admiral's sailor*), Edgar "Blue" Washington, Lionel Pape, Jane Crowley, Maureen Roden-Ryan.

SYNOPSIS

On the ship Glencairn, the death-obsessed crew unite to send Ole Olsen, who is still young and not yet detached from the land and the living, back to Sweden. Ole is the only one among them who has the chance of going home again, and they finally succeed in spite of the death of one man, the sacrifice of another, and the relentless pull to ship out again. The fog and storm are

main characters in this expressionistic film of Eugene O'Neill's play.

The men of the ship *Glencairn* are obsessed with (and each in his own way, in search of) death. Set in the beginning of World War II, the surface narrative concerns of *The Long Voyage Home* are so tangential to the central obsession with death that the viewer is left with an impression of moody, sensual shots rather than the story. The dangerous journey to England while loaded with ammunition, the "evidence" that Smitty is a traitor, the enemy plane that strafes the ship—these are incidental to Yank and Smitty's death, Donkeyman's severance of his ties with land, and above all , the love/hate relationship the men have with their fate.

Death is a nearly physical presence in *The Long Voyage Home*, and is so sensually compelling that the men ignore the beautiful, sexy (*very* sexy, for 1940) women who come on board in favor of the rum they bring. Smitty especially, who has already given up a family, a commission, and forsaken his homeland—England—forever for drink, moodily brushes off the girl who responds to his unhappiness and wants to be "his girl." The others grab the women the way they would pick up a football, and put them down to fight each other. Finally a man is cut with a bottle, and the captain stops the fight and sends the women off without pay, since they incited the fight by bringing the rum. This is the first instance in which the men are seen to have virtually no control over the events of their lives. If certain events are put into motion, others will follow. Central to this of course is the notion that it is their fate to continually ship out when all want most to go "home."

Gregg Toland's dark, expressionistic, foggy, and above all, long depth-of-field photography provides the sensual element for the men that the women cannot. Through its moodiness and darkness, which often reduces the men to faceless, nameless shadows, this sensuality is linked with death. The most compelling conversations are between Donkeyman—a ghost figure, caught between the life of the land and the loss of memory he yearns for—and Smitty, when they speak of death in the soft, dark night during the dance with the women. Another is below when Driscoll (Thomas Mitchell) reads Smitty's letters and Ford cuts to strange and exciting close-ups of the men with half and one-quarter light on their faces. Smitty is also shot in close-up, gagged and in anguish as his living death is revealed to them all. At the end of this sequence, Driscoll turns out the light and shoos the men away; Smitty returns to the deck in silhouette and answers Ole's call of "All's well."

To say that there is a strong current of homosexuality in *The Long Voyage Home* might be true. Certainly the men demonstrate stronger and more emotional attachments to each other than to any

Sensuous native women bring rum and fruit on board the ship *Glencaim*.

The energy of the dance turns to unfocused chaos and finally to violence.

Dris comforts Smitty after the men have violated his privacy by reading his letters, thinking he was a spy.

Through the moody darkness of the lighting, sensuality is linked with death.

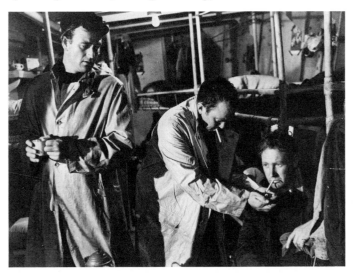

Ward Bond as Yank and Thomas Mitchell as Dris.

Yank's death.

The *Almindra* agent gets the men drunk to shanghai Ole.

women. The exception is Smitty who still loves the wife and family he nonetheless left forever, but Donkeyman points out that Smitty is different from the very first—something on land still has a hold on him. Yank's death scene with Drisc could be seen as homosexual; Yank recalls women they have known as indications of their bond to each other, but those homosexual implications fail to get to the heart of the film. The overhead shots of the men lying quietly on the deck are indeed the most sensual in the film but more central is their yearning towards their own destruction. They are each simply going through the cycle—however many times it takes for them to be released from it —into death.

Ole (John Wayne) is the innocent. Young, healthy and not subject to the others' passions for destruction, he functions rather like the opposite of a sacrificial lamb for the rest of them. He does not die that they may live; rather, he lives that they might die. To get him off the ship and home to his farm is the goal of them all; it will redeem them indirectly in a way they are incapable of accomplishing for themselves. Ole is truly different, and must be saved. He does not take part in the drinking, the dancing, and more importantly, in the "trial" of Smitty. Perhaps Ole can go home because he doesn't have the "memories" that plague the rest of them—the land is the home of memories and pain, and Donkeyman says it must be given up. Only Ole, through his very health and simplicity (which make him less interesting than the bitter, driven Smitty or any of the others) can actually make "the long voyage home." For the others, "home" is death.

Ole's innocence makes him vulnerable, and the skipper of the *Almindra* picks him out of the group to be shanghaied. When he is, it is the responsibility of all the men to save him, but this is not done without cost. Once Ole is delivered into the jaws of death—as indeed he would have been since the *Almindra* is torpedoed—the men must provide a substitute to free him. Drisc takes his place when he pauses to gloat over the rescue, and sails off on the "devil ship." The interrelatedness of Ole's going home, Drisc sailing to his death on the *Almindra,* and the rest of the crew returning to the *Glencairn* is not accidental, but is indeed casual.

The men are propelled by a fate which causes them to continually ship out. They are shanghaied, they spend all their money, and however it happens, they find themselves at sea again. Only

The men always find themselves at sea again.

Ole is rescued from the *Almindra*.

Donkeyman has given up the struggle to go back to the land. But none of the men—except Ole, with the help of all of them—is able to return. Indeed, watching the last half hour of the film in which the men get drunk and are led around by the agent of the *Almindra* knowing full well that this is a repetition that will get them all—Ole included—back on ship, is a difficult experience. The men are too helpless—or too unwilling—to break out of this destructive pattern which will result in their deaths. It is not that they are incapable of struggle, but that the mise-en-scene of the film makes such struggle useless. Death is expressed in the dark, foggy streets, and is ultimately more attractive than the life of the land, contaminated by women, war, and families. Their death at sea—like Yank's and Smitty's—draws them, through booze and fights, away from women and land, through its sensual expression in the film. Rather than struggle against their fate, they embrace it.

The dark lure of death is expressed in the mise en scene.

Death at sea? Yank is mortally injured in the storm.

THE FUGITIVE
1947

Henry Fonda and Dolores Del Rio in *The Fugitive*: visual expression is dominant.

CREDITS

Production company: Argosy Pictures–RKO Radio. *Director:* John Ford. *Producers:* John Ford, Merian C. Cooper. *Associate Producer:* Emilio Fernandez. *Scenarist:* Dudley Nichols, from the novel, THE LABYRINTHINE WAYS (or THE POWER AND THE GLORY), by Graham Greene. *Photography:* Gabriel Figueroa. *Special effects:* Fred Sersen. *Art director:* Alfred Ybarra. *Set decorator:* Manuel Parra. *Music:* Richard Hageman. *Sound:* Eugene Grossman, Roger Heman. *Editor:* Jack Murray. *Executive assistant:* Jack Pennick. *Directorial assistant:* Melchior Ferrer. *Assistant director:* Jesse Hibbs. Filmed in 47 days on locations in Mexico and at Churubusco Studios, Mexico City. 104 minutes. *Released:* November 3.

CAST

Henry Fonda (*the fugitive*), Dolores Del Rio (*Mexican woman*), Pedro Armendariz (*police lieutenant*), Ward Bond (*El Gringo*), Leo Carrillo (*chief of police*), J. Carroll Naish (*police spy*), Robert Armstrong (police sergeant), John Qualen (*doctor*), Fortunio Bonanova (*Governor's cousin*), Chris Pin Martin (*organ player*), Miguel Inclan (*hostage*), Fernando Fernandez (*singer*), Jose I. Torvay (*a Mexican*), Melchior Ferrer.

SYNOPSIS

After a revolution which makes priests criminals in a Latin American country, one priest becomes a fugitive to continue serving his people. A madonna-like woman and an American criminal help him escape. He is tricked into returning to administer last rites to the dying American. Captured and executed, the priest is martyred.

Films made from literary sources present unique problems to both the audience and the critic. There is the almost irresistible urge to compare, especially if the literary source is well known and highly regarded, and inevitably the novel or play will be the standard against which the comparison is made. Thus it is often the case that the very best a director can do is to be "faithful" to the source, and any change is regarded only in terms of its effect on the original material. It seems obvious that this is an inadequate way to interrogate a film: the difference in audience, mode of expression, and necessary length necessitate that a new work is going to be created, not simply a novel or play filmed. The difference between visual and verbal expression is so great that "faithfulness" becomes a very relative notion, yet this urge to comparison is nearly impossible to refuse. *The Fugitive* is a particularly compelling case, because most admirers of Ford agree that in spite of his own satisfaction with the film (he has called it his only perfect film), it is among his very worst. A natural place to look for some of the causes of that failure is in the material from which the story was taken, Graham Greene's *The Power and the Glory*. Michael Wilmington in *The Velvet Light Trap*, No. 5, Summer 1972, locates the failure of the film in the "whitewashing" of the priest. This removal of his "stink of humanity" renders him an insipid character, and removes the duality of a priestly yet sinful character that provides much of the tension in the book. While I am in total agreement with Wilmington and others who find this film inferior to Ford's standard, the place to look for the failure is not in a change from the novel's central character, but in the film. The most basic change which determines the world view of the film is found in the visual form. The effect can best be seen against the form of the novel. The structure and language of the book stresses the everyday misery and suffering of the priest and the people he meets. His humanity—his stinking humanity—and their own is insisted upon relentlessly: his hunger, filth, and drunkenness fill the book. Detail is heaped upon detail until the poverty and degradation of the people and of the priest are almost physically felt by the reader. The priest is never depicted as noble or saintlike, and the peo-ple are never beautiful in their need of him and his religion. Indeed, they often fear his presence or ill-use him. The film not only *changes* this characterization, it portrays a *different* one. To compare them is illuminating; to place a value judgment on the difference has no relevance because they are simply two different products.

Ford uses his visual style to carry out a process of abstraction which immediately removes the film and the priest and people in it to a level very different from the dreary, detailed, everyday level of the novel. The film is photographed in the most expressionistic style he has ever used: the angles, lighting, and composition are so beautiful and so

The priest abstracted through visual style: the meaning is almost exclusively in the mise-en-scene.

The visual expression gives the church and the people purity, beauty and nobility.

dramatic that they sometimes look like Eisenstein's most symbolic work, or like German Expressionism, which presents its meaning almost exclusively in the mise-en-scene. Both priest and peasants are thus given a religious purity, beauty, and nobility that abstracts them from the poverty, filth, and degradation of the world of the novel. In one sequence, the priest appears in silhouette in the church, the people walk in beautiful lines carrying candles which softly illuminate their beautiful faces, and the church is transformed into a holy room of light and shadow. There is no stink

of humanity here; it is the first extended scene in the film, and sets the emotional tone. Music contributes to the effect as well, swelling magnificently as a woman goes to ring the bell to call the people to mass, and softly modulating the later nearly soundless deathbed scene.

The suffering of the people likewise is rendered noble through abstraction. We see it primarily in the beautiful woman who first meets the priest and later helps him escape. She is the mother of the police lieutenant's child (not the priest's, as in the book) and must dance in the cantina to sup-

264

(*Opposite page*) The church is transformed into a holy room of light and shadow.

The unwed mother is a Madonna figure.

port herself and the child. There is of course the indication of prostitution here: both in the police lieutenant's reaction to her, which assumes her guilt, and in her manipulation of his body through her dancing to protect the priest from the police. She is thus the totality of Woman: the other, the beautiful bearer of sexuality, and the prostitute. She is the madonna. Ford extends her role as protector and finally agent of the priest's escape. The child is a babe in arms, not the vicious little girl of the novel, and the way Ford frames the mother and child demonstrates not only a change from the book, but the creation of a new character. The priest is transformed into a saintly, other-worldly figure, the woman and child into an image of the madonna, and the people into beautiful supplicants.

The structural and thematic connections between the two other major figures from the novel perform this same function of abstracting the level of action in the film. After the first extended scene in the church, the film fades to El Gringo,

the American criminal whose flight through Mexico parallels the priest's. He is followed by the police lieutenant, whose brutality and guilt are immediately apparent. He tells the people, "I'm an Indian just like you," as his troops overrun the crowd and take hostages to be shot. The lieutenant rides into the church on his horse, laughing at the altar in an act of desecration, only to be stopped by the cry of a child—his child. The madonna stands in the church; his desecration is extended to all things religious and *natural*. His guilt stems from his own inadequacy with regard to "his" woman and their child. The tensions in the film are thus changed from the material to the personal and emotional: his motive is guilt which is extended to a vendetta against the church and the priest. In the novel Greene separates religion from the priest, thus allowing him to be both a sinful man and still a vessel of the church. He further separates the revolution (its exact nature is never made clear) from the lieutenant, allowing it an independent, non-personal existence. This

separation does not take place in the film: the priest must embody the church and the lieutenant must encompass the weaknesses and petty cruelty of the revolution. The personal realm, thus becomes the larger forces of the novel, not the rationale in the film. Ford unites these two in character, and the duality of the book is no longer operative.

The connection between the priest and the criminal is more personal in the film. They never meet before the fatal end in *The Power and the Glory,* but there are two earlier encounters in the film in which the Gringo assumes a protective role towards the priest: first in the cantina after the priest has been released from jail. The Gringo calls him "father," thus establishing a bond of recognition between them, and later when the priest escapes, the Gringo covers the escape with his gunfire and is fatally wounded. The web of sacrifices in the film is thus based on *personal* not theoretical contact and commitment. When the priest, having escaped to a safe state, is asked by

The troops of the "revolution" repress religion and brutalize the people.

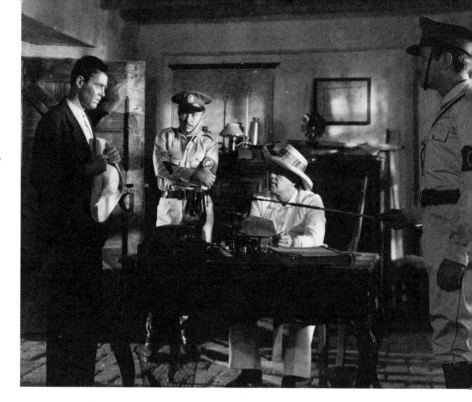

The Priest and the Lieutenant.

Painterly classical composition engrandizes the film and abstracts its themes.

the traitor to minister to the dying Gringo, there is still a sense that he knows he is going to his own martyrdom and is choosing it, but the personal connection between himself (as a man, not only as a priest) and the dying man mediates the selflessness of the act in the book. After the priest has been shot, another priest appears in silhouette to the people: he closes the door behind him and the image of the cross is cast in light through the door. This is so much like the first scenes, and the people's beautiful faces as they watch the first priest die are shot so melodramatically, that it seems much like a miracle—the first priest embodied the church; when he dies, another priest is sent. The church does not exist independently of its servants: this abstracted unity of the symbol—the church—and its sign—the priest—is created by Ford's visual style and completely differentiates his film from Greene's novel.

The personal dimension is carried out to the very end: the woman lifts her beautiful, rain-soaked face to the priest's window on the dawn of his death; the lieutenant reacts as if he himself had been shot when the priest dies; the Gringo "blesses" the priest; and the people watch, hushed and worshipful. The level of the everyday, the horror, the poverty, the filth, even the sin, has been left out of the film, and only an assumption that a film should incorporate all elements of another form can base its failure in this change.

The priest responds to the religious needs of his people even when it could mean his death.

The priest in prison awaiting death.

The people are transformed into beautiful, spiritual supplicants by the lighting and composition.

MOGAMBO
1953

CREDITS

Production company: MGM. *Director:* John Ford. *Producer:* Sam Zimbalist. *Scenarist:* John Lee Mahin; from the play, RED DUST, by Wilson Collison. *Photography* (in Technicolor): Robert Surtees, Fredrick A. Young. *Art director:* Alfred Junge. *Costumes:* Helen Rose. *Editor:* Frank Clarke. *Second-unit directors:* Richard Rosson, Yakima Canutt, James C. Havens. *Assistant directors:* Wingate Smith, Cecil Ford. Exteriors filmed in Africa. 116 minutes. *Released:* October 9.

CAST

Clark Gable (*Victor Marswell*), Ava Gardner (*Eloise Y. Kelly*), Grace Kelly (*Linda Nordley*), Donald Sinden (*Donald Nordley*), Philip Stainton (*John Brown Pryce*), Eric Pohlmann (*Leon Boltchak*), Laurence Naismith (*Skipper*), Dennis O'Dea (*Father Joseph*), Asa Etula (*young native girl*), Wagenia Tribe of Belgian Congo, Samburu Tribe of Kenya Colony, Bahaya Tribe of Tanganyika, M'Beti Tribe of French Equatorial Africa.

SYNOPSIS

An explosive triangle of a big game hunter, a proper lady, and an earthy unrepressed woman comes together in an African safari.

Mogambo is something of an anomaly in Ford's oeuvre. It contains fewer typically "Fordian" elements than any of his films of the forties or fifties, uses none of his "stock company" of actors, and has relatively few recognizable stylistic motifs. The sexual triangle is never grounded in the larger contexts of the character's lives. Yet it is well made and satisfying, providing a sense of closure so complete that the world of the film seems to cease to exist after the end credits. Nothing is left ambiguous either in action or intention. No character loses anything for what he/she ultimately gains. This element of neat completeness

John Ford directing Clark Gable on the set of *Mogambo*.

is most unlike Ford, whose characters generally have to make and live with as messy and complex decisions as do we all.

Mogambo is a remake of Victor Fleming's *Red Dust* (1932), also starring Clark Gable. Jean Harlow played Ava Gardner's role as Kelly, and Mary Astor was the aristocratic, repressed Linda (Grace Kelly in *Mogambo*). None of these characters is a typical Fordian "type." Gable's Victor Marswell is a "leader of the boys." Like a Howard Hawks character, he is well integrated into the masculine world of action, and in need of being shown what he really wants by an aggressive woman. Kelly is that woman—intensely Hawksian with her hardy, direct sexuality. She is a woman without ambiguity, who always knows what she wants—Vic. She can be "one of the boys" and can take care of herself. Kelly is contrasted with Linda, who is fragile and brittle. With her, sexuality is repressed just enough to entice Vic. Linda has no predecessor in Ford's repeated use of women.

The film's "foreignness" extends beyond the locale and character types. It is situated between *The Sun Shines Bright* (1953) and *The Long Gray Line* (1955), two of Ford's most emotionally rich, excessive films. This proximity exaggerates its lack of a personal dimension. But this is not to say that the picture is inadequate. As Andrew Sarris observes, the sexual dynamic of the three characters is even more charged than in the earlier picture. Kelly and Linda's verbal sparring perfectly demonstrates their opposed sexuality and its different appeal for Vic. Kelly is vulgar, earthy, sensual and obvious. Linda is refined, repressed,

272

and, in the most exaggerated sense of the word, prim. Kelly is associated with bright, sensual colors, with animals (a baby elephant primarily for comedy, panthers and leopards for her sexuality), with flowing easy movement—and is integrated into nature. Linda is always at odds with the uncontrolled elements of nature and of herself, but when her own sexuality breaks forth, it is with a brittle excited force. Her barely repressed sexuality is more exciting to Vic than is Kelly's earthiness. As in a Hawks film, he must pursue the unhealthy ideal in order to learn to accept the healthy one. The comedy and tension of the film are structured beautifully. When Kelly jumps off the departing boat to stay with Vic—who has as much trouble asking her as does a Hawks hero—all the tensions have been brought to resolution. The ending is as complete and satisfying as the sexual dynamic was predictable.

The white hunter structures the foreign locale.

Clark Gable as Vic and Ava Gardner as Kelly.

Vic and Kelly: she is a woman who can take care of herself.

Ava Gardner and John Ford.

DONOVAN'S REEF
1963

John Wayne as "Guns" Donovan and Lee Marvin as "Boats" Gilhooley.

CREDITS

Production company: Ford Productions–Paramount. *Director-producer:* John Ford. *Scenarists:* Frank Nugent, James Edward Grant; from story by Edmund Beloin, adapted by James Michener. *Photography (in Technicolor):* William Clothier. *Art directors:* Hal Pereira, Eddie Imazu. *Set decorators:* Sam Comer, Darrell Silvera. *Costumes:* Edith Head. *Music:* Cyril J. Mockridge. *Editor:* Otho Lovering. *Assistant director:* Wingate Smith. Filmed on the island of Kauai in the South Pacific. 109 minutes. *Released:* July.

CAST

John Wayne (*Michael Patrick "Guns" Donovan*), Lee Marvin (*Thomas Aloysius "Boats" Gilhooley*), Elizabeth Allen (*Amelia Sarah Dedham*), Jack Warden (*Dr. William Dedham*), Cesar Romero (*Marquis Andre De Lage*), Dorothy Lamour (*Miss Lafleur*), Jacqueline Malouf (*Leilani Dedham*), Mike Mazurki (*Sgt. Menkowicz*), Marcel Dalio (*Father Cluzeot*), Jon Fong (*Mister Eu*, Cheryline Lee (*Sally Dedham*), Tim Stafford (*Luki Dedham*), Carmen Estrabeau (*Sister Gabrielle*), Yvonne Peattie (*Sister Matthew*), Frank Baker (*Captain Martin*), Edgar Buchanan (*Boston notary*), Pat Wayne (*Navy lieutenant*), Charles Seel (*Grand Uncle Sedley Atterbury*), Chuck Robertson (*Festus*), Mae Marsh, Maj. Sam Harris (*members of family counsel*), Dick Foran, Cliff Lyons (*officers*), and Ford's yacht, THE ARANER.

SYNOPSIS

"Boats" Gilhooley jumps ship for Haleokaloa, a Polynesian island, to join his old war buddy "Guns" Donovan for their mutual birthday brawl. When they learn that Doc Dedham's Boston daughter Amelia is coming to Haleakaloa, they decide to conceal his three Polynesian children from Amelia until the Doc can return and explain his second family. Donovan covers for Doc by

posing as the father of Lukie, Sarah, and Leilani. A comedy of errors develops as Amelia and Donovan fall in love, and finally Leilani and Amelia are joined as sisters during a Polynesian ceremony.

In 1962 Ford made *The Man Who Shot Liberty Valance,* a black-and-white, visually austere film. It is a narratively direct expression of Ford's themes of loss of meaning from past to present, disillusion with the cultural structures of order, and repression of the values that are most attractive and compelling by necessary ordering that destroys all meaning. The film is the clearest, least ambiguous statement Ford ever made. *Donovan's Reef,* made a year later, was dismissed by critics at the time as a lush, slapstick comedy about two war buddies carousing on a Polynesian island. Actually, *Donovan's Reef* deals with the same basic concepts as does *The Man Who Shot Liberty Valance,* but in ways so indirect, both visually and in the narrative, that it was "out of touch" with its audience in 1963 and is still a misunderstood film even among Ford admirers.

After *The Last Hurrah* in 1958 all Ford's films set in America were Westerns, a genre which provides a built-in distancing device in its structure. He made either films set in other countries or Westerns; each gave him the space he needed to explore the bleak vision which was necessarily rooted in his own culture. In the Westerns a structure was already provided which could give form, and, above all, reconciliatory comfort to despair, but in *Donovan's Reef,* he had to create his own structure. The setting itself, a mythical island of Haleakaloa (itself a recognizable combination of Haleakala and the Hawaiian suffix loa) is immediately removed from any reality. The characters are often comic parodies of film archetypes: John Wayne as "Guns" Donovan and Lee Marvin as "Boats" Gilhooley cannot keep from beating each other up on their mutual birthday. The comedy is very broad. The Chinese continue to play a broken slot machine, the Padre believes it is a juke box, the governor dictates his letter of request for transfer based on the hardship of the island life as a line of beautiful dancers sway by him bearing food. His right-hand man caricatures the educated, insufferable Chinese to the hilt, while the "Limeys" enthusiastically engage Boats and Guns in a brawl, and comic rivalry between Guns and Amelia (Elizabeth Allen) ritualizes their courtship. All these broad comedy elements are laid over the intensely serious and dark obsessions of the film.

These themes are Ford's constant ones, but woven together and hidden in *Donovan's Reef.* They are family, culture, the relationships among these elements, and the meaning that they give to their members. The family relationships are most readily accessible: there are two biological families, Doc Dedham's (Jack Warden) family in Boston and his family in Haleakaloa. There are cultural associations with each: cold, dark, visually formal and imposing with the Boston family. Our only view of them is of a business meeting in which all colors are toned down, all portraits—with the same face—are unattractive, and all people are either repressed or senile. (Mae Marsh smiles meaninglessly to herself, erupts into action, and lapses back into uncomprehending geniality.) Amelia, whose character parodies the masculine characteristics that the head of the family might require in such a society, brings her culture to Haleakaloa in an attempt to get the controlling shares away from the father she has never met. The cultural associations with the Polynesian family are of course gentler: the music of Hawaii Ford uses so well, the graceful and feminine population, the water, and the lush, relaxed scenery.

But it is not so simple as this, because at the next stage of "family" the cultural associations become mingled and the relations between the elements, rather than the elements themselves, are important in the construction of value. Guns,

Slapstick action comedy: the "Limeys" in Donovan's Reef just before a fight breaks out.

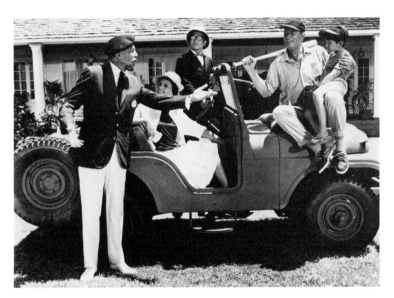

Cesar Romero as the Marquis Andre DeLage and Jon Fong as Mister Eu, with Guns and Amelia.

Guns and Boats: "sibling" rivalry with a brawl on their mutual birthday.

Lailani, Amelia and Guns with the monument to the princess Manulani.

Amelia—Elizabeth Allen—invades the male sanctuary of Donovan's Reef carrying her Boston culture even in her "tropical" dress.

Boats, Doc, and even the governor came to Haleakaloa during the war when their boat was torpedoed. Doc was their commanding officer and continues to function as a father figure for Guns and Boats, and their sibling relationship based on the war is signified in their mutual birthday, December 7, which is Pearl Harbor Day. Thus the family has a military base—always significant in Ford's oeuvre—but has further a functional and cultural grounding in the everyday life of the island, and in its past. The dead and now mythic Manulani, granddaughter of the last hereditary prince of the islands, also fought the Japanese with the men, and then married Doc. She is not only mother to his children and wife/mother to the men, but a sort of cultural queen to the entire island. When Amelia is trying to find out Manulani's identity she sees traces everywhere: in the monument to their fight with the Japanese; in the hospital which is named for Manulani; in the cemetery where the grandest grave, covered with red, white and blue leis is hers; and above all, in her father's house in the portrait that Ford frames potently above and behind Amelia and Doc as they have tea. Manulani then, as a continuing presence, provides a grounding for one biological family, all of the symbolic families, and for the culture into which all are intermingled. The work of the film is to fit Amelia into this loose structure, and it is not done through her union with Guns Donovan, but through her union with her sister and "mother" Manulani.

It is actually the relations among the women that are crucial in *Donovan's Reef*, and the men inadvertently complicate these relations. Leilani is the key to the film. She is the first character we see, diving from the canoe into the water. A beautiful, just barely adolescent girl, she is the perfect mixture of white and Polynesian cultures. We realize at the end of the film that, like her mother Leilani is the hereditary princess of all the islands. With news of Amelia's coming, Guns devises a scheme to prevent the proper Boston lady's discovery of her father's "half-caste" (her own term) children. Guns takes the three to his house to pose as his own. Leilani receives this information, circled by five men, looking helpless and in a way brutalized by them. She finally understands, saying, "It's because I'm not white!" and runs from the room. Guns follows her and comforts her in an oddly sexual scene in her bedroom, but the result is expulsion from her own home. The camera tracks in front of the party as they walk from their house to Gun's above the saloon. Leilani is often visually separated from her sister, suffering from it, as she is later framed behind fishnets, watching sadly as Amelia arrives in Haleakaloa. This relationship, watched over by the myth of Manulani, expresses the most important individual themes of the film: the racism which is critiqued, and the union of the two women and the cultures they represent which nearly miraculously "heals" all the breaks—comic or otherwise—of the community. Their relationship is an intangible mixture of mother/daughter and sibling, as Leilani is identified with her mother Manulani who would be a mother to Amelia, especially since the portrait looks startlingly like Amelia. But Amelia acts as mother to the girl as well, and in the final scene when Leilani bows and Amelia calls her sister, their union embraces all these levels. It is only after this that the slot machine gives up its money, which will go to build a roof for the church; Donovan gives the bar to Gilhooley, who then agrees to marry Miss Lafleur (Dorothy Lamour). Leilani tells Amelia to at least say good-bye to Guns and this results in their union, and the family walks in procession back to Doc Dedham's house.

The racial issue is dealt with in as elliptical a manner as the rest of the themes. Mister Eu (Jon Fong) speaks to the stereotyped Chinese "in their barbaric tongue" and they relentlessly put money in the broken slot machine; the Polynesians run down to the beach to sway and sing in their colorful costumes as every boat arrives. Racial types are as broadly drawn as the comic caricature of Boats Gilhooley playing with his electric train. But there are two places at least in which the racial comment seems to burst through the surface distancing devices. First is the character of Manulani and Leilani themselves; both are queens to their people, white, Asian, and Polynesian. In Manulani—and therefore in Leilani—is combined the religion, the history (both traditional and since World War II) and the cultural heritage of the island. Not only do they have a dignity unrealized by the rest of the characters, but it is only their presence and implied (explicit in the final ceremony) lending of the meaning they embody that orders the society and gives meaning to any other character. From the fact that Amelia looks like Manulani to the extremely civilized and gracious interracial home of the Dedhams, to the final unifying ceremony, the racism expected of Boston's representative is critiqued. But what is

The Polynesians of Haleakaloa greet Gilhooley.

more, the expectation of that racism is also critiqued: it is Donovan and Gilhooley who take the children from their home, and long after there is any external reason to maintain the fiction (since Doc neither wants the stock nor the fiction) it is maintained not out of need, but out of the men's expectation of that need. They act out of their own exaggerated sense of racism.

The other moment in which the comedy, the racial issue, and the religious dimensions of the film come together is in the Christmas pageant. In spite of the ridiculousness of the King of the United States (Gilhooley) and the infidelity to the Christmas legend of the three wise men, the attitude of the people, the music—mostly Hawaiian—and the visual style, which is very slow and stately, combine to make the ritual deeply moving. Visual jokes on the order of a cut to John Wayne immediately following the first close-up of Pat Wayne, and the rain which drenches everyone, cannot destroy the richness of the texture. It refers to a realm of idealized rather than depicted, realized meaning, similar to that in *The Man Who Shot Liberty Valance*. Missing are the reasons and the compensatory values that the Western presents. Indeed, perhaps the single most important function of the farcical narrative structure is to drain away the meaning that this film of cultural and familiar uniting might otherwise have. The meaning is based in the Polynesian culture, alien to Ford and to us, and is reproduced in the rela-

277

The Christmas pageant is both ridiculous and deeply moving: Guns and Amelia.

Guns and Amelia: often more like squabbling siblings than lovers.

278

Guns Donovan and Amelia Dedham.

tions between people. Thus Guns's place in the Dedham family is more "real" than it would be if he were an actual son, because in the cultural and functional relationships he already is a son and father. These kinds of bonds create a more meaningful system than the kinship system, perhaps because in a parodied, alien culture Ford can fantasize an ideal bonding system. Certainly the most traditional relationship (the courtship of Donovan and Amelia) is the most absurd and ritualized, as they compete in business, in sports, and in speech.

Ford creates a fantasy world in *Donovan's Reef* that is both built upon and belittled by the farcical comedy of the film. The deep structures of meaning, family culture, and perhaps most important of all, the relationships of the women in the film, are both cloaked and devalued by their juxtaposition to slapstick humor. His approach to the deepest levels of meaning is never very direct. That meaning is generally situated in the past so that it can be alluded to, rather than directly expressed, but in Ford's late films it becomes more and more necessary for him to mediate that approach. He does it through genre conventions, through displacing a film to another culture, through highly stylized comedy, and formally through exaggeration of color which falsifies the mise-en-scene, or through use of black and white and virtual TV shooting styles. In a situation so remote and foreign from our own, Ford can point toward the direction in which these issues can be found. In *Donovan's Reef* the realm of meaning is indicated only indirectly, because it is "foreign," and because it is lacking. The neat summing up of the "problems" of the film, complete with yet another comic fall and slap for Amelia, only bare the triviality of their dynamic. Only the embrace of Amelia and Leilani refers to an area which can enrich their lives; their cultures, their families, and it is only a fleeting moment, followed by more humor which functions to abstract the meaning. *Donovan's Reef* is as bleak as Ford's other late films, but the bleakness is nearly veiled.

SEVEN WOMEN
1966

John Ford and Anne Bancroft on the set of *Seven Women*.

CREDITS

Production company: Ford-Smith Productions–MGM.
Director: John Ford. *Producer:* Bernard Smith. *Scenarist:* Janet Green, John McCormick; from the story
"CHINESE FINALE," by Norah Lofts. *Photography* (in
Metrocolor and Panavision): Joseph LaShelle. *Art directors:* George W. Davis, Eddie Imazu. *Set decorators:*
Henry Grace, Jack Mills. *Costumes:* Walter Plunkett.
Music: Elmer Bernstein. *Editor:* Otho S. Lovering. *Assistant director:* Wingate Smith. 87 minutes. *Released:*
January.

CAST

Anne Bancroft (*Dr. D.R. Cartwright*), Sue Lyon (*Emma
Clark*), Margaret Leighton (*Agatha Andrews*), Flora
Robson (*Miss Binns*), Mildred Dunnock (*Jane Argent*),
Betty Field (*Florrie Pether*), Anna Lee (*Mrs. Russell*),
Eddie Albert (*Charles Pether*), Mike Mazurki (*Tunga
Khan*), Woody Strode (*Lean Warrior*), Jane Chang
(*Miss Ling*), Hans William Lee (*Kim*), H.W. Gim
(*Coolie*), Irene Tsu (*Chinese girl*).

SYNOPSIS

In China of 1935, a Christian mission is threatened
with destruction from without by the marauding bandit
Tunga Khan, from within by the presence of a new
doctor who brings life and sexuality to the cloistered
religious order. The doctor sacrifices herself to save the
missionary women and the new baby born in the midst
of death and chaos.

> "I'm always reaching for something that isn't
> there. God isn't enough. God help me, He isn't
> enough."
>
> *Miss Andrews to Dr. Cartwright*

A central concern, perhaps *the* central obsession, of art is the search for the production and
location of meaning. A classical artist in a stable
society can find it in the structures of that society,
its rituals and its values. An artist in a decadent
culture can locate it in the individual and his/her
internalized structures of value, however alienated from the cultural context, and a modern, self-conscious artist creates its lack, thereby validating the quest for meaning even while denying its
existence. Ford found himself in at least all three
of these possible categories during his career, and
although such schematization is never really accurate, we can see a sort of culmination with
traces of all three in his later pictures. In *Cheyenne Autumn* Ford explodes not only the values
of society, but the inner worth (and therefore union) of its individuals, creating a bleak world peopled by lesser individuals whose values are false
or nonexistent. Any attempt to locate meaning in
either the external structures of society—government, religious, military—or the inner values of
the pallid lovers (Thomas Archer and Deborah
Wright) is doomed to be absurd.

In *Seven Women* Ford immediately removes
these external structures by setting the film in as
foreign a culture and as faraway a country as he
could: China of 1935; and then by hollowing out
the missionaries' dedication to religion and to
family. The little world of the mission could be
seen as a greatly schematized version of his former groundworks of value, all cut off from their
source of creation and thus from their significance. Miss Binns (Flora Robson) has never even
been *home* to England, and when the women
speak of traditions of Christmas and Thanksgiving in their prison, their isolation from a cultural
base is poignant. The obvious artifice of the
MGM sets further deteriorates any authenticity
and visual realism that could have been easily

279

The obvious artifice of the MGM sets makes no attempts at authenticity.

Margaret Leighton as Miss Andrews: rigid and inflexible.

Anne Bancroft as Dr. Cartwright: sensuous and flexible.

created had Ford wanted to ground *Seven Women* in any familiar context—physical, spiritual, or emotional. It is the most removed and alien of his films; he relies on a very schematic visual representation and narrative story, and lack of genre associations to create a canvas, curiously blank in many traditional ways, upon which to express some of his most abstract ideas of law, religion, sexuality, and chaos.

The central metaphor of *Seven Women* is the dialectic between order and chaos. Ford uses religion (even militarism in religion) law, repression, sexuality, and healing to explore this relationship. In a simple structural diagram, Miss Andrews (Margaret Leighton) as architect of her mission, repressed lesbian, and irrational believer in the law, rules, and the symbolic power of American government, represents order by both internalizing and enforcing these values. Dr. Cartwright (Anne Bancroft), agent of healing, liberator of sexual repression, rule breaker whose belief is in reality rather than scripture or law, is eventually led to carnal participation in a nightmare vision of chaos. She is thus structurally opposed to Miss Andrews—an agent of chaos. From her arrival at the mission, Dr. Cartwright threatens Miss Andrews' authority and finally even her sanity as other missionaries, a plague outbreak, the Mongols led by Tunga Khan, and finally a new life invade her stronghold, stripping her of power. Finally she loses her own most personal hold on order—her mind. But such a simple opposition requires the reshaping of the picture which ignores subleties and perhaps most profoundly, the essential similarity of the two women. As in other Ford films (*The Searchers, The Whole Town's Talking*), they are alter egos in many ways, but it is difficult to name the ego and the shadow.

The antagonism is set up between them at their first meeting: Miss Andrews on the porch—in a visually superior position—standing very stiff and rigid; Dr. Cartwright below, relaxed, gesturing freely, moving impulsively. It is through authority, healing, and possibly sexuality that the women first interact and feel each other's strength. Miss Argent has earlier complimented Miss Andrews on her medical skill despite a lack of training, and Miss Andrews has accepted the compliment with a comment on the skills necessary to run a mission. This is definitely her area, and she moves through her compound dispensing graciousness, semipaternalistic authority, and gifts. In the script of *Seven Women* she is ungracious and unkind to her underlings; her need for total authority is much less ambiguous. But her need to heal stops at Florrie Pether (Betty Field). Miss Andrews' aversion to the pregnant woman is clear before the doctor ever arrives. Florrie Pether is clearly a battleground, first of authority and power, later of sexuality and chaos. First to be involved is the question of religion. Charles Pether (Eddie Albert) tells the doctor he brought his wife to China because the lay mission was as close to a ministry as he could get, and he continues to place his "calling" above his wife's safety until it is too late. Most significantly, he quotes Scripture to her to the effect that God will take care of Florrie, and when she answers that she has never seen God take care of anyone in a hospital, he quotes, "Though he may slay me, yet still will I trust him." He is following Miss Andrews in denying their real need for the expertise of the doctor, who knows that Florrie requires greater medical attention. Pether can do no more than impotently die when he finally takes responsibility for himself and his wife's well-being. Florrie herself refers to giving birth "like an animal" in a ditch, and Dr. Cartwright accuses Miss Andrews of punishing Florrie for a sexual act in the sacred mission. While this is clearly part of Miss Andrews' aversion to the pregnancy and her derangement at the birth, it is not simply the sexuality of the process. Miss Andrews' militant order, in which rules are more important than people, resists any change or chaos, and the entrance of new life—especially male life into her female mission—is certainly disorder.

It is in Florrie and in Emma (Sue Lyon) that the ground of sexuality becomes a source of tension and possibly competition between the central figures of power until the Mongols arrive to bring the tension out into the open. Miss Andrews can barely control her compulsion to touch and to dominate Emma: in the girl's room Miss Andrews seems driven beyond her power to control herself to touch Emma's hair and arm, yet in this scene (and in a later one in which the hostility and threat from Dr. Cartwright are located in Emma as Miss Andrews warns the girl against the doctor's evil). Visually Miss Andrews is trapped by her own movements. She is framed generally center frame, alone in the shot and unable to permit any sharing. Ford cuts between one-shots of the two women, but even when they are together in the frame something (like the door in the office scene) intrudes between them and acts as a

Mike Mazurki as Tunga Khan: symbol of chaos, violence and savagery.

The antagonism between Dr. Cartwright and Miss Andrews is immediate.

The clinic: inoculating against cholera.

Charles and Florrie Pether—her pregnancy and its implied sexuality is a match to ignite the forces of chaos.

Sue Lyon as Emma Clark, and Miss Andrews: barely repressed desire.

boundary for Miss Andrews. Dr. Cartwright can touch Emma and move easily about her; she even liberates the girl to the extent that she can speak more naturally and move more freely. The struggle for Emma is obviously in Miss Andrews' mind and in her own need to retain power: Dr. Cartwright does not engage at all. It is the more fundamental concept of chaos that drives Miss Andrews insane, although the metaphors she seizes upon are Biblical and sexual. She calls Dr. Cartwright a whore, and is even led to a not very subtle racism tinged with jealousy when she says to no one in particular, "He only wants her because she's white and he's yellow."

If chaos is the central metaphor of the film, and if meaning is the *"ding an sich,"* then questions of where the chaos comes from, what it represents, and who, what, or how it is ordered become central. The first is easiest: chaos comes from inside the mission itself. Miss Andrews' repressive, militaristic measures seem to draw the forces of chaos, metaphorically unleashing them from the repressed natures of her staff. Charles Pether, as impotent, emasculated a male as Ford had created, *fathered* a child which ultimately became the major force in the hysteria with which Miss Andrews marked her own insanity. Miss Argent (Mildred Dunnock), admirer and loyal servant, found her own strength as Miss Andrews lost hers. Emma was drawn to life rather than repression with the baby's birth. Thus, the doctor had virtually nothing to do with the seeds of chaos in this highly abstracted film: in fact, she is the most able to order the chaos, although it does destroy her. Dr. Cartwright disrupts the careful order of the dinner table, but can order the chaos of the plague — a time in which Miss Andrews is most visually out of control of both her own body and the surrounding area, until her breakdown. The doctor takes care of Florrie as God doesn't seem to, actually "selling herself" for the medical bag that will ease the difficult birth. Further, once the baby is born she is able to move the women to a better·place, and eventually out of the mission altogether. She controls Tunga Khan physically, ordering both him and his lieutenant around with the force of her body and her tone. She even kills him, Tunga Kahn, the incarnation of all that civilization (or perhaps woman) has to fear in a concretized form of the dark unknown. And unlike Miss Andrews, who loses all power (even over Miss Argent, who finally tells her to shut up, and over herself), Dr. Cartwright controls her own

Dr. Cartwright's arrival creates dissension and distance between Emma and Miss Andrews.

death. In the brilliant gold and red kimono Tunga Khan makes her wear, the doctor is the first startling burst of color in the film which has been kept carefully muted, in tones of brown. Until this moment, *Seven Women* is nearly a black, white, and brown movie. Suddenly Dr. Cartwright's sensuality is in full bloom, and moreover, the change in costume does not affect her own bearing. Ford isolates her in beautiful silhouette as she walks down the corridor, then tracks rapidly away from her after she drinks her potion. She is alone, isolated, and far away from both the people of the film and from us, but she is still the orderer of chaos.

The nature of the chaos is more difficult to determine. Miss Andrews says with her grace the first night at dinner, "Only thou, Lord, knowst what is good for us." It does indeed seem that in many ways the chaos is healing, terrifying as it may be. The repression of the mission has skewed people's priorities to the extent that Miss Argent repeats rules to the doctor as though they had precedence over Florrie's life, and Florrie wants a baby because "all my chums have them." Charles wants to be in China because it is as close to a pulpit as he can have, so he winds up earnestly preaching Scripture at uncomprehending little boys. The Chinese people—adults and children—of the mission are barely noticed by anyone: everyone there has a reason of her/his own that has nothing to do with them. When the British missionaries come, Miss Andrew's lack of Christian charity and abundance of petty denominational hostility is not even surprising. And these women too are questionable servants of God: Miss Russell (Anna Lee) is a missionary only because of her drunken husband, and seems to lust after the bloody violence and degradation of Tunga Khan and his men. Only Miss Binn, who in the film's script actually teaches the missionary children pride and respect for their own country's culture and history, seems a dedicated missionary who understands both her own work and the doctor's. It is she who tells Emma that Dr. Cartwright is dedicated to saving human lives, implying that this vow is as sacred as their own.

Life in the mission has also led to an almost amusing, but symptomatically dangerous and groundless attitude. When we hear the first mention of Tunga Khan, Miss Andrews, with Miss Argent parroting her, states that no savages would dare to harm the mission because they are American citizens. Their complete loss of touch with

John Ford directing Margaret Leighton and Sue Lyon.

Dr. Cartwright's arrival does not create the tension at the mission, but helps to unleash it.

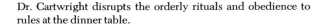

Dr. Cartwright disrupts the orderly rituals and obedience to rules at the dinner table.

reality, which goes along with their walled-in mission and unconcern with the Chinese people, is in need of correction, especially as it is a manifestation of inner disturbances in the personal lives of the people. In a hauntingly beautiful scene Dr. Cartwright and Miss Andrews discuss

Tunga Khan's men: the incarnation of unrepressed violence.

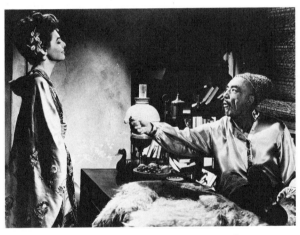

Dr. Cartwright is capable of control over Tunga Khan.

women's lives at night in a moment of calm in the plague. To the inspired blues score by Elmer Bernstein, Miss Andrews admits that something is missing from her life that work and God cannot fill. The implication is that something of the same is true for the doctor, and we later learn she was jilted by a married man, but somehow her advice that Miss Andrews should have married and had sons ("That's real living") seems inadequate for both of them. We never know what would be; one dies and the other loses her mind, but for both, clearly, something is missing. Otherwise they would not be there, each drawing the forces of chaos that will destroy them both.

The chaos that comes into the world of the mission destroys very little that is good in the life of the mission. The Chinese are not represented as a people, rather, simply a locale. They do not even figure in the life of the mission. Illusions are destroyed, the repressive, antisexual regime of the church is lost, and the walled-in mission is opened. New life is born, and only Dr. Cartwright is lost. In a beautiful subjective tracking shot, she sees the others off in the wagon which leaves her behind. For both Miss Andrews and Dr. Cartwright, there was nowhere else to go. Miss Andrews is lost in the broken order of her own mind, and Dr. Cartwright is dead by her own choosing. As the camera pulls back from her, alone and isolated and surrounded by darkness and death, we can examine the forces that brought her here and her complicity in her fate, but we find no answer when we ask why. All the reasons have been used up and wiped out: only a vague kind of romantic existentialism or a high-minded loyalty and sacrifice attempt insubstantial answers. Both have already been sought and rejected: Miss Binns suggests that the doctor is giving her own life to save the baby's and the emotional and visual closure offered by the suicide is inviting. But neither reconciles with the rest of the film, which has offered and rejected all the answers it has. We are left in the end with a bittersweet hollowness: bitter by virtue of her death and our inability to understand and make it meaningful, sweet by virtue of the beautiful music and tracking shot, but lacking utterly a grounding for her, the rest of the women, and the world of the film itself. Ford has presented as desolate, distanced, and artificial a repudiation of the values and sources of meaning our culture has, yet at the same time managed to enrich and invest this vision with the deeply healing power of art.

Irrational, terrifying chaos: Tunga Khan's men murder the Chinese peasants and their children.

Mr. Pether preaches scripture to uncomprehending Chinese children.

John Ford directing Jane Chang as Miss Ling.

John Ford directing a scene of the women held captive while Mrs. Pether's baby is born.

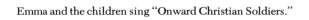
Emma and the children sing "Onward Christian Soldiers."

IN CONCLUSION

John Ford did not think of himself as an artist, but his industry, his audience, and his colleagues do. When he died August 31, 1973, he had been named best director three times by the Director's Guild of America, received four Academy Awards for best direction, and been honored with the D. W. Griffith Award. The American Film Institute gave him their "Life Achievement Award." Months before his death, then-President Nixon presented him with the U.S. Medal of Freedom and this citation:

> In the annals of American film, no name shines more brightly than that of John Ford. Director and filmmaker for more than half a century, he stands preeminent in his craft—not only as a creator of individual films of surpassing excellence, but as a master among those who transformed the early motion pictures into a compelling new art form that developed in America and swept the world. As an interpreter of the nation's heritage, he left his personal stamp indelibly imprinted on the consciousness of whole generations both here and abroad. In his life and in his work, John Ford represents the best in American films and the best in America.

Today Ford's critical reputation is so secure that *Film Quarterly* (Summer 1975) felt it time to *re*consider his oeuvre. His films are the subject of college courses and regularly appear on "Ten Best" lists. In *Action*, publication of the Director's Guild of America (November-December 1973), European as well as American film artists pay him tribute:

JEAN RENOIR: Talent is rare. Technical skill is not common. Leadership on a set is not found on every street corner. A quality even more scarce is nobility. John Ford was a king; he knighted all those who had the immense luck to work with him.

SATYAJIT RAY: In my youth I admired John Ford for almost exactly the same reasons that I admired Beethoven: for his strength and simplicity; for his warmth, his lyricism and his breadth of vision; for his heroic stance, and his unbounded faith and optimism.

FRANCOIS TRUFFAUT: John Ford was one of those artists who never used the word "art" and was one of those poets who never used the word "poetry."

STANLEY KRAMER: The film speaks for itself. That's what we face in discussing John Ford. There is nothing to be said—his films roar through our times.

FRANK CAPRA: John Ford was the Compleat Director, undoubtedly the mightiest and most versatile in films. A megaphone was to John Ford what a chisel was to Michelangelo: his life, his passion, his cross.

FEDERICO FELLINI: What I like most in John Ford is the artist in a state of purity . . . For all this I esteem him, I admire him, and I love him.

But even though Ford is recognized by the public, the critics, the theorists, and fellow artists, the depth and scope of his artistic vision has barely begun to be seen. His films reward the return viewer as only the greatest of art can—they can never be exhausted, only more fully appreciated. Today it is still his most accessible films that are widely known: *Stagecoach, The Grapes of Wrath, The Searchers, The Quiet Man.* The bittersweet beauty of *The Sun Shines Bright,* the profoundly radical vision of *The Wings of Eagles,* the truly modern alienation of *Seven Women:* these are still to be experienced by most of the film audience. Ford is the Shakespeare of the cinema.